The Mills of Medieval England

Plate 1 A fourteenth-century windmill. (British Library Stowe Ms. 17 fo. 89v). Reproduced by kind permission of the British Library.

The Mills of Medieval England

Richard Holt

Basil Blackwell

Copyright © Richard Holt, 1988

First published 1988

Basil Blackwell Ltd
108 Cowley Road, Oxford, OX4 1JF, UK

Basil Blackwell Inc,
432 Park Avenue South, Suite 1503
New York, NY 10016, USA

British Library Cataloguing in Publication Data
Holt, Richard,
The Mills of Medieval England.
1. England. Watermills, 600 – 1500
2. England. Windmills, 600 – 1500
I. Title
621.2'1

ISBN 0 – 631 – 15692 – 5

Typeset in 11 on 12 pt Goudy
by Pioneer Associates Ltd., Perthshire
Printed in Great Britain by
Bookcraft Ltd, Bath, Avon

To Vanessa,
and to Alice and Thomas (who bought
me a book so I should know what to write)

Contents

Preface

This book is the outcome of a programme of research into English medieval mills which began at Birmingham University in 1983 and continued until 1987. Arising originally out of John Langdon's interests and research into medieval technology, it began with a five-month pilot project headed by Christopher Dyer and financed by the Economic and Social Research Council to examine the documentary evidence for the mills of the West Midland region. At the completion of this phase, the Leverhulme Trust most generously took over responsibility for supporting the project for another two years and nine months.

The project began with the proposition that although mills represented the most complex of the technical innovations of the Middle Ages, they have not hitherto received the detailed attention they deserve from historians. The history of technology has tended to develop as an independent subject, and one moreover which is studied with great enthusiasm and often written with grand flourishes. Technological historians are attracted towards the pioneering heroism of the inventors, and in the main they have set out to demonstrate that technical innovation lay at the root of wider social changes. Our aim, by contrast, was to examine mills within the context of medieval society, expecting to find that they developed to satisfy the specific needs of the people who built, managed and used them. For example, as labour-saving devices was their primary function to free manpower for other tasks? And if such a relationship existed, did the spread of mills fit into the well-known cycle of medieval population history which changed from a shortage of labour to a glut in the seven centuries up to 1300, and then back to shortage again in the succeeding two centuries? To what extent were mills built to raise toll revenue for feudal lords who imposed the obligation to perform suit of mill on the local peasantry? Or was the mill-builder more of an entrepreneur, gambling on the profits to be gained from the market value of the service that the mill provided? How was the mill regarded by the people for whose apparent benefit it had been built and worked: an admirable convenience, or an oppressive nuisance? Or did it perhaps provoke a more complex mixture of attitudes? The problems posed by mills are numerous, and no single research programme can attempt to give each of them full consideration.

Dr Langdon began work by looking at the mills of the West Midland region, building on the existing body of knowledge and information at Birmingham. His theme was the rise and decline of mill numbers, from the already high level achieved in the eleventh century to a peak around 1300, followed by a falling away in the later Middle Ages. The results of this research are in preparation. He is now also working on the distribution pattern of English mills using a large national sample taken from the inquisitions *post mortem* of the early fourteenth century.

After nine months Dr Langdon left the project to take up an assistant professorship at the University of Alberta, and his place was taken by Richard Holt. Because of the work that had already been completed, he concentrated on mills from outside the West Midland region. His research on documentation from the south-west led to an article on the mills of the Glastonbury Abbey estate, and further published work is planned using the large body of data that has been collected. An article by Dr Holt on the question of medieval technological innovation is currently in preparation. Throughout the project, and in all these publications, the three participants have worked closely together, and the continuing role of Christopher Dyer in guidance and criticism has been invaluable.

Many people contributed directly to the project. Our colleagues in the School of History gave advice and support, whilst our friends of the Friday Evening Seminar patiently listened to papers on mills and gave them their accustomed searching and sober consideration. Bruce Campbell gave freely of his deep knowledge of Norfolk manorial records, and also provided us with a platform at the Anglo-American Seminar at Norwich in July 1986. Helena Graham, Sandra Raban, Rodney Hilton, Philip Rahtz, Julia Barrow, Robert Swanson, Miri Rubin, Steven Bassett and Chris Wickham contributed unpublished material or references, and Bob Smith provided many insights into aspects of milling in the traditional peasant societies of Eastern Europe.

Without financial support the project could not have gone ahead. We should therefore like to express our gratitude to the Leverhulme Trust and the Economic and Social Research Council for enabling this research to be undertaken.

Christopher Dyer
John Langdon
Richard Holt

1
The Watermill

O stay your busy hands, ye girls that grind at the mill;
Let not the cock that heralds dawn disturb your sleep.
The river-nymphs are bidden by Demeter's will
To do your work; and on the topmost wheel they leap
And turn the axle's winding spokes, upon whose coil
Concave Nisyrian millstone's weight revolves anon.
A golden age has come again; for free from toil
We learn to taste what fruits from Mother Earth are won.

Thus the poet Antipater, writing in the first century BC, welcomed the watermill in words that leave little doubt of its novelty in the Mediterranean world.[1] It was at approximately the same time, around 25 BC, that the Roman engineer Vitruvius noticed the new machine, and entered the earliest precise reference to it into his notebook with a description of how mill wheels could be turned by water, their motion being conveyed by means of two interlocking gearwheels to the revolving millstones.[2] Yet in apparent contradiction of these and other references that suggest that the watermill was known at a variety of locations by the end of the first century AD, historians have for long insisted that the watermill was little used by the Romans. Despite Antipater's extravagant praise of its labour-saving qualities, the essential task of grinding corn into flour by hand would for centuries continue to be the daily work of women and girls. Only in the medieval centuries, it is said, did the use of waterpower at last displace the handmill or quern.[3]

[1] L. A. Moritz, *Grain-Mills and Flour in Classical Antiquity* (Oxford, 1958), p. 131.
[2] Vitruvius, *On Architecture*, 2 vols, ed. F. Granger (London, 1931–4), II, pp. 305–7.
[3] M. Bloch, 'Avènement et Conquêtes du Moulin à Eau', *Annales E.S.C.*, vii, (1935), pp. 538–63; trans. J. E. Anderson as 'The Advent and Triumph of the Watermill', in M. Bloch, *Land and Work in Medieval Europe* (London, 1967), pp. 143–6; T. S. Reynolds, *Stronger than a Hundred Men: A History of the Vertical Water Wheel* (Baltimore, 1983), pp. 48–9.

In fact this view has been shown to be erroneous, having arisen largely from an over-reliance on literary references to the mill — or rather the noted lack of them; the slowly accumulating body of archaeological evidence has until recently been neglected. Now the Swedish archaeologist, Örjan Wikander, has started anew to present all of the available evidence for the Roman watermill, and it has become clear that the beginning of the period during which the mill was becoming widely accepted throughout Europe dates not from the early Middle Ages, but rather from the third century or before.[4]

For Britain, archaeological evidence of the use of waterpower in the Roman period is as plentiful as it is for subsequent epochs, with eight watermills having so far been identified or excavated at locations in Kent, Essex, Hampshire, Wiltshire and on Hadrian's Wall. In addition, of the twenty-four instances of the finding of large millstones from the Roman world that Wikander has so far been able to identify, a dozen were from British sites. As there is no way of distinguishing a stone used in a watermill from one used in an animal-powered mill, none of these can individually be taken as proof of the existence of a watermill; nevertheless, at least half were found close to running water, or actually in the beds of streams. At two sites in Britain iron mill spindles of the fourth and fifth centuries have been found in hoards of ironwork.[5]

The large number of references to mills in the Frankish kingdom that was established after the end of the Roman Empire in the West has been taken to indicate that they were more common there than elsewhere. It is much more likely, though, as Wikander has suggested, that this is a false impression induced by too great a dependence on literary sources, there being no archaeological evidence for any unusual concentration of mills in northern Gaul in the sixth and seventh centuries.[6] And if such a situation was normal, it confirms not only that the watermill must have been widely used during the later years of the Empire; it also shows how little the collapse of Roman authority had affected everyday activities such as corn milling.

[4] Ö. Wikander, *Exploitation of Water-Power or Technological Stagnation? A Reappraisal of the Productive Forces in the Roman Empire* (Scripta Minora Regiae Societatis Humaniorum Litterarum Lundensis, Lund, 1984); 'Archaeological evidence for early water-mills — an Interim Report', *History of Technology*, 10 (1985), pp. 151–79.

[5] Wikander, 'Archaeological evidence for early water-mills', pp. 155–6, 163–4.

[6] Reynolds, *Stronger than a Hundred Men*, pp. 49–50; Wikander, 'Archaeological evidence for early water-mills', p. 157; *Exploitation of Water-Power*, pp. 15–23.

It is pertinent to ask what implications this might have for the continued use of the watermill in Dark Age Britain. After all, the mill was as well established in Romano-British society as it was elsewhere in the Empire, and so why should we not suppose that it survived the invasions as it so clearly did on the other side of the Channel? The lack of any evidence for the watermill during these centuries is not by itself proof that it had been forgotten; many aspects of life at this time are similarly unverifiable. What makes its survival unlikely is that the level of disruption of civil life was far worse in Britain than it was on the Continent, with the combination of barbarian raids, political struggles and economic crisis having brought about an apparent state of chaos long before the establishment of the English kingdoms could restore a measure of stability.[7] The disappearance of even such a basic commodity as pottery testifies to a fragmented society in which the humblest of crafts could no longer be pursued profitably, and the demise of the relatively complex mechanism of the watermill may have followed inexorably from the loss of the millwright's skill. Nevertheless, the possibility that the watermill remained in use in at least a few locations can not be excluded.

If the mill was lost to Dark Age Britain, it was reintroduced relatively quickly. The earliest documentary reference to an English mill comes in a charter dated 762, issued by AEthelberht, the king of Kent, and which concerned an already existing mill in the village of Chart; thereafter references in charters occur relatively frequently.[8] As might be expected, archaeology points to earlier use of the mill, with the massive machine excavated at Old Windsor in 1957 now having been firmly dated by dendrochronology to the late seventh century. How common the mill was in England by 700 there is as yet no way of telling, although seventh-century mills have been found in Ireland, the earliest being similarly dated to 630.[9] Enough Irish examples from succeeding centuries have been excavated to demonstrate how common the mill was there, and its place in Irish life was recognized

---

[7] P. Salway, Roman Britain (Oxford, 1981), pp. 454-501.

[8] Cartularium Saxonicum, ed. W de Gray Birch (London, 1885–99), 191; Anglo-Saxon Charters, P. H. Sawyer (ed.), (London, 1968), 25; P. Rahtz and D. Bullough, 'The Parts of an Anglo-Saxon Mill', in P. Clemoes (ed.), Anglo-Saxon England, 6 (Cambridge, 1977), pp. 18–19.

[9] 'Medieval Britain in 1957', Medieval Archaeology, 2 (1958), pp. 184–5; M. Baillie, 'Dendrochronology – the Irish view', Current Archaeology, 73 (August 1980), pp. 62–3.

when the codification of traditional Irish law, the *Senchus Mor*, referred to it in such a way as to accept that it was frequently the subject of disagreement and litigation.[10] Folk legend, for what it is worth, declared that the first mill had been built in Ireland by a prince anxious to preserve the charms of his favourite slave-girl from her daily task at the quern: accordingly he had sent for a millwright from over the sea – a story which perhaps embodies a distant memory that the mill had been introduced initially from Britain.[11]

The mill in general use in Ireland was quite unlike that described by Vitruvius, being the horizontal mill.[12] This is a simple yet effective machine, in which the wheel lies horizontally and drives the grinding stone above directly by means of a vertical shaft. There is no gearing, therefore, and little or no iron need be used in its construction. The reasons why some societies have preferred the horizontal mill to the Vitruvian or vertical model, and the circumstances surrounding its disappearance from England by the thirteenth century, will be examined in chapter 8; for the moment we shall consider the evidence for its origins and its use in England before the Conquest.

Many writers, assuming that the horizontal mill's presence along the north-western fringes of Europe was a sign of its having been spread by the Vikings, have called it the 'Norse mill'; alternatively, its use in the eastern Mediterranean has earned it the name of 'Greek mill'.[13] Neither name is appropriate. As we have seen, the Irish were already building horizontal mills at least 150 years before they saw a Viking, and in the South their use was certainly not confined to the Hellenic lands. Late Roman horizontal mills have been excavated at Gannes in France and at Chemtou in Tunisia, and it is probably a mistake to look for a separate pattern of diffusion for this more basic design.[14]

---

[10] *The Ancient Laws of Ireland, vol. 1: Introduction to Senchus Mor* (Dublin and London, 1865), pp. 124–5.

[11] R. Bennett and J. Elton, *History of Corn Milling*, 4 vols (London and Liverpool, 1898–1904), ii, pp. 81–2.

[12] A. T. Lucas, 'The horizontal mill in Ireland', *Journal of the Royal Soc. of Antiquaries of Ireland*, 83 (1953), pp. 1–36.

[13] Bennett and Elton, *History of Corn Milling*, ii, pp. 6, 12; L. Syson, *British Water Mills* (London, 1965), pp. 89–1; W. A. McCutcheon, 'Water power in the north of Ireland', *Trans. Newcomen Soc.*, 39, (1966–7), p. 67; R. Wailes, 'The "Greek" and "Norse" waterwheels', *Trans. Fourth Symposium of the International Molinological Soc.* 1977 (1982), pp. 163–4.

[14] Wikander, 'Archaeological evidence for early water-mills', pp. 157, 159.

Undoubtedly both types of mill were known to the ancient millwright, and knowledge of both spread to all parts of the Roman Empire and beyond. The horizontal mill was certainly not a sign of technical regression, or of cultural backwardness: the Irish used it by choice, just as they chose also to build vertical mills at Little Island, county Cork, in the seventh century, and at Morett, county Laoise, at the beginning of the eighth.[15]

In England, too, both types were known, although it is impossible to tell which of them predominated as so few early mills have as yet been discovered on this side of the Irish Sea. The mill at Old Windsor, on the Thames, has already been mentioned: it was an ambitious construction, employing three vertical water-wheels. Interestingly, after its destruction in the ninth or tenth century, it was replaced by a horizontal mill like the one excavated at Tamworth and now known to have been built in the 850s. The casual find at Stroud in Gloucestershire of what appears to be part of the wheel of another horizontal mill completes the sum of the evidence for the use of this pattern of mill in England.[16] Yet the evidence for the use of the vertical mill is no more substantial. It is not clear what sort of wheel drove the Anglo-Saxon mill at Wharram Percy in Yorkshire, although a vertical wheel was used in the eleventh-century mill at Castle Donington in Leicestershire.[17]

It is the meagreness of the hard evidence for Anglo-Saxon mills that makes such a marked contrast with their massive presence, by the eleventh century if not long before, in practically every part of England. The treatise describing the duties of the reeve of an estate and known as Gerefa takes it for granted that among the cares of the reeve will be a mill and its servants, whilst Domesday Book, compiled in 1086, confirms the ubiquity of the watermill.[18] Designed to record manor by manor those items which contributed to a lord's revenues, Domesday Book thus contains details of ploughlands, ploughteams, the number of peasant tenants, assets such as woods and fisheries, and mills. Several modern writers have extracted all of these references, and

[15] Ibid., p. 155.

[16] P. A. Rahtz, 'Medieval milling', in D. W. Crossley (ed.), Medieval Industry (Council for British Archaeology Research Report 40, London, 1981), p. 6.

[17] J. G. Hurst, 'The Wharram research project: results to 1983', Medieval Archaeology, 28 (1984), pp. 101–2; P. Clay, 'Castle Donington', Current Archaeology, 102 (Nov. 1986), pp. 208–11.

[18] W. Cunningham, The Growth of English Industry and Commerce during the Early and Middle Ages (Cambridge, 1905), pp. 571–6; Domesday Book (London, 1783).

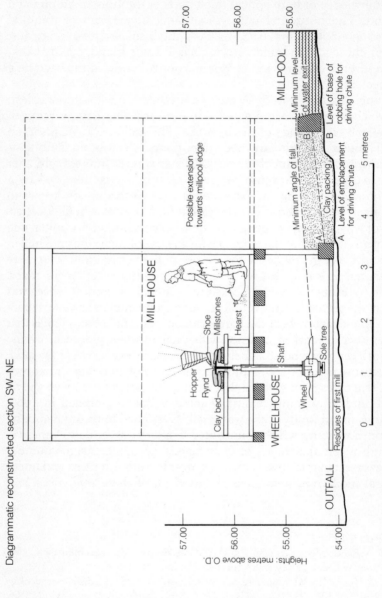

Diagrammatic reconstructed section SW–NE

MILLHOUSE

Possible extension towards millpool edge

MILLPOOL

Hopper
Rynd
Shoe
Millstones
Clay bed
Hearst
Shaft
WHEELHOUSE
Wheel
Sole tree
Residues of first mill
OUTFALL

Minimum level of water exit
Minimum angle of fall
Clay packing
Level of base of robbing hole for driving chute
Level of emplacement for driving chute

Heights: metres above O.D.

57.00
56.00
55.00
54.00

57.00
56.00
55.00

0   1   2   3   4   5 metres

Figure 1 Tamworth 1971 'The Second Mill'. Reproduced by kind permission of the excavator, Philip Rahtz.

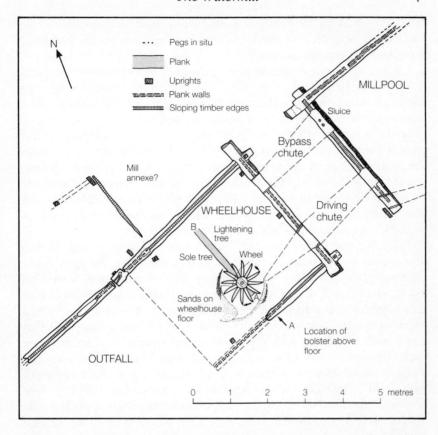

Figure 2 Tamworth 1971 'The Second Mill', restored plan of wheelhouse and foundation timbers. Reproduced by kind permission of the excavator, Philip Rahtz.

presented them in tabular form: Bennett and Elton listed the mills county by county in the 1890s; Margaret Hodgen enumerated and mapped them in 1939; and Sir Henry Darby and his associates similarly counted and mapped the entries for mills in the course of each of their county analyses.[19] Darby's totals are far more accurate than Hodgen's — which for some counties are seriously wrong — although it is her

[19] Bennett and Elton, *History of Corn Milling*, ii, pp. 150–80; M. Hodgen, 'Domesday water mills', *Antiquity*, 13 (1939), pp. 261–79; H. C. Darby, *The Domesday Geography of Eastern England* (Cambridge, 1952), pp. 72–4, 136–8, 188–90, 248–9, 307–9, 344–6; H. C. Darby and I. B. Terrett, *The Domesday Geography of Midland England*

total of 5,624 mills which is more often quoted than his better
calculation of 6,082. Nevertheless the distribution map she prepared
(see figure 3) remains useful.[20]

Of the northern counties only parts of Yorkshire were properly
surveyed in 1086, and so the distribution pattern is trustworthy only
for England south of the Humber. Notable concentrations are at once
apparent, as are districts from which the mill was entirely absent, or
where it was at best a rarity. Perhaps the most marked feature of the
map is the contrast between much of Norfolk, where there was a high
density of mills, and the neighbouring Fenland region of west Norfolk,
north Cambridgeshire, Huntingdonshire and south Lincolnshire where
there were none at all. Other regions with few recorded mills included
the Somerset Levels and the Weald, whilst there were concentrations
in the Cotswolds, in Suffolk and in Dorset.

Believing that within this distribution pattern lay concealed clues to
the course of the mill's diffusion in earlier centuries, Hodgen made
three suggestions: firstly that if geographical density of mill-sites be
taken as evidence of age, then the mill appeared first in Norfolk and
Lincolnshire; secondly if the many mill clusters, or sites where several
mills were to be found, were the oldest sites (on the assumption that
extra mills had been added only when experience had shown they
were needed), then Kent, Lincolnshire and Norfolk had seen the
earliest concentration of mills in England; thirdly if the number of
mills held as fractions denote age (on the assumption that they were
the outcome of sub-division through inheritance), then again Norfolk,
Lincolnshire, and now Wiltshire, were areas where the mill was longest
established.[21]

Although all three hypotheses stem from the mistaken assumption
that the watermill was still a relatively recent introduction to England
from the Continent, they should not simply be dismissed. Reginald

---

(Cambridge, 1954), pp. 41−2, 98−100, 147−9, 202−5, 257−8, 299−301, 344−6,
375−7, 407−9; H. C. Darby and I. S. Maxwell, *The Domesday Geography of Northern
England* (Cambridge, 1962), pp. 71−4, 150−2, 221−3, 268−70, 319−21, 376; H. C.
Darby and E. M. J. Campbell, *The Domesday Geography of South-East England*
(Cambridge, 1962), pp. 39−41, 83−5, 129−31, 174−6, 224−7, 269−71, 345−7,
394−6, 458−61, 540−3; H. C. Darby and R. W. Finn, *The Domesday Geography of
South-West England* (Cambridge, 1967), pp. 45−9, 112−15, 190−4, 276−8, 334.

[20] The Domesday mills are totalled in H. C. Darby, *Domesday England* (Cambridge,
1977), p. 361.

[21] Hodgen, 'Domesday water mills', p. 276 and *passim*.

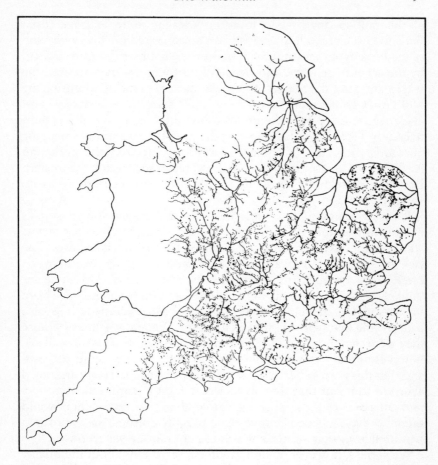

Figure 3 Sketch map of Domesday water mills and river systems.
Source: Antiquity, 1939, 13.

Lennard, too, wondered if the remarkably small total of mills in Cornwall — only six — and in Devon, west of the Exe, might not have been a sign that in 1086 the mill had only just begun to penetrate these most westerly counties.[22] Attractive as the thought may be that Domesday Book might have caught the bow-wave of the process of diffusion in its stately progression westwards, the image of a moving front of technical innovation can not now be sustained. For knowledge

[22] R. V. Lennard, *Rural England 1086–1135* (Oxford, 1959), p. 280.

of the mill to have taken four centuries or more to travel from
Berkshire to Cornwall is not credible; nor is it credible that with both
of the basic types of watermill in use on the southern coast of Ireland
by the seventh century, knowledge of it should not have crossed the
sea. In any case, the notion of a regular pattern of diffusion during the
Middle Ages becomes ever more dubious as the archaeological
evidence for early mills continues to mount. The isochronal pattern
traced by Terry Reynolds, showing the use of the watermill spreading
outwards from 'the few pockets' where it survived the barbarian
invasions of Gaul and northern Italy, to reach southern Italy, western
Britain and Ireland only in the ninth and tenth centuries, has no
validity.[23]

If we are searching for explanations for the uneven spread of mills
in eleventh-century England, we should do better to look for factors
which might have had a direct bearing on the use of waterpower. The
lack of mills in Cornwall can be accounted for in several ways:
carelessness on the part of the surveyors is one, though it seems
unlikely, as the settlements were recorded and there should have been
no reason for the mills alone to have been excluded. It is also
conceivable that Cornish mills escaped the Domesday survey because
they were somehow outside demesne ownership. What is more likely,
however, is that the watermill really was as rare as the record suggests,
and that this is an indication not that the peasants had some irrational
aversion to it but that they were accustomed to eating their corn —
particularly oats — as porridge rather than as bread. They would
therefore have needed only to have roughly crushed the grains in a
handmill or mortar — a task which did not require waterpower.

We should, however, maintain some reservations about the quality
of the evidence. In the case of the Weald, the apparent absence of
settlements and mills reflects the inadequacies of the work of the
surveyors rather than the situation as it was.[24] In general, however, the
distribution map does reveal genuine differences in the use of waterpower, as in the case of both the Fens and the Somerset Levels which
were clearly unsuited to the watermill. It was not lack of water that was
their problem, but lack of running water. There was one mill in the
Lincolnshire Fens, and none in the Fens of Cambridgeshire; only one
mill was to be found in the two hundreds of Flegg in the similar terrain

---

[23] Reynolds, *Stronger than a Hundred Men*, pp. 48–51.
[24] P. H. Sawyer, *Medieval Settlement* (London, 1976), pp. 1–4.

of the Norfolk Broads.[25] Counties with high densities of population, such as Norfolk and Lincolnshire, were served by large numbers of mills, although the counties with the greatest milling capacity per household were particularly those in the south-west: Somerset, Dorset, Wiltshire and Hampshire.[26] Here the annual rainfall and terrain together favoured the watermill, unlike the dry, flat eastern counties where the ripple of flowing water is rarely to be heard. In the populous hundred of Lothingland in Suffolk, only three villages out of thirty had mills; further inland in the hundreds of Hartesmere and Thedwestry mills were to be found in only seven out of fifty-three vills. The same picture is to be seen in the hundreds of Edwinstree and Odsey in Hertfordshire, and in large areas of Buckinghamshire.[27]

The geographical density of mill-sites and the many mill clusters which Hodgen found in Norfolk and Lincolnshire were most plausibly, then, the result of nothing more than the pressure of demand on a relatively limited number of streams that were suitable for milling. The same factor could also account for the abnormally high number of mills in shared tenure, if lords found it advantageous to develop scarce water resources in co-operation with their neighbours.

The only detail that Domesday Book records for each mill is its value. In Oxfordshire, to take the example of one county, there were 196 mills in 1086 and eleven tenurial fractions, which probably added up to a further seven or eight mills. Darby calculated a total of 203 mills for the county, which is quite acceptable.[28] For each of the 196 mills with single owners a cash rent is specified, in all amounting to £101 14s 3d, or an average of 10s 4½d per mill. Actually, the average figure conceals a wide variation in mill values between the lowest of 1s 8d, at Brightwell, and the highest, at Cowley, of £2 and £1 15s. In all there were twenty-eight mills valued at £1 or over, amounting to £30 17s 6d, whilst as many as forty-nine were worth 5s or less. All together, this latter group were worth only £8 8s 9d to their owners.

In Cambridgeshire the situation was very similar. Domesday Book recorded 124 mills, with a further ten halves and a sixth. Darby's total of 132 seems on balance to be correct, as only six of the halves can be

---

[25] Darby, *Domesday Geography of Eastern England*, pp. 75, 138, 309.

[26] Darby, *Domesday England*, p. 361.

[27] Darby, *Domesday Geography of Eastern England*, p. 190; *Domesday Geography of South-East England*, pp. 85, 175.

[28] *Domesday Book*, fols 148b, 154–61; Darby and Campbell, *Domesday Geography of South-East England*, pp. 224–7.

matched up.[29] Adding together the cash rents of the 127 mills we can be sure of, their value amounts to £78 5s, or an average of 12s 4d per mill. Again, thirty-one of the mills all together worth £44 1s 6d were each valued at £1 or more; eighteen others were worth 5s or less, and together were worth only £2 1s 4d. Cambridgeshire, therefore, had proportionately more valuable mills than Oxfordshire, and proportionately fewer mills of low value.

Huntingdonshire had thirty-six mills, a figure which Darby uncharacteristically miscounted as thirty-seven.[30] Their total value came to £42 13s 8d, giving a high average of £1 3s 8½d. Most of this was accounted for by the mills worth £1 or more, of which there were twenty-three worth together £37 7s; with the exception of six mills worth intermediate sums, the remaining seven of the county's mills were valued at 5s or less, and all together at only £1. The contrast between the high-value and the low-value mills was thus much higher than in Oxfordshire and Cambridgeshire.

The question of the significance of these and other mill values will recur in later chapters. For the moment it is only necessary to point out that some of the factors contributing to a mill's high value in these three sample counties were perfectly straightforward. In Oxfordshire high-value mills were to be found in and around Oxford itself, and in Cambridgeshire and Huntingdonshire the same clustering of high-value mills around the population centres of the county towns can be seen. More importantly, they tended to be on the major rivers. This is most obvious in Huntingdonshire, where all of the high and intermediate value mills were on the rivers Ouse and Nene, whilst all of the low-value mills were situated on the county's less significant watercourses. Even with elaborate systems of leats and water storage, streams like this can have provided very little power; as we shall see, it was these very mills which in later centuries, and particularly after the invention of the windmill, would be at a disadvantage. Marginal enterprises on inadequate streams were not uncommon in the eleventh century, and in Suffolk, Cheshire and Shropshire there were mills described in Domesday Book as 'winter mills' — situated presumably on streams which in the drier months of the year failed altogether.[31]

[29] *Domesday Book*, fols 189–203b; Darby, *Domesday Geography of Eastern England*, pp. 307–9.

[30] *Domesday Book*, fols 203–7c; Darby, *Domesday Geography of Eastern England*, pp. 344–6.

[31] *Domesday Book*, fols 255b, 263b, 265; ii, fols 304, 359, 359b, 361b, 365.

Rental values in later centuries were much higher, but do not show such a wide range: Anglo-Saxon lords were prepared to tolerate their mills paying little or no rent in a way that later lords clearly were not.

The potential power of each mill was not, of course, the only determinant of its value. As Reginald Lennard asked, with regard to a pair of these Huntingdonshire manors: how can it have been that Hartford, with twelve plough teams, had two mills worth £4, whilst Kimbolton, with thirty teams, had one mill worth 5s?[32] Hartford, on the Ouse, had greater potential as the site of a mill than did Kimbolton on the tiny River Kym; nevertheless, we might expect there to have been more demand for milled flour in Kimbolton than in Hartford. The conclusion, inevitably, is that, whereas a mill such as Kimbolton's processed only local grain, those on the major rivers drew much of their undoubtedly greater volume of custom from outside their localities, perhaps from a considerable distance.

To an extent this provides an answer to the question that needs to be asked not only for the eleventh century but for the later medieval centuries as well: what happened in those manors where there was no mill? How did the inhabitants of districts where mills were scarce, like the Fens, or parts of Essex, or the New Forest, contrive to grind their corn? Usually it has been assumed that the peasants must have continued with their traditional use of handmills, although the frequent finds of quernstones made by archaeologists on Anglo-Saxon sites cease to be a feature of sites dated to the later period.[33] This does not exclude the handmill from the reckoning, but suggests, as with the example of Hartford, that by the eleventh century the inhabitants of many villages had become accustomed to carrying their corn to mills outside their lordships.

What Domesday Book illustrates above all is that the rise of the watermill in England was an achievement of the centuries before the Conquest. As we shall see, watermills would continue to be built in those parts of the country where water resources outstripped the population, but otherwise any increase in their numbers would be slight. Yet, even in the eastern counties, milling capacity was not a static quantity. Already by the eleventh century there were mills going out of use, presumably while others were being built in better positions. The occasional references in Domesday Book to derelict mills, or to the sites of former mills, acquire more substance in the detailed folios

[32] Lennard, *Rural England*, p. 280.
[33] P. A. Rahtz, 'Medieval milling',

of Little Domesday Book, the volume that covers Norfolk, Suffolk and Essex. In these counties thirteen, eleven and sixteen villages respectively had, it was said, lost mills since 1066. Unfortunately it is not specified what proportion of the 1,014 mills in the three counties had been constructed within the same period.

It is possible to gain some insight into the rate at which there was a turnover of mills by looking forward into the next century, at one of the very earliest of the estate surveys. The manors belonging to Peterborough Abbey in the East Midlands were surveyed between 1125 and 1128, and the abbey is shown to have owned twenty-one mills, rented out for a total of £26 2s 4d.[34] Forty years earlier, these same manors had been served by an identical number of mills, but there had been more changes in the intervening years than this would suggest, with four of the twenty-one Domesday mills having disappeared by the 1120s and four others having been built.[35] Those that had gone were a mill worth 5s at Peterborough itself, a mill at Kettering, and two mills worth £1 at Collingham in Nottinghamshire; meanwhile a third mill at Alwalton and a second mill at Castor had been built, while both Great Easton and Fiskerton had acquired mills, apparently for the first time. As only £14 4s 4d had been collected in rent in 1086, it is also the case that the abbey had succeeded in the same period in almost doubling its revenue from this source (see table 1).

The same trends of mill sites going out of use while new ones appeared, coupled with growing values and now a continued modest rise in the overall number of mills, can be seen if we compare the twenty-three West Country manors of Glastonbury Abbey which possessed mills either in 1086 or when the abbey's lands were surveyed a century later in 1189.[36] The underlying congruity of the two surveys is apparent, with the twenty-eight mills of 1086 becoming thirty-one by the time of the later survey; the accumulation of changes over this longer period is of course more obvious than on the Peterborough estates, with only nine manors having the same number of mills that were attributed to them in Domesday Book. In this wetter, more undulating landscape, there was still a clear trend towards greater use

[34] *Chronicon Petroburgense*, ed. T. Stapleton (Camden Soc., old ser., 47, London, 1849), pp. 157–83.

[35] *Domesday Book*, fols 221–2, 231, 284, 345b.

[36] *Liber Henrici de Soliaco: An Inquisition of the Manors of Glastonbury Abbey of the Year 1189*, ed. J. E. Jackson (Roxburghe Club, London, 1882), *passim*; *Domesday Book*, fols 59b, 66b, 67b, 72b, 90, 90b, 165.

Table 1   Mills on seventeen Peterborough Abbey Manors:
1086 and 1125

Manor	1086 Number	Value	1125 Number	Rent
Kettering	2	20s	1	20s
Tinwell	2	24s	2	35s
Oundle	1	20s	1	40s
Pilsgate	1	10s	1	4s
Collingham	2	20s	0	
Cottingham	1	3s 4d	1	20s
Great Easton	0		1	13s 4d
Warmington	1	40s	1	60s
Alwalton	2	40s	3	82s
Peterborough	1	5s	0	
Pytchley	1	8s	1	26s
Ashton	2	40s	2	60s
Castor	1	8s	2	60s
Fiskerton	0		1	3s
Scotter	2	8s	2	20s
Irthlingborough	1	18s	1	20s
Stanwick	1	20s	1	59s

of the mill. Only three manors had lost all of their milling capacity, whilst seven or eight had acquired it during the century, probably for the first time. The rise in Glastonbury's income from milling was in line with Peterborough Abbey's, the total of mill rents having more than doubled from £10 19s to £21 15s 4d (see table 2).

In both of these cases, it is the profitability of milling that highlights the lack of any major increase in the provision of mills after 1086. Clearly demand was not stagnant, and it can only be concluded that with few exceptions all viable streams and rivers had indeed already been exploited. In East Anglia and elsewhere there was little possibility of any increase in the number of mill-sites, and so only those communities that were already favoured could benefit from a more efficient use of water resources. If Domesday Book demonstrates the extent of the triumph of the watermill in Anglo-Saxon society, it also

The Watermill

reveals its limitations: that because of its uneven distribution, waterpower alone would never be sufficient to mill the flour that the people of medieval England needed.

Table 2   Mills on twenty-three Glastonbury Abbey Manors:
1086 and 1189

Manor	1086 Number	Value	1189 Number	Rent
Pilton	2	10s	2	21s 4d
Batcombe	1	5s	1	18s
Ditcheat	1	7s 5d	1	16s
Butleigh	0		1	13s 4d
High Ham	0		1	6s
Westonzoyland	0		1	20s
Shapwick	0		1	3s
Street	Not in Domesday Book		1	11s 2d
East Brent	0		2	40s 6d
Winscombe	1	5s	1	10s
Wrington	3	14s 2d	3	54s
Pucklechurch	2	8s 4d	1	4s
Nettleton	3	22s 6d	3	26s
Christian Malford	2	40s	2	55s
Ashbury	2	22s 6d	2	20s
Badbury	1	3s 4d	0	
Winterborne Monkton	1	15s	0	
Idmiston	0		1	20s
Damerham	4	20s	3	55s
Sturminster Newton	3	40s	2	19s
Kentlesworth/Marnhull	1	3s 9d	1	20s
Buckland Newton	0		1	3s
Kington St Michael	1	2s	0	

2

The Windmill

As well as counting the mills of each county in the separate volumes of *The Domesday Geography of England*, Sir Henry Darby and his assistants frequently drew attention to those regions where the number of mills was far below what might be expected. Particular attention was drawn to Cornwall and Devon, but parts of ten other counties were identified that had a disproportionately low number of mills compared with their population: the East Riding of Yorkshire, Cheshire, Norfolk, Suffolk, Essex, Middlesex, Hertfordshire, Buckinghamshire, Kent and Sussex.[1] The inhabitants of these districts had no choice but to mill at some distance from their homes, or to rely on handmills. Only a new source of power altogether could prove a satisfactory remedy for their acute lack of usable water courses.

It is not clear when horsemills began to be used in medieval England. Ubiquitous throughout the Ancient World, and in their simplest form little more than large handmills, there is no technical reason why beast-driven mills should not have been employed in Anglo-Saxon England.[2] This was, after all, a culture able to cope with the considerably more complex mechanisms of the watermill, and we may suspect, therefore, that horsemills were in use long before the earliest known reference to one, at Oxen-le-Flatts in county Durham in 1183.[3] If the Domesday commissioners had regarded them as domestic devices they would as a consequence have been ignored, and so their apparent absence from Domesday Book would be explained. Neither should

[1] Darby and Finn, *Domesday Geography of South-West England*, pp. 276–8, 334; Darby and Maxwell, *Domesday Geography of Northern England*, pp. 222, 376; Darby, *Domesday Geography of Eastern England*, pp. 138, 190, 249; Darby and Campbell, *Domesday Geography of South-East England*, pp. 131, 85, 175, 461, 543.

[2] Moritz, *Grain Mills and Flour in Classical Antiquity, passim*. For a discussion of the use of horsemills mainly in the modern period, see F. Atkinson, 'The horse as a source of rotary power', *Trans. Newcomen Soc.*, 33 (1960–1), pp. 31–55.

[3] *Boldon Book*, ed. D. Austin (Chichester, 1982), p. 61.

the lack of identifiable remains be taken as proof of their non-existence; when so few pre-Conquest watermills have been excavated, it is hardly surprising that the much less substantial and probably less recognizable structures of horsemills should have escaped the notice of archaeologists.

In this context it may be worth reconsidering the curious complex of buildings which formed part of the Anglo-Saxon palace of Cheddar, in Somerset, and to which the excavator, Philip Rahtz, assigned the title of Structure X. In use during the tenth century, when the palace was a favourite residence of the Wessex kings, Structure X consisted of a circular building some eighteen or nineteen feet across, to which were attached on the north and the south two rectangular buildings nineteen feet by eleven. The three buildings had interconnecting doorways, and the circular building had at its centre a roughly circular platform eight feet in diameter, raised about one foot above the surrounding floor. This was interpreted as a hen-house by Professor Rahtz (following the pattern of two circular buildings for hens and geese shown on the ninth-century plan of the monastery of St Gall in what is now Switzerland), with the southern rectangular building, which had contained an oven, being the residence of the man responsible for the birds.[4]

Professor Rahtz's original interpretation of this structure as a mill is surely better fitted to the evidence. There was a circular track, suitable in size for a horse to walk around, whilst fenced off in the centre was space for the simple mechanism. The building adjoining could then more plausibly be interpreted as a bakehouse.[5] Evidence for the corn-milling that took place somewhere within the palace precincts was provided by the several pieces of rotary quernstone that were found, and by the fragment of a stone, four feet ten inches in diameter, that was far too large to have been used in any but a mechanical mill of some description.[6]

Without any more definite indication of the existence of horsemills in England before 1183, it is fruitless to speculate on the extent to which they may have served the needs of the many people who during the eleventh and twelfth centuries still had no easy access to a

[4] P. A. Rahtz, *The Saxon and Medieval Palaces at Cheddar: Excavations 1960–62* (BAR, British ser., 65, London, 1979), pp. 124–32.

[5] P. A. Rahtz, 'The Saxon and medieval palaces at Cheddar', *Medieval Archaeology*, 6–7 (1962–3), pp. 61–2.

[6] Rahtz, *The Saxon and Medieval Palaces at Cheddar*, pp. 234–6.

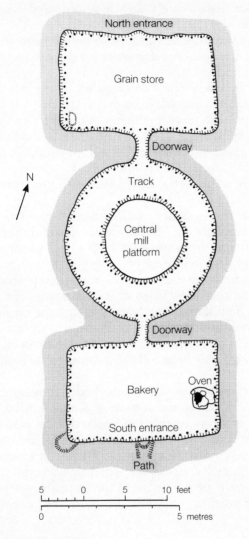

North entrance

Grain store

Doorway

N

Track

Central
mill
platform

Doorway

Oven

Bakery

South entrance

Path

5   0   5   10 feet

0   5 metres

Figure 4 Cheddar Corn Mill
Source: Medieval Archaeology, 1962–3, 6–7.

watermill. The community dwelling at Peterborough Abbey apparently had their flour milled by hand in 1125, there being then two kitchen servants retained solely for that purpose; in 1251, though, it was taken for granted that the bakers and the villeins of Wisbech, in the absence of any manorial mill, would very likely have provided themselves with their own horsemills.[7]

But it was the windmill that proved to be the inspired solution to the problem of the lack of waterpower, to the extent that within a century of its introduction, recorded first in 1185, it had become a common sight in many parts of England. There are in fact two references to English windmills from that year: one to an existing mill at Weedley, near South Cave, in the East Riding of Yorkshire, and the other to a mill built since 1180 at Amberley in Sussex by Bishop Seffrid II of Chichester. We are told of a third windmill, at Dinton in Buckinghamshire, around 1187, and then follows an explosion of references, with a further twenty windmills that can be dated confidently to the 1190s.[8]

Together with the evidence of twelfth-century estate surveys — such as that of the Ramsey Abbey manors, made during the 1160s, and the Glastonbury Abbey survey of 1189 — that windmills were not yet in use, the sudden occurrence of this group of references indicates that the first windmill had indeed been constructed probably not long before 1185, and that knowledge of it had rapidly spread.[9] Found before 1200 on both sides of the North Sea and the English Channel — along the south and east coasts of England, and in Flanders and northern France — and only in those locations, we can be certain that the windmill's origins lay here and not in southern or eastern Europe, or in Asia.

European historians have always assumed a continental origin for the windmill. In fact, in so far as its origins may now be traced, it is equally likely that it was invented in England, most plausibly in East Anglia. The impressive number of references to English windmills from before 1200 compares with at most five continental examples that have been quoted, the earliest apparently being the mill at Sainte Martin de Varreville, near Liesville in the Cotentin, referred to in an undated charter assigned, somewhat arbitrarily, by Léopold Delisle to

[7] Chronicon Petroburgense, p. 167; Brit. Lib., Cotton Claud. Cxi, fols 74, 76.

[8] E. J. Kealey's assertion that the windmill was recorded in England as early as 1137 cannot be sustained by the evidence he cites: Harvesting the Air: Windmill Pioneers in Twelfth-Century England (Woodbridge, 1987), pp. 59–78, and passim. Full details of all the windmills to which there are references dating from before 1200 may be found in Appendix 1.

[9] Cartularium Monasterii de Rameseia, 3 vols, ed. W. H. Hart and P. A. Lyons (Rolls Series, London, 1884–94), iii, pp. 241–90; Liber Henrici de Soliaco, passim.

1180.[10] A second reference quoted by Anne-Marie Bautier to a windmill at Pontieu, near the mouth of the Somme, dates from 1191−2.[11] Paul Bauters in 1982 cast doubts upon Delisle's dating of the Norman mill, and for the earliest references pointed instead to three mills all in Flanders − at Wormhoudt, Silly and Ypres − recorded in 1183, 1195 and 1197.[12]

A-M. Bautier understandably saw as further evidence of the French origins of the windmill a well-known decretal of Pope Celestine III (1191−8), which affirmed that windmills were liable to payment of tithes. According to the final version of the decretal, the original query had been addressed to the papal court by a Breton cleric, the archdeacon of Dol de Bretagne, who complained that a knight had built a windmill in his parish and refused to pay tithes on it; an examination of earlier texts, however, has recently shown that the papal order that the knight should be made to pay was addressed to the Abbot of Ramsey and the Archdeacon of Ely.[13] Wherever the complainant had his church, then, it was not at Dol, but at some place in eastern England whose name had been corrupted by the Italian copyist.[14]

Doubtless there remain to be discovered more references of this sort on both sides of the Channel, which may in time illuminate further the windmill's earliest years. Evidence from the thirteenth century indicates that however wide its initial diffusion it was not adopted in any great numbers for some time. Perhaps the design had yet to be perfected, and there were still technical difficulties; perhaps many lords felt it not worth investing precious capital in what was still a

---

[10] L. Delisle, *Études sur la Condition de la Classe Agricole et l'État de l'Agriculture en Normandie au Moyen Age* (Évreux, 1851/Paris, 1903), p. 514, n. 17.

[11] A-M. Bautier, 'Les Plus Anciennes Mentions de Moulins Hydrauliques Industriels et de Moulins à Vent', *Bulletin Philologique et Historique*, 2 (1960), p. 611.

[12] P. Bauters, 'The oldest references to windmills in Europe', *Trans. of the Fifth Symposium of the International Molinological Soc., 1982* (Saint-Maurice, 1984), pp. 111-19.

[13] Bautier, 'Les Plus Anciennes Mentions de Moulins', pp. 613−4; M. G. Cheney, 'The Decretal of Pope Celestine III on Tithes of Windmills, JL 17620', *Bulletin of Medieval Canon Law*, New ser., 1 (1971), pp. 63−6.

[14] Mary Cheney's tentative suggestion that the archdeacon in question was Burchard, the archdeacon of Durham, *Dunelm'* having been misread by the copyist, is a rather eccentric one given the identity of the addressees. E. J. Kealey, in *Harvesting the Air*, accepts the identification far too readily, and fails to indicate how improbable it is: pp. 180−2, 216.

speculative venture. Fortunately, although manorial and other evidence for the number of windmills is copious only from around 1250 onwards, the documentation of one or two estates makes it possible to identify the crucial decades when most windmills were being built.

The bishopric of Ely held some fifty manors, chiefly in Cambridgeshire, but also in Norfolk, Huntingdonshire, Suffolk, Hertfordshire and Essex. Not surprisingly, given the character of these counties, few of the manors had watermills in 1086: in all there were twenty-two situated in just twelve of the manors.[15] In short, this was just the sort of estate that we might expect to have welcomed the windmill with enthusiasm. Yet when it was surveyed in 1222, thirty-seven years after the first record of an English windmill, there were only four listed, at Pulham and Terrington in Norfolk.[16] Maybe these were pilot projects, the performance of which was being carefully monitored, because what the evidence shows is that it was soon after this date that the building of windmills on the bishop's manors began in earnest. When the estate was surveyed again in 1251 there were now thirty-two windmills, nine of them being described as new to account for the lack of available information as to their profitability.[17] The conclusion that the 1230s and particularly the 1240s had been a time of intense windmill-building activity is inescapable, but all the signs are that by 1251 the main force of this activity had abated. Although for a further five manors still without mills it was noted that there could be a windmill if the lord wished, in the event only four of these mills were

[15] The mills belonging to Ely in 1086 had been at Hatfield (4) in Hertfordshire; at Balsham and at Great Shelford (2) in Cambridgeshire; at Littlebury (4) in Essex; at Feltwell, Bridgeham (2), Northwold (2) Pulham and Dereham in Norfolk; at Bramford (2), Glemsford, and Barking in Suffolk: *Domesday Book*, fols 135, 190, 191b; ii, fols 19, 213, 213b, 214b, 227, 281b, 289b, 382, 382b.

[16] Two windmills at Pulham were worth £5 a year, and two mills at Terrington were worth £2 17s 4d. These were probably windmills, as they were quite clearly not low-value watermills that would be replaced by the two windmills recorded for the manor in 1251: Brit. Lib., Cotton MS Tib. Bii, fols 184, 236v, 86–241.

[17] Brit. Lib., Cotton MS Claud. Cxi, fols 25–312. The windmills described as new were at Downham, Littleport, Doddington, Wisbech, Triplow and Little Gransden in Cambridgeshire, Totteridge and Hadham in Hertfordshire, and Walpole in Norfolk. The other twenty-three were at Ely (2), Linden End, Willingham, Ditton and Balsham in Cambridgeshire; Somersham (3) in Huntingdonshire; Kelshall in Hertfordshire; Rettendon in Essex; Terrington (2), Pulham (2), Dereham, Shipdham (2) and Feltwell in Norfolk; Rattlesden, Hitcham, Wetheringsett and Brandon in Suffolk.

built, and only eight more windmills would appear on the estate before the end of the century.[18]

Between 1222 and 1251 the number of the bishop's watermills apparently remained steady, at twenty.[19] Evidently the watermill and windmill were not in competition, and on the manors where there had been powered milling during the eleventh century there were no more than six windmills built during the thirteenth century.[20] Only at Pulham and at Balsham, Cambridgeshire, was waterpower abandoned in favour of the windmill, and in the latter case there was no direct replacement: the mill that had been worth as little as four shillings in 1086 had gone by 1222, and the windmill there was built after that date.[21]

The situation on the other large estates of eastern England seems to have been similar, although none of them is documented by two such comprehensive surveys made so opportunely to register the windmill's arrival. As Pope Celestine's decretal of the 1190s had been addressed to the Abbot of Ramsey, we can be quite sure that the abbey, with its manors lying principally in the fenlands of Huntingdonshire, was before 1200 aware both of the windmill's existence and of its potential value. Just as on the neighbouring Ely manors, watermilling capacity was inadequate, with only eleven Ramsey manors possessing in 1086 fourteen mills between them; this figure was to fall within a very few years, as low-value mills at Wistow and Broughton in Huntingdonshire

[18] At Leverington, Wells, and Hardwick in Cambridgeshire; at West Walton in Norfolk; at Hartest in Suffolk (ibid.). By 1298 windmills had appeared on all these manors with the exception of Wells, and eight more had been built at Stretham, Tydd and Wisbech in Cambridgeshire; Terrington and Walpole in Norfolk; Glemsford and Barking in Suffolk: PRO, SC 6/1132/10.

[19] In 1251 there were watermills at Great Shelford, Fen Ditton and Triplow in Cambridgeshire; Hatfield (2) and Hadstock (2) in Hertfordshire; Littlebury (2) in Essex; Dereham (2), Feltwell, Bridgeham (2) and Northwold (2) in Norfolk; Barking, Glemsford and Bramford (2) in Suffolk: Brit. Lib., Cotton MS. Claud. Cxi, fols 25–312. The mills at Fen Ditton, Hatfield, Feltwell, Glemsford and Bramford were not recorded in 1222, but as Domesday Book recorded watermills for all but Fen Ditton, it would be rash to assume that the situation around 1250 was substantially different from that of earlier years: Brit. Lib., Cotton MS Tib. Bii, fols 86–241.

[20] At Balsham, Pulham, Dereham and Feltwell by 1251, and at Glemsford and Barking by 1298: Brit. Lib., Cotton Claud. Cxi, fols 121v, 202, 215, 246v–7; PRO, SC 6/1132/10.

[21] Domesday Book, fols 190; ii, 214b; Brit. Lib., Cotton MSS Tib. Bii, fols 126v–9v, 184; Claud. Cxi, fols 121v, 202.

and at Barton in Bedfordshire went out of use and were not mentioned in the twelfth-century surveys of the estate.[22] Again, though, this great ecclesiastical lord was at first cautious of the new device, and surveys of several of the manors made around 1200 show no sign of its introduction. Perhaps it was a windmill that Wistow possessed in 1216, there being certainly one there in 1252. Elsworth in Cambridgeshire also had a windmill later in the century, and there, too, we may suppose that the mill first recorded in 1216 had been powered by wind.[23] By 1252 at least six of the abbey's manors had windmills and another, at Burwell, was built in 1259.[24] When the next full survey of the estate was made in 1279 Ramsey had thirteen watermills and now twenty-one windmills.[25] Interestingly, only one of the windmills directly replaced a watermill: that at Holm in Norfolk, which the abbot in 1243 allowed a free tenant there to build on the site of the former watermill.[26]

So far we have looked only at the situation in the eastern counties. Elsewhere in England both the debut and the wider adoption of the windmill would come rather later, and the sharp contrast at the end of its first century between the windmill's acceptance in the east and the caution still being shown in relatively well-watered counties is nowhere seen to better advantage than in the Hundred Rolls of 1279. Now surviving only in fragmentary form, this great survey commissioned by Edward I was intended, like the Domesday survey of two centuries previously, to reveal the true extent of personal and institutional holdings of land. Much more elaborate than Domesday, each hundred was to be surveyed systematically, village by village, the tenants of each manor enumerated, and their holdings and obligations described. The enrolments we have, as printed by the Record Commissioners in 1818, cover most of the counties of Oxfordshire, Cambridgeshire and

---

[22] In 1086 there had been mills belonging to Ramsey Abbey at Burwell (2) in Cambridgeshire; Broughton, Elton (2), Hemingford, Houghton, Wistow and Wyton in Huntingdonshire; Shillington, Pegsdon (2) and Barton in Bedfordshire; Brancaster in Norfolk: *Domesday Book*, fols 192b, 204, 204b, 210b; ii, fols 215b; *Cartularium de Rameseia*, iii, pp. 241–90.

[23] Ibid., i, pp. 354, 273–4; ii, p. 217.

[24] Broughton, Wistow, Stukeley, Ringstead and Holm, Cranfield and Ripton: ibid., i, pp. 333, 354, 397; ii, 313–17; PRO, SC 6/740/7; 875/6. For the Burwell windmill see *Cartularium de Rameseia*, ii, pp. 227–8.

[25] Ibid., i, 267–80. E. J. Kealey dated this survey to around 1250, but it was obviously compiled in 1279, at the same time as the details of Ramsey's properties were included in the Hundred Rolls.

[26] Ibid., ii, p. 313.

Huntingdonshire, and provide most valuable source material for many aspects of English social and economic history.[27] For present purposes, the holdings of mills they record for each village enable a territorial milling pattern to be established.

So far as Oxfordshire is concerned, there are adequate enrolments of eleven of the fourteen hundreds, together with one for the town of Oxford. It is plain that the windmill had in 1279 as yet made very little impact on the county, there being just four of them, at South Stoke, Bucknell, Launton and Kirtlington — against a total of 144 recorded watermills.[28] At the end of its first century the windmill was thus of only marginally greater importance in Oxfordshire than the horsemill — of which there were two listed, both in Oxford itself.[29] By contrast the surviving enrolments for eight of Cambridgeshire's fifteen hundreds give notice of the windmill's triumph. Here there were thirty-one watermills, but fifty windmills.[30] In the dry parts of the county especially — the hundreds of Chesterton, Papworth, Northstow and Longstow, to the north and west of Cambridge — the transformation was most marked: there the only two watermills of 1086 had both disappeared, to be replaced by thirty-nine windmills.[31]

If the surveys of the Cambridgeshire Fens which comprised the two hundreds of the Isle of Ely had survived, then the extent to which the windmill had come to predominate would have been even more apparent. Not surprisingly, in 1086 this region that accounted for half of the land area of the county had had no mills at all, its flat, waterlogged terrain being quite unsuitable for the application of waterpower.[32] This was where the Bishop of Ely and the Abbot of Ramsey were great lords and, as we have seen, by the 1270s their commitment to the windmill was assured, with ten of their fenland manors together having thirteen windmills and two horsemills.[33]

[27] *Rotuli Hundredorum*, ii, ed. W. Illingworth and J. Caley (Record Commission, London, 1818). Material from the Hundred Rolls has been presented and interpreted most effectively by E. A. Kosminsky, *Studies in the Agrarian History of England in the Thirteenth Century* (Oxford, 1956).

[28] Ibid., pp. 750, 826, 832, 839 and pp. 688–877, *passim*.

[29] Ibid., pp. 788, 791.

[30] Ibid., pp. 356–590.

[31] Ibid., pp. 402–12, 446–82, 507–40. *Domesday Book*, fols 195, 201.

[32] Darby, *Domesday Geography of Eastern England*, p. 309.

[33] The ten manors were Chatteris, Ely, Downham, Littleport, Stretham, Linden End, Doddington, Wisbech, Leverington, Tydd: *Cartularium de Rameseia*, i, p. 276; Brit. Lib., Cotton MS Claud. Cxi, fols 26, 35, 39v, 44v, 54v, 74; PRO, SC 6/1132/9, 10.

Enrolments for all four Huntingdonshire hundreds are extant, and complete the picture of what had happened in and around the Fens. Twenty-eight watermills were recorded, with most of the county's milling capacity provided by the one horsemill and forty-eight windmills.[34]

It is the drawback of the Hundred Rolls that as they cover so little of England it is impossible to use them to construct generalizations with more than a local application. The question of where at the end of its first century the windmill was already in widespread use, and where it had as yet made little impact, is not to be answered by the obvious contrast between Oxfordshire on the one hand and Cambridgeshire and Huntingdonshire on the other. Fortunately, a spread of manorial documentation from several other counties is available to provide comparative data. By far the best of this is for Suffolk. An extensive survey known as the Itinerary of Solomon of Rochester, and preserved in two cartularies of the Abbey of Bury St Edmunds, has been shown to date from 1279 or 1280; to be in fact derived from, or otherwise associated with, the now lost Hundred Rolls.[35] Intended as a permanent record of the tenurial status of all the abbey's holdings of land, it is as a consequence not just a survey of its manors in the western part of Suffolk but describes even those manors in which the abbey had only a marginal interest. Mills were recorded in seventy-one villages in the hundreds of Hartesmere, Babergh, Thedwestry, Thingoe, Blackbourn and Lackford, and perhaps predictably by this date almost two-thirds were windmills — sixty-five as against thirty-four watermills. On the eastern side of the county, on eighteen manors belonging to the Earl of Norfolk, documentation from around 1270 shows that the proportion was exactly the same, with nineteen windmills to ten watermills.[36]

The Norfolk evidence tells the same story. Five manors belonging to Norwich Cathedral Priory are documented for this period, together with nine belonging to the Bishop of Ely, four belonging to the Abbot

---

[34] *Rotuli Hundredorum*, ii, pp. 591–687.

[35] *The Pinchbeck Register*, 2 vols, ed. F. Hervey (Brighton, 1925), ii, pp. 30–281; for the dating of this survey see Kosminsky, *Studies in the Agrarian History of England in the Thirteenth Century*, p. 8.

[36] The manors were Bungay, Hollesley, Hoo, Kelsale, Peasenhall, Walton, Clopton, Cratfield, Dunningworth, Hacheston, Moulton, Nayland, Soham, Sproughton, Staverton, Stonham, Syleham and Framlingham: PRO, C 132/38/17; SC 6/994/14, 27; 995/15; 998/11; 1002/17; 1003/1; 1004/1; 1005/6, 7, 24, 1006/29; *Medieval Framlingham: Select Documents 1270–1524*, ed. J. Ridgard (Suffolk Recs. Soc., 27, Woodbridge, 1985), pp. 22, 27.

of Ramsey and sixteen belonging to the Earl of Norfolk.[37] During the 1270s these thirty-four manors possessed thirty-four windmills and seventeen watermills, in the same ratio of two to one as was to be found in Suffolk and Huntingdonshire, and doubtless in Cambridgeshire too. Eight Hertfordshire manors had between them, in by now familiar proportions, six windmills and three watermills, but as we move further into the Midlands the number of windmills falls away sharply, so of the thirty mills whose existence can be traced in Bedfordshire around 1279 only six were windmills, and of thirty-six known mills in Buckinghamshire ten were windmills.[38] The situation in the West Midlands counties, however, was still not identical to that in Oxfordshire, the unpublished Hundred Rolls for the two Warwickshire hundreds of Stoneleigh and Kineton listing ten windmills in five locations. The far less comprehensive documentation for the other counties records four windmills in Gloucestershire by the 1270s, although none as yet in Worcestershire.[39]

[37] The manors were Eaton, Hindolveston, Hindringham, Plumstead and Sedgeford: Norfolk CRO, DCN 60/8, 18, 20, 29, 33; Terrington, Walpole, West Walton, Pulham, Dereham, Shipdham, Bridgeham, Feltwell and Northwold: Brit. Lib., Cotton MS Claud. Cxi, fols 174, 184v, 191v, 202, 215, 227v, 241, 246v–247, 251v; PRO, SC 6/1132/9; 1132/10; Popinho, Brancaster, Hilgay and Walsoken: PRO, SC 6/942/12; *Cartularium de Rameseia*, i, p. 277; Banham, Ditchingham, Forncett, Hanworth, Acle, Attleborough, Bressingham, Caistor-cum-Markshall, Earsham, Framingham, Halvergate, Loddon, Lopham, Senges, Suffield and Walsham: PRO, C 132/38/17; SC 6/929/1, 14; 931/21; 932/11, 26; 934/12, 39; 935/20, 37; 936/2; 937/22, 27; 943/10; 944/1, 21, 31.

[38] The Hertfordshire manors were Kelshall, Hatfield, Totteridge, Little Hadham, Standon, Stevenage, Weston and Therfield: Brit. Lib. Cotton MS Claud. Cxi, fols 142v, 146, 152, 153v; PRO, SC 6/1132/9, 10; 868/17, 19; 870/9; 873/13; 872/19. Details of the Bedfordshire mills come from the fragment of the Hundred Rolls for the county, and from the manors of Shillington, Cranfield and Barton: *Rotuli Hundredorum*, ii, pp. 321–33; *Cartularium de Rameseia*, i, pp. 276–7. Details of the Buckinghamshire mills are drawn similarly from the Hundred Rolls and from the manors of Ivinghoe and West Wycombe: *Rotuli Hundredorum*, ii, pp. 334–55; Hampshire CRO, Winchester Pipe Roll 1283–4, Eccl. ii, 159306.

[39] PRO, E 164/15. The Gloucestershire windmills were at Wytewell, Tockington, *Linkeholte* and Henbury-in-Salt-Marsh: *Abstracts of Inquisitions Post Mortem for Gloucestershire*, iv, ed. S. J. Madge and E. A. Fry (British Rec. Soc., 30, London, 1903), pp. 27, 73; *Historia et Cartularium Monasterii Sancti Petri Gloucestriae*, ed. W. H. Hart (Rolls Ser., 3 vols, 1863–7), iii, p. 42; *Red Book of Worcester*, p. 403. I am grateful to J. L. Langdon for providing me with these details from his work on the mills of the West Midlands.

In south-western England the windmill's existence had scarcely been noticed. The twenty Hampshire manors and boroughs of the Bishop of Winchester had but two windmills to thirty-six watermills, and eleven manors in Wiltshire had between them one windmill and fourteen watermills.[40] Further to the west, it seems that windmills were to be found only in Somerset, as the sixteen manors and boroughs of the earldom of Cornwall that were surveyed in 1296 had none, and on eight manors in Devon and Dorset only eleven watermills were to be found.[41] All four of the Somerset windmills on a sample of twenty-eight manors had been built by Glastonbury Abbey on the Levels;[42] on the uplands of the county only the watermill was in use, a situation confirmed by evidence from the years before 1300 of fifteen more Somerset manors. Apart from two windmills at Yatton, another low-lying settlement, and nearby Congresbury, these manors had twenty-four watermills.[43]

It is the Glastonbury evidence that demonstrates just how little interest there was in the windmill in this region, despite the clear need

[40] The Bishop's windmills were at Burghclere and at Hambledon: Hampshire CRO, Winchester Pipe Roll 1283 – 4, Eccl. ii, 159306; the Wiltshire windmill was at Winterborne Monkton, and the other Wiltshire manors in this sample were Idmiston, Badbury, Damerham (4), Longbridge Deverill (2), Monkton Deverill, Nettleton (3) and Christian Malford: Longleat MS 11,244; *Rentalia et Custumaria Michaelis de Ambresbury, 1235 – 1252, et Rogeri de Ford, 1252 – 1261*, ed. C. J. Elton (Somerset Rec. Soc., 5, 1891), p. 166; Brit. Lib., Add. MS. 17450, fols 186, 189v, 212v, 215; Egerton MS 3321, fols 238v, 239, 248.

[41] *Ministers' Accounts of the Earldom of Cornwall, 1296 – 1297*, ii, ed. L. M. Midgley (Camden 3rd ser., 68, 1945), *passim*; the Devon manors in this sample were Exminster, Tiverton (3), Yarcombe and Uplyme, and the Dorset manors were Marnhull or Burton, Sturminster Newton (2), Buckland Newton and Maiden Newton: K. Ugawa, 'The economic development of some Devon manors in the thirteenth century', *Trans. Devonshire Assoc.*, 94 (1962), pp. 644, 657; Devon CRO, CR 1436; Brit. Lib., Add. MS 17450, fols 221v, 195v, 197, 201v.

[42] The twenty-eight manors were Butleigh, Othery, High Ham, Walton, Glastonbury, Westonzoyland, Ashcot, Ditcheat, South Brent, Shapwick, Lympsham, Berrow, Wrington, Doulting, Baltonsborough, Meare, Mells, East Brent, Middle Zoy, Street, Marksbury, East Pennard, Pilton, Batcombe, Minehead, Dunster, Taunton, Rimpton: *Rentalia et Custumaria*, pp. 5, 23, 152; Longleat MS 10,762; Brit. Lib., Add. MS 17450, fols 106v, 120 – 32, 138v, 140v, 141v, 155, 190, 204, 221, 230; Longleat MS 11,244; Somerset CRO, DD/L P1/1; Hampshire CRO, Eccl. ii, 159306.

[43] Banwell, Blackford, Cheddar, Chew Magna, Claverton and Bathampton, Compton Bishop, Congresbury, Evercreech, Huish Episcopi, Wellington, Wells, the borough of Wells, Wiveliscombe, Wookey and Yatton: PRO, SC 6/1131/3, 4, 6.

for it. For instance, those manors of Glastonbury Abbey that were situated on the Somerset Levels had as little recourse to the watermill in 1086 as did the Fenland settlements of the east, yet they were slower to take up the new device. Writing in the next century, the abbey's chronicler, Adam of Domerham, praised the abbot elected in 1234, Michael of Amesbury, for his determination to restore Glastonbury's fortunes; amongst his reforms, according to Adam, was a programme of mill-building, the progress of which can be traced independently through the abbey's records.[44] A series of surveys of his manors made for Abbot Michael, apparently to reveal the condition of the estate's resources at the time of his appointment, reveals the existence of only one windmill, at Westonzoyland in the heart of the Levels.[45] By the time of the first surviving annual account for the estate, that for 1258, there were windmills also at Glastonbury and at South Brent, though away from the low-lying marshlands the necessity was less, and so we find at both Pilton and Wrington, at the southern and northern fringes of the Mendips, new watermills built since 1189.[46]

Glastonbury Abbey's circumspect approach to the windmill continued, with only two more being built by 1274.[47] Obviously the abbey administration still had reservations about its performance, and when the Westonzoyland mill went out of use, sometime before 1274, it was eventually replaced not by another windmill but by a horsemill.[48] This continued attachment to the horsemill, seen also on some of the Ely manors, was not to be demonstrated anywhere else on the Glastonbury estates, although the Westonzoyland mill proved satisfactory enough for the windmill there not to be rebuilt until sometime after 1316. Even then the horsemill was retained for grinding malt, and was still in use in 1335.[49]

---

[44] Historia de Rebus Gestis Glastoniensibus Adami de Domerham, 2 vols, ed. T. Hearne (Oxford, 1727), ii, pp. 502–8; see also R. A. Holt, 'Whose were the profits of corn milling? An aspect of the changing relationship between the abbots of Glastonbury and their tenants 1086–1350', Past and Present, 116 (1987), pp. 3–23.

[45] Rentalia et Custumaria, pp. 1–178. There had been a mill recorded for this manor in 1189, but given the early date of that survey, the terminology employed and the absence of any other evidence the earlier mill must be presumed to have been a watermill: Liber Henrici de Soliaco, p. 49.

[46] Longleat MS 10,762.

[47] At Winterborne Monkton, Wiltshire, and at Middle Zoy: Longleat MS 11,244.

[48] Ibid.

[49] Longleat MSS 10,766; 10,656; 10,632.

We must not be mistaken in assuming that this distribution pattern of the windmill at the end of its first century is anything other than a snapshot — and a blurred one at that — of a subject in full motion. The year 1279 is a somewhat arbitrary choice, determined principally by the existence of the Hundred Rolls; a different date, were there the documentation, would produce a slightly different picture as the windmill continued its progression westward. The next seventy years would see many more windmills built where none had been before, so that by the fourteenth century no region would be entirely without them. Even in Cornwall, where the windmill was never to establish more than a marginal presence, there were two described as newly-built at Fowey in 1314, and a mill of the Black Prince at Tewyngton which in 1356 was described in such a way as to indicate that it was a windmill.[50]

The better evidence for Somerset also shows new windmills being built, but perhaps it is significant that these should all have been on Glastonbury Abbey manors. By 1301 a new windmill had been built at Othery, and a second had appeared at Middle Zoy.[51] At Berrow-on-the-Shore a windmill was built in 1306, and by 1325 there were windmills at Ashcot and at Shapwick.[52] As we have seen, a new windmill, supplementing the existing horsemill, was built at Westonzoyland between 1316 and 1332, and the last act of this expansive phase was a windmill erected at Walton in 1342.[53] Moving northwards, the number of windmills in the West Midland counties was similarly rising. By 1300 there were seven recorded for Worcestershire, a genuinely recent development if the judgment of the local jury at Hanbury is to be taken literally, for although the manor had a windmill in 1299, in the survey made some ten years previously it was reported that there was no mill 'because there is no water for one'.[54]

By the fourteenth century there is at last some indication of how far the windmill had penetrated the less-well documented counties of

---

[50] C. Henderson, *Essays in Cornish History* (Oxford, 1935), p. 209; *Register of Edward the Black Prince*, 4 vols (HMSO, London, 1930–3), ii, p. 104.

[51] Longleat MS 11,272.

[52] Longleat MS 11,246; Brit. Lib., Egerton MS 3321, fols 190v, 53v, 23v.

[53] Longleat MS 10,766; 10,761; 10,801.

[54] The windmills were at Hanley Castle, Bushley, Elmley Castle, Stoulton, Kempsey, Ripple and Hanbury: *Inquisitiones Post Mortem for the County of Worcester*, i, ed. J. W. W. Bund (Worcs. Hist. Soc., 1894), pp. 56, 63, 64; *Red Book of Worcester*, pp. 62, 151, 172, 184. I am grateful to J. L. Langdon for providing me with these references.

northern England. Both the survey made in 1183 of the Bishop of Durham's manors, known as Boldon Book, and a vacancy account of the bishopric of around 1300 which lists the annual values of the estate's mills, display a marked reticence as to numbers and types of mill to be found in each manor.[55] Only through Bishop Hatfield's Survey of about 1380 can we begin to discover some consistent detail other than totals of mill rents for this most northerly part of the country, and coming at a time when mills were becoming less profitable and beginning to decrease in numbers this evidence is not ideal. What it shows is windmills at only six locations in the Bishop's manors in Northumberland and Durham, as well as one at Wearmouth for which the tenants of six vills were individually paying, ostensibly to farm, and which probably in fact had ceased to exist.[56] Again, the overwhelming proportion of the Bishop's mills were watermills, and so despite the windmill's early appearance in the region at Newcastle-upon-Tyne in 1196 this had not been followed by any great enthusiasm for it.

In Yorkshire, the windmill made considerably more progress after its early start, recorded first at Weedley in 1185; already by 1245 there was one in the West Riding, at Hemsworth, and nearby, at the eastern end of the vast manor of Wakefield, three more windmills had appeared by 1270.[57] If they were not already a common sight around Wakefield and Pontefract they would be so after 1300: the Earl of Lancaster owned windmills here in the 1320s on his manors of Tanshelf, Ackworth, Elmsall, Campsall, Owston, Scales, Cridling Stubbs and Altofts, and there is a scatter of fourteenth-century references to windmills throughout the vicinity.[58] There were wind-mills, too, on the Earl's manors of Whitgift and Cowick, on the low ground around the Aire and the Ouse; and although this is poorly documented it would seem that a large part of the low-lying East Riding was dependent on windpower.[59] A number of medieval

---

[55] Boldon Book, ed. D. Austin (Chichester, 1982); PRO, SC 11/1012.

[56] The windmills were at Gateshead, Boldon, Easington, Hameldon, Sedgefield and Hartlepool: Bishop Hatfield's Survey, ed. W. Greenwell (Surtees Soc. 32, 1857), pp. 89, 100, 131, 139, 188, 198, and passim. For other instances of rents paid for non-existent mills, see chapter 3.

[57] M. L. Faull and S. A. Moorhouse, West Yorkshire: An Archaeological Survey to A.D. 1500, iii (Wakefield, 1981), pp. 703, 717.

[58] Ibid., p. 718; PRO, SC 6/1145/21.

[59] PRO, SC 6/1145/21.

windmill sites in the county have already been identified by archaeologists, and there is no suggestion that the tally is as yet at all complete.[60] In the well-watered uplands the situation was quite different, there being no evidence of anything other than watermills being used at this time in the Pennine regions of either Yorkshire or Lancashire; on the lowlands to the west, however, windmills again appear, being found in the early fourteenth century at Upton-in-Widnes in Lancashire, and Haulton in Cheshire.[61]

If the number of windmills in the west and north was continuing to grow after 1300, what was happening in the east? The evidence, such as it is, confirms that, as has already been suggested, the impressive investment in windmills during the middle decades of the thirteenth century had been sufficient to meet demand. By 1279 windmill-building had to all intents finished, and from now on there would be no significant increase in numbers. For example, nineteen Cambridge-shire manors of the Bishop of Ely and of Ramsey Abbey had altogether in 1279 seventeen windmills; by 1300 or so the number had risen slightly to nineteen, and there were still nineteen twenty years later.[62] In Norfolk, ten manors of Norwich Cathedral Priory, the bishopric of Ely and of Ramsey Abbey saw only a modest rise, from nine windmills around 1279 to eleven fifty years later.[63] Twenty-one Suffolk manors saw a more noticeable increase from seventeen windmills in 1279 to twenty-two windmills in and around 1300.[64] Evidence for a handful of

[60] J. R. Earnshaw, 'The site of a medieval post mill and prehistoric site at Bridlington', *Yorks. Archaeol. Journal*, 45 (1973), pp. 39–40.

[61] *Two Compoti of the Lancashire and Cheshire Manors of Henry de Lacy, Earl of Lincoln, 24 and 33 Edward I*, ed. P. A. Lyons (Chetham Soc., old ser., 112, 1884), *passim*; PRO, DL 29/1/2; C 134/22.

[62] The nineteen manors were Graveley, Elsworth, Burwell, Chatteris, Ely, Downham, Littleport, Stretham, Linden End, Doddington, Wisbech, Leverington, Willingham, Fen Ditton, Balsham, Great Shelford, Thriplow, Hardwick, Little Gransden: *Cartularium de Rameseia*, i, pp. 273–6; PRO, SC 6/767/12, 19; 766/23; 765/6, 7, 8, 20; Brit. Lib., Cotton MS Claud. Cxi, fols 26, 35, 39v, 44v, 54v, 62, 74, 83v, 111v, 115, 121v, 132, 135v, 139; PRO, SC 6/1132/9, 10.

[63] The ten manors were Hilgay, Popinho, Eaton, Hindolveston, Hindringham, Plumstead, Sedgeford, Terrington, Walpole, West Walton: *Cartularium de Rameseia*, i, p. 279; PRO, SC 6/937/14; 942/12; 943/5; Norfolk CRO, DCN 60/8/3, 14; 60/18/1, 13, 27; 60/20/3, 22; 60/29/2, 24; 60/33/1, 27; Brit. Lib., Cotton MS. Claud. Cxi, fols 174, 184v, 191v; PRO, SC 6/1132/9, 10, 13.

[64] The twenty-one manors were Redgrave, Palgrave, Brockford, Melford, Chevington, Saxham Parva, Elmswell, Culford, Lawshall, Glemsford, Hartest, Rattlesden, Barking,

these manors from succeeding decades suggests, however, that there was very little increase after that date.[65] Nine Huntingdonshire manors showed only a gentle expansion of milling capacity during this period, from seven windmills in 1279, to eight at the turn of the century, and to nine in the 1330s.[66]

In conclusion, two points emerge which require particular emphasis because of their wider implications.

First, of the limited number of genuinely medieval inventions the windmill was perhaps the most important economically; it is therefore fortuitous that we can observe so much of its progress through the English countryside, and it is particularly satisfying that we can be so very precise as to the details of its early years. In comparison with our profound ignorance of the conditions under which the English watermill spread during the Anglo-Saxon centuries or before (so that we can only guess at the identity or motivations of its earliest builders), the clear chronology which can be established for the windmill's development illustrates perfectly the essential role played by seigneurial investment. Whatever its origins in the 1170s or 1180s, by 1200 it was known the length of eastern England from Newcastle-upon-Tyne to Sussex, a pattern which indicates a transparent need in many places for a satisfactory source of power for milling, coupled with the almost proverbial strength and reliability of the winds on the east coast. It is also a reasonable supposition that an awareness of this new device was diffused in the first instance by sea-borne travellers — most plausibly those engaged in coastal traffic rather than in trade across the North Sea — especially as the concept of a wind-driven machine would have been grasped far more readily by communities already familiar with

---

Wetheringsett, Brandon, Bromford, Cratfield, Dunningworth, Hollesley, Hoo, Walton: *Pinchbeck Register*, ii, pp. 30, 32, 68, 155, 185, 209, 220; *Cartularium de Rameseia*, i, p. 278; Brit. Lib., Cotton MS Claud. Cxi, fols 255v, 263, 269, 284v, 292, 300v, 306v; PRO, SC 6/994/27; 995/16; 998/8; 999/6; 1007/4, 19. For these manors in the period after 1300 see Brit. Lib., Harley MS 230, fols 144–56v, *passim*; Add. MS 14848, fol 52; PRO, SC 6/995/8, 22; 999/1, 15, 16; 1001/8; 1007/19; 1132/10.

[65] For instance at Elmswell, Culford, Redgrave, Palgrave, and Lawshall: Brit. Lib., Add. MS 14849, fols 3v, 19v, 32v, 52; PRO, SC 6/1001/12.

[66] Ripton Abbots, Broughton, Warboys, Wistow, Somersham, Weston, Elton, Hemingford and Bythorn: *Rotuli Hundredorum*, ii, pp. 600–2, 605, 629, 656, 680; *Cartularium de Rameseia*, i, pp. 267–73; PRO, SC 6/875/10, 16, 19; 877/2; 878/14; 882/18; 885/18, 19, 22, 30, 31, 33; 1135/8.

the sailing ship. But it was only when the lords of these communities became convinced that the windmill could most profitably meet the existing need did building begin in earnest.

So it was that, after a cautious start, it was in those regions shown to be most short of milling capacity in 1086 that the windmill was brought into use on a major scale from the 1230s onwards, with the result that within a generation the counties of East Anglia and the south-east midlands had satisfied in full measure their long-felt need. Diffusion of the windmill westwards seems to have taken a good half-century, so that even on the marshlands of Somerset it remained a rarity until at least 1250; then, because of the greater availability of waterpower in western England, far fewer windmills were built. The major phase of construction in the west came not before 1300 but after, and there is nothing to suggest that it was on anything like the scale it had been in the east.

The second point to be emphasized, therefore, is that the windmill came to supplement the watermill, not to supplant it. The latter's greater strength and consistency, reflected in the often higher revenue it generated, meant that adequate waterpower, when it was available, was always preferable to windpower. It is significant that it was rare for an established watermill to be replaced by a new windmill during the thirteenth century, this usually only happening where the existing mill was on a poor watercourse, as at Holm in Norfolk, or at Fiskerton, Lincolnshire, where a clearly unsatisfactory mill worth only three shillings in 1125 had by 1231 been replaced by a windmill and a horsemill.[67] Sometimes, too, windmills were built to replace tide-mills, dependent as they were on an unsatisfactory power source which, moreover, from time to time demonstrated its capacity for destructiveness.[68] Windmills, we may be sure, presented their own technical problems that made them unacceptable except where the alternative

[67] *Cartularium de Rameseia*, ii, p. 316; *Chronicon Petroburgense*, p. 164; Soc. of Antiquaries Lib., MS 60, fol 201. As no mill was recorded for Fiskerton in Domesday Book, Edward Kealey would presumably argue that the mill built between 1086 and 1125 must have been a windmill, being identical with that recorded in 1231. At Great Easton in Leicestershire, too, there was an apparently recently-built mill in 1125, and only a windmill in 1321. These would then predate his supposed earliest English windmill at Wigston Parva by some twelve years: *Domesday Book*, fols 231, 345b; *Chronicon Petroburgense*, p. 159; Brit. Lib., Add. MS 39758, fol. 125; *Harvesting the Air*, pp. 227–8 and *passim*.

[68] For examples of this see chapter 8.

was even less acceptable. As we have seen, not only were the horsemills that had been perhaps widely used in the twelfth century retained on some manors, but new ones were constructed: clearly they were viable, economic alternatives to a machine whose power source was free to all, but whose maintenance costs were evidently considered extraordinarily high.

3

The Mill and the Manor

Historians agree that it was a feature of the feudal economy that mills, like other valuable assets, were firmly in the hands of manorial lords. Moreover, through their legal right to force their tenants to use the manorial mill, and to extort an excessive fee for the privilege, the owners could ensure the profitability of the investment that only they could make. As a consequence the peasantry were often resentful, it is accepted, of a labour-saving machine that nevertheless seemed more a curse than a blessing.[1] But it has now become clear that whilst this judgement on the medieval mill still, in essence, stands, it does need considerable modification. In particular some of the more extravagant assertions that have been made need to be refuted, and there are a host of misunderstandings to be corrected. The most important of these — that in fact there were many mills which in practice did not operate under the control of the manor, and whose existence has previously been noted only in passing — will be dealt with in the following chapter.

Stressing the role played by lords throughout northern Europe in constructing and operating mills, the French historian Marc Bloch felt able, on the evidence he presented, to write in 1935 that 'all the mills whose history we can more or less follow were in fact seigneurial in origin.'[2] He pointed to the failure of continental peasant communities to co-operate in the construction of mills, and assigned to the greater monastic communities the major role in the harnessing and utilization of waterpower — initially for their own use, but already during the early Middle Ages as a source of profit. Grinding facilities were offered to the peasants of their own estates and round about, and although there was during the ninth and tenth centuries as yet no obligation on the part of the peasants to use their lord's watermill, this would soon

[1] H. S. Bennett, *Life on the English Manor* (Cambridge, 1937), pp. 129–33.
[2] Bloch, 'Advent and triumph', p. 151.

begin to change. The growing control over local justice that the French aristocracy was acquiring at the expense of the degenerating machinery of the state enabled lords to establish monopoly rights over a range of communally used facilities, of which the village wine-press, the bread-oven and above all the mill were the most profitable. Indeed, such were the profits to be made from a judicious exploitation of these *banalités* — that is, rights arising from the lord's *ban* or powers of private justice — that they began to take on an ever greater significance in the total of seigneurial incomes. So potentially lucrative was the monopoly over the mill, especially, that it came to be regarded as one of the perquisites of *haute justice*, as one of the greater judicial privileges that minor lords often did not possess; as a result the lord's mill had often to be used, not just by everyone within a particular lordship, but also by the inhabitants of neighbouring lordships.[3]

It has been customary to assume, as did Bloch himself, that a seigneurial monopoly of milling was one of the customs introduced to the English manor during the imposition of feudal law and relationships that followed the Norman Conquest of 1066 — though Bloch quite correctly insisted that legal monopolies were never to be as important here as they were in France.[4] In actual fact there is no specific evidence at all for this assumption, and the evidence of Domesday Book suggests that, to the contrary, close seigneurial control of milling must have been a feature of English life before 1066. Judging by the greater amount of detail for the situation before the beginning of Norman rule which is provided for the eastern counties in Little Domesday, the overwhelming majority of the 6,000 mills of 1086 had been built before the Conquest. Although we can now be certain that mill rents were additional to the stated value of each manor, nevertheless there is no suggestion that they were paid to anyone other than the person named as lord.[5] Of course, despite having invested so heavily in mills, Anglo-Saxon lords may not have forced their use on their tenants; however, until it can be demonstrated that there was a free market in milling before 1066, it is surely reasonable to suppose that on many or most manors there was not. No trust can be placed in Bennett and Elton's insistence that the lack of any reference in Domesday Book to

---

[3] Ibid., pp. 152–3; G. Duby, *Rural Economy and Country Life in the Medieval West* (London, 1968), pp. 187–8, 213, 239n, 252.

[4] Bloch, 'Advent and Triumph', p. 156.

[5] Lennard, *Rural England*, p. 281, n. 1; J. McDonald and G. D. Snooks, *Domesday Economy: A New Approach to Anglo-Norman History* (Oxford, 1986), p. 89.

tenants being compelled to use their lords' mills indicates that the practice was still in 1086 unknown, as so many of the obligations of the peasant that we may be sure did exist went unrecorded in a survey designed to record the essential elements of a lord's income and not the minutiae. Their further insistence that milling sokes or legal monopolies did indeed exist in England before the Conquest serves only to confuse the issue.[6]

Whilst they are not common, allusions to milling monopolies are frequent enough in twelfth-century charters to show that whatever the situation had been previously, the lord's ability to compel his tenants to use his mill was not now legally in question. From the 1130s comes perhaps the earliest example, in a grant from Cecily de Rumilly of her mill in Silsden, Yorkshire, to Embsay Priory.[7] With the mill went the service or suit to it of the villagers, who had no choice in the matter and who were expressly forbidden either to use their own mills (including handmills) or to go to any other mill on pain of confiscation not only of their corn but also of the horse that carried it. When the twelfth-century burgesses of Tewkesbury, Newcastle, Cardiff and doubtless elsewhere were allowed by their lords to use handmills, this was represented as a special concession, and certainly was a privilege never granted to rural communities.[8]

From the middle years of the thirteenth century onwards there survives detailed evidence from manor courts to put flesh on these few bones. A diligent search of any set of court rolls will provide some case or other to add to the general picture; it will suffice to quote only a very small but representative selection of instances. At a court held in 1275 in Bledlow, Buckinghamshire, a manor belonging to the Abbey of Bec, Hugh Wiking was fined a shilling for not doing suit of the lord's mill, and six years later Walter de Fraxino was fined sixpence.[9] Matilda, the wife of Robert Sarle, and William Thesorch, both of Chatteris, Cambridgeshire, were fined sixpence each in 1287 and 1288 respectively, for not using Ramsey Abbey's mill. The following year, however, clemency was shown to John Andrews whose fine was

[6] Bennett and Elton, *History of Corn Milling*, ii, pp. 122−3; iii, pp. 206−7.

[7] Ibid., i, p. 211; *Early Yorkshire Charters, vol. vii: The Honour of Skipton*, ed. C. T. Clay (Yorks. Archaeol. Soc. Rec. Ser., Extra Ser. 5, 1947), pp. 55−6, No. 4.

[8] A. Ballard, *British Borough Charters 1042−1216* (Cambridge, 1913), p. 96.

[9] *Select Pleas in Manorial and Other Seignorial Courts*, ed. F. W. Maitland (Selden Soc. Pubs., 2, 1889), pp. 27, 30.

waived in view of his poverty.[10] Sixpence appears to have been the usual fine for this misdemeanour, and was a considerable sum when a penny — or at most twopence — was a labourer's daily wage.[11] John Edrich of Halesowen, Worcestershire, paid it in 1280, and Richard of Sharnbrook did so at Chalgrave, Bedfordshire, in 1289. At the same court, though, Alice, described as the daughter of the late William Brid and thus presumably an unmarried woman, paid only threepence for evading suit of the mill.[12] At Wakefield, Yorkshire, Alice at the Bar had to pay sixpence in 1275, as did three men of Raistrick in the same manor in 1315.[13]

What the simple charge of failing to perform suit of the lord's mill usually fails to make clear is that it actually covered two quite separate transgressions. On the one hand there was the offence of taking corn to a mill that was not the lord's, for which Richard Plombe of Houghton, Huntingdonshire, was fined sixpence in 1310, and of which Richard, son of Amiscia of Illey, was guilty when he was caught bringing home a sackful of flour from the mill of Frankley, outside the lordship of the abbot of Halesowen.[14] But then on the other hand there were those who ground at home with their own handmills, like three men at Raistrick in 1286, or Elias the Carpenter at Chalgrave in 1297, or Andrew Saladyn at Elton, Huntingdonshire, in 1331, and who were also fined sixpence.[15] Ralph Motiga of Aldborough, Yorkshire, had his own millstones, it was alleged in 1338, and the court there, obviously having no clear idea of whether this was an isolated case or not, then went on to issue a general order for the arrest

---

[10] *Court Rolls of the Abbey of Ramsey and of the Honour of Clare*, ed. W. O. Ault (New Haven/London, 1928), pp. 273, 275, 280.

[11] J. E. Thorold Rogers, *Six Centuries of Work and Wages* (London, 1884), p. 170.

[12] *Court Rolls of the Manor of Hales*, iii, ed. R. A. Wilson (Worcs. Hist. Soc., 1933), p. 71; *Court Roll of Chalgrave Manor, 1278–1313*, ed. M. K. Dale (Bedfords. Hist. Rec. Soc., 28, 1950), p. 24.

[13] *Court Rolls of the Manor of Wakefield*, vol. i: *1274–1297*, ed. W. P. Baildon (Yorks. Archaeol. Soc., 29, 1901), p. 128; *vol. iii: 1313–1316, and 1286*, ed. J. Lister (Yorks. Archaeol. Soc., 57, 1917), p. 121.

[14] *Ramsey Abbey Court Rolls*, p. 253; *Court Rolls of the Manor of Hales*, i, ed. J. Amphlett (Worcs. Hist. Soc., 1912), pp. 102–3.

[15] *Wakefield Court Rolls*, iii, p. 164; *Chalgrave Court Roll*, p. 38; *Elton Manorial Records 1279–1351*, ed. S. C. Ratcliff (Roxburghe Soc., Cambridge, 1946), pp. 299, 303.

of all the other tenants of the manor who might own handmills.[16]

Cases as specific as these are comparatively unusual, and as defendants were most frequently accused only of failing to perform suit of mill, there is no easy way of telling which of the two practices was the greater threat to the lord's monopoly. Neither should it be necessarily assumed that lords themselves knew which to fear most. Many presentments may have arisen only through the vigilance of the miller or the jurors in observing that a household which was known to bake or brew did not also use the mill, or used it infrequently: there may have been no one willing to testify as to how the household had obtained its flour. At its most illicit, milling went on in concealed establishments like those run by two men in Ogbourne, Wiltshire, who in 1296 had millstones in their houses which they operated for profit, taking toll from their customers.[17] Were these handmills or horsemills? The court record does not say. As the decision of the court that the millstones should be seized was perhaps inevitable, all we can be sure of is that their owners had expected to be able to continue their activities long enough for the enterprise to be worthwhile.

A number of disputes arising from the enforcement of suit of mill have been quoted so frequently as to become common currency amongst historians. Pre-eminent is the long struggle between the abbots of St Albans and the people of the town, which has often been recalled as an illustration, not only of the attachment of the people to their handmills, but also of the implacable and vindictive nature of seigneurial authority. For Marc Bloch the contest between town and abbey was an epic illustration of his thesis that the common people of the Middle Ages used their lords' mills only when coerced; left to themselves they would have continued to mill by hand.[18]

Yet a reconsideration of the St Albans case calls into question just how typical this quarrel was. From its recorded beginnings, in 1274, it was much more than just a dispute over milling. At issue was the nature of the relationship between the inhabitants of this urban

---

[16] Extracts from the Court Rolls of the Manor of Aldborough 1338–9, ed. T. Lawson-Tancred and J. W. Walker (Yorks. Archaeol. Soc. Rec. Ser., 74, 1929), p. 41.

[17] Select Pleas in Manorial Courts, p. 47.

[18] Thomas Walsingham, Gesta Abbatum Monasterii Sancti Albani, 3 vols, ed. H. T. Riley (Rolls Ser., London, 1867–9), i, pp. 410–23; ii, pp. 149–260; iii, pp. 285–372; Bloch, 'Advent and Triumph', pp. 157–8. Bennett and Elton were clearly convinced that the St Albans quarrel arose entirely from the ambition of the burgesses to mill by hand: History of Corn Milling, i, pp. 215–16.

community and their lord, for had St Albans belonged to the Crown or to a lay magnate then long before the end of the thirteenth century its people would have been able to secure, for a consideration, a charter of liberties enshrining their right to commercial and administrative self-government. The great ecclesiastical corporations, in contrast, looked to the future and scorned short-term advantage: they were not so easily persuaded to renounce for ever the profits from their towns in return for a fixed annual rent and a single payment, however substantial that might have seemed to those who offered it. For this reason the burgesses of St Albans were increasingly locked into a struggle with their lord. After years of growing bitterness there was open insurrection in 1326, to be followed by an uneasy truce. In this context the defiance shown by some eighty of the people in using their own handmills, and the determination of the abbot to stop them, take on new meaning, with the question of the seigneurial monopoly of milling being quite obviously not so much an end in itself as a pretext. Here was the ground on which both sides had determined to do battle, and so the victory at law won by the abbot in 1331 and his confiscation of the millstones was not to be followed logically by their destruction or their sale. To commemorate the event these triumphal ornaments were to be used to pave the monks' parlour. Fifty years later, seizing the opportunity of the Peasants' Revolt of 1381, the people of St Albans once more rose up in insurrection, and attacking the abbey they hacked up the hateful floor. Again this was a symbolic act, for they had no intention of using the shattered stones; instead they distributed the fragments amongst themselves as tokens of their mutual solidarity. Thomas Walsingham, the chronicler of these events, cannot have been alone when he likened this to the sharing of the sacramental bread.[19]

Other disputes over handmills are quoted, for instance that between the abbot and people of Cirencester, another of these unchartered towns with a merchant and artisan population struggling to be free of their lord's officials.[20] Although it was a prosperous cloth manufacturing centre, the inhabitants were denied the commercial and tenurial

[19] Bloch, 'Advent and triumph', pp. 157—8. The social context of the events of 1381 in St. Albans was considered by R. H. Hilton, *Bond Men Made Free* (London, 1973), pp. 198—202.

[20] Bennett and Elton, *History of Corn Milling*, i, pp. 216—18. An extraordinary error of presentation obscured their account of the events in Cirencester, which were described as if they were a later phase of the St Albans quarrel.

privileges of burgage tenure, being instead forced to hold their property in villeinage, a matter which had caused ill-feeling for some considerable time when around 1300 the use of handmills became a point of contention. It seems to have come to a head with the coming of the justices of the commission of trailbaston into Gloucestershire in 1305; appointed specifically to deal with violent and hooligan behaviour which was felt to be contributing to a general state of lawlessness, the commission's broad remit and the harsh penalties prescribed for those convicted was an encouragement to many, it was claimed, to use the sessions to pursue private quarrels.[21] The people of Cirencester accordingly saw their opportunity. The abbot's bailiff and his men had at various times in recent years forcibly entered the houses of five named men to seize their millstones, and now they were presented by the local jury as trailbastons, or troublemakers. The outcome, not surprisingly, was that the town was ordered to pay the abbot £66 13s 4d compensation for a false complaint, and the matter was not raised again.

Only by looking at the whole of this struggle, however, with an urban population constantly seeking grounds to attack an already unpopular lord, can we understand that the dispute over handmills was a relatively trivial affair, and certainly not in itself the deeply-held grievance it might otherwise appear. The town's resistance would last for three centuries, always taking a different shape. By 1312 the abbot was being sued for illegally levying tallage, a suit that ended in 1321. In 1343 the townsmen began to claim that the abbot was usurping dues from Cirencester that rightfully belonged to the king, and then they ingeniously presented what they said was a copy − the abbot having burnt the original − of an unfortunately patently spurious charter of liberties granted to the town by Henry I. During the middle years of the century the Trinity gild was founded, undoubtedly as a focus of communal liberty against the abbot, and in 1400 the town rose in insurrection, the people binding themselves together by a communal oath. Refusing to pay any dues to the abbot, they now began to send their corn to be milled at a mill that was outside the lordship. This was far from being the end of the quarrel, which

[21] *The Cartulary of Cirencester Abbey*, 2 vols, ed. C. D. Ross (London, 1964), pp. xxxiv−xl, no. 349; E. A. Fuller, 'Cirencester − Its Manor and Town', *Trans. Bristol and Gloucestershire Archaeol. Soc.*, 9 (1885), pp. 298−344; *The Political Songs of England, from the Reign of John to that of Edward II*, ed. T. Wright (Camden Soc., old ser., 6, London, 1839), pp. 231−6.

through such issues as the town's right to establish a merchant gild, and its ability to levy rates to pave the streets, continued until the abbey was dissolved in the sixteenth century.

In the countryside, too, we should be aware that use of the mill might be only one, and not the most important, of the vexed questions between lord and peasant. Consider the example of the manor of Halesowen in Worcestershire, which saw during the latter decades of the thirteenth century a string of prosecutions in the lord's court for failure to perform suit of mill. None of the cases specifically mentioned handmills, all of the offences apparently arising from the use of mills situated outside the lordship. Richard the son of Amiscia of Illey was, as we have already seen, in 1278 caught red-handed on his way home from the mill of neighbouring Frankley, though when the bailiff of the Abbot of Halesowen, the lord of the manor, seized both his sack of flour and his mare, Richard resisted by raising the hue and cry. Two years later, in 1280, ten men were fined for grinding at a mill other than the abbot's, and a further two were fined later in the same year.[22]

Once more we need to take into account the context in which these cases were brought to court. Since at least the 1240s the abbey and its tenants had been locked in a contest in which suit of mill had latterly become one of the points at issue — perhaps in part because there had been no demesne mill in the manor before the foundation of the abbey in 1215 or for some time after; until relatively recently, therefore, the tenants had ground their corn wherever they pleased.[23] But at the heart of the struggle lay far more important issues: the abbot's design, successful by the 1270s, to substantially increase the labour services his tenants performed, and his insistence, confirmed by the royal courts in 1286, that they were villeins of servile status and thus subject to his will. Roger Kettle, the abbot's chief adversary of the 1270s, was one of the men who refused to do suit of mill in 1280, and an aspect of this case which we can be sure escaped neither him nor the abbot was that free men could mill where they pleased.[24] Only customary tenants

[22] *Hales Court Rolls*, i, pp. 102–3, 136; iii, pp. 67, 68, 71.

[23] Ibid., i, p. 225, n. 1; for details of the dispute between Halesowen Abbey and its tenants, see R. H. Hilton, *A Medieval Society* (London, 1966), pp. 159–61, and Z. Razi, 'The Struggles between the Abbots of Halesowen and their Tenants in the Thirteenth and Fourteenth Centuries', in T. H. Aston, P. R. Coss, C. Dyer and J. Thirsk (eds), *Social Relations and Ideas: Essays in Honour of R. H. Hilton* (Cambridge, 1983), pp. 151–67.

[24] G. G. Coulton, *The Medieval Village* (Cambridge, 1925), p. 57.

— those whom the abbot was insisting were unfree — had no choice where they milled, and so, conversely, for a tenant to do suit of mill could be taken, or at least held up in court, as an admission of servile status. This was as true in Cirencester in 1305 as it was in Halesowen in 1280.

At Darnhall, too, in another celebrated case, the tenants of this Cheshire manor of the Abbey of Vale Royal came together by arrangement one night in 1329 and agreed not to grind at the abbot's mill.[25] Again this seems to have been rather a gesture of defiance than a protest directed against the mill itself; their other claims and demands, even as reported by the monk who recorded all this, were intended to prove that they were free men and not the abbot's bondmen. If the peasants thought that a boycott of the mill would be an effective economic sanction they were sadly mistaken, and when confronted by the abbot in court all but ten of them lost their nerve and submitted. Following a period during which the whole village was no doubt cowed by the harsh punishment inflicted on the ten, who were put in fetters and fined heavily, the resentment once more came to the surface in 1336. Despite the tenants' new tactic of pleading their free status in a series of extraordinary appeals to the king, the queen and parliament, they met with no success. Their last desperate throw, a violent attack on the person of the abbot which left his groom dead of an arrow wound, was of no avail, and again they suffered humiliating defeat. This time there had been no protest against suit of mill, a clear enough indication that however irritating it might have been to the Darnhall tenants, its removal was not one of their fundamental objectives.

In reassessing these conflicts, there is no intention of dismissing suit of mill as something that was of little importance. Even if it was not so bitterly opposed as historians have usually insisted, the frequent evasions brought before manorial courts leave no doubt that peasants objected to it, and that lords remained convinced that it contributed to the profitability of their mills. In the exercise of their seigneurial rights, however, they often showed a degree of flexibility which has usually gone unremarked. Abbot Richard of St Albans, Bloch's 'terrible leprous abbot', was within two years of his reputedly crushing victory over handmilling in the town licensing the use of handmills in his

---

[25] Ibid., pp. 131–5; *The Ledger Book of Vale Royal Abbey*, ed. J. Brownbill (Lancs. and Cheshire Rec. Soc., 68, 1914), pp. 31–2, 37–42.

manor of Codicote, eight miles away.[26] He well knew that the value of his two watermills there (farmed out for £6 annually) was not threatened by his allowing Stephen le Bray to use a handmill in his house for a penny a year, or John Dolitel to do likewise for twopence. And he was certainly not alone in realizing that to insist on his tenants using his mill was not the only way to profit. Lords everywhere may have been willing to commute suit of mill for an appropriate payment, as the Abbot of Glastonbury did in the 1330s when he allowed a tenant of his manor of Pennard to mill outside the lordship in return for a payment of a bushel of wheat, worth in most years sixpence or rather more.[27] The Bishop of Norwich was content that two tenants of his manor of Honingham, Norfolk, should each pay sixpence in 1325 for release from suit of his mill there; forty-five years later there were two men paying a shilling each for permission to do the same.[28]

Of course, what is at once striking about these fees is that they were charged at the same level as the fines for evasion of suit: sixpence was most common in both circumstances, and we may be forgiven for asking whether the courts always distinguished between the two. The cases cited were taken from account rolls, where they were included to explain additional items of revenue. It is not impossible that the court rolls followed a set formula, and that sometimes the accounts are the more truthful record.

Sometimes a township paid collectively, like the Earl of Norfolk's men of Sutton in Suffolk who together paid 6s 8d, so that they should not have to use his mill at Hollesley.[29] Perhaps it was knowledge of such cases that persuaded a number of lords to take commutation to its logical conclusion, and do without a mill altogether. At Winscombe in Somerset we find that in 1345 the villeins together paid 13s 4d to be released from suit of the windmill, and still did so in 1493, despite the fact that during all this period there seems to have been no windmill. Moreover, in Somerset in the fourteenth century every customary tenant of the manor of Minehead paid a shilling for the right to mill where he chose — this providing, apparently, a more satisfactory income for their lord than a mill would have done.[30] In the Bishop of

[26] Bloch, 'Advent and triumph', p. 158; Brit. Lib., Add. MS 40,734.
[27] Longleat MS 10,761, m. 10d.
[28] PRO, SC 6/1141/1, m. 2; SC 6/1141/2, m. 6A.
[29] PRO, SC 6/998/24.
[30] Somerset RO, DD/CC 110739/2; DD/CC 110739/3; DD/CC 110739/8; DD/CC 13194/7; DD/CC 110739/22; DD/L P62/2.

Winchester's manor of Woodhay, Hampshire, the tenants together paid 10s in lieu of suit of the non-existent windmill, and for the same privilege the villagers of High Clere and Ashmansworth contributed 4s 7d.[31] Examples of this sort demonstrate just how far some lords had been able to extend their claims to suit of mill, because at the beginning of the thirteenth century the evidence is that it was owed only to a working mill. Where a lord had no accessible mill his tenants were free of suit, like the men of Halesowen.[32] When a mill ceased to work, whether for want of repairs or for want of wind or water, those who were obliged to use it were after one or two days free to go elsewhere. They also had permission to grind where they wished if the miller could not cope with the volume of custom, as might happen in late summer when the new harvest could coincide with a shortage of water.[33]

The way in which these lords had been able in the first place to exact such dues is, therefore, not immediately clear, although from the terminology used it would appear that in each instance there had been a mill originally. It is plausible enough that following on a mill's destruction — and this was common enough with windmills, which were prone to damage by the wind — a tacit agreement might be reached whereby the lord forbore to rebuild and his tenants paid a fixed levy instead. He would no longer have the unpredictable burden of maintenance to consider, and they would gain access to cheaper milling elsewhere. Possibly an arrangement of this sort was developing during the 1330s in the manor of Berrow, Somerset, although on this occasion the lord concerned, the Abbot of Glastonbury, does appear to have been unreasonably greedy. Perhaps he was simply establishing a position from which to negotiate. For when the abbey's windmill was blown down after twenty-seven years of useful life, its demise was noted in the reeve's account of the manor for 1335 with a declaration that the homage of Berrow owed £2 for its farm, and must continue to pay each year until they re-erected the windmill at their own expense.[34] As previous accounts confirm that the mill had not been at farm

[31] Hants CRO, Winchester Pipe Roll 1283−4, Eccl. II, 159306.

[32] *Hales Court Rolls*, i, p. 225, n. 1.

[33] *Final Concords of the County of Lincoln 1244−1272*, ed. C. W. Foster (Lincoln Rec. Soc., 17, 1920), p. 25; *Cartularium Monasterii de Rameseia*, 3 vols, ed. W. H. Hart and P. A. Lyons (Rolls Ser., London, 1884−94), i, pp. 472−3 ii, p. 313.

[34] Brit. Lib., Egerton MS 3321, fol 190v; Longleat MS 11,215, mm. 35−8; 10,761, m. 22d.

before being blown down, we are presented with a lease granted on an already derelict windmill that was due to end as soon as the lessee had rebuilt it — a curious agreement indeed, and one that cannot have been freely entered into.[35]

Surely this was a spurious device inflicted on the peasants of Berrow, apparently with the intention of establishing that the multure they had been wont to pay was not simply a fee paid when they milled, but a due to which the abbot was entitled whether his tenants ground or not. Unfortunately, much as one would like to know more about this matter and its outcome, lack of further documentation draws a veil over the subsequent course of events. Our understanding of the practical operation of suit of mill would have been greatly extended had we known whether this affair resulted in the resumption of milling at the tenants' or the abbey's expense, or whether the 'farm' became institutionalized as an annual payment, at a level grudgingly agreed on by both parties. Something of the kind seems to have come about at Feltwell in Norfolk, where the single mill of 1086 was described in 1251 as being at farm to the whole vill for £1 12s, whilst the lord, the Bishop of Ely, had meanwhile built a windmill. In 1298 the windmill was at farm for £2 10s and the customary tenants now paid £1 12s simply to be released from suit of the watermill, a form of words which strongly suggests that this mill had in fact ceased to work.[36]

Instances of peasants paying for the privilege of not having to use a non-existent mill, and of lords finding the arrangement more advantageous than bringing a mill into use, together serve to highlight those questions concerning milling which have deep implications for any discussion of technological innovation during the Middle Ages. For if the manorial mill was regarded by both its users and its owners as little more than a means of transferring wealth from the former to the latter, it thereby follows that its ubiquity was the result not of any merits it had as a labour-saving device, but of the nature of the relationship between the aristocracy and its tenants. Without the coercive authority that each lord had at his disposal, the medieval peasant would have preferred to save the fee payable for grinding in favour of expending his efforts (or more correctly those of his wife and daughters) working at the handmill. At any rate, this was the argument

---

[35] Longleat MS 10,632, mm. 12, 12d.
[36] *Domesday Book*, ii, fol 213b; Brit. Lib., Cotton MS Claud. Cxi, fols 246v, 247; PRO, SC 6/1132/10.

advanced by Marc Bloch, who went on to suggest that the example of the watermill — introduced initially to save labour, but subsequently imposed on the rural population — was not without its parallels, and could serve as a model for the way in which technical progress has historically come about.[37]

For Pierre Dockès the matter was even more clear cut: the handmills to which the peasants clung were actually more efficient and economical in use, whilst technical progress was and remains 'a by-product of social struggles', being no more than an incidental feature of man's exploitation of man.[38] By means of an ingenious set of calculations, designed, as he insisted, not to be taken literally but at least to question the simple contention that the lord's mill must have brought some economic benefit to the peasantry, Dockès demonstrated that the time spent milling by hand could be set against the disadvantages of the manorial mill. For as well as the multure the miller took for grinding, there was the proportion of the corn he stole, and also to be taken into account were the time the peasant spent travelling to the mill, the cost of any animal transport used, and the possible risks involved. On these grounds alone (and Dockès forbore to include the time that the peasant must often have spent hanging around at the mill waiting for his corn to be ground) handmilling could, it seems, have produced flour for all or most peasant households more cheaply than did the lord's mill.

How far does the evidence for the way in which the manorial mill operated actually bear this out? Is it really so that England's corn mills brought economic benefit only to their aristocratic owners? To start to answer such an important question we must first return to Dockès, who, despite his calculations based on assumptions of crop yields, consumption, multure, grinding times and labour productivity, placed more faith in the empirical evidence he had seen. 'Only the long struggle waged against the mill stands as proof of its disadvantages for the overwhelming majority of the peasant population', he insisted.[39] The evidence of this long struggle, however, was almost entirely restricted to that provided by Bloch's single article which, however accurate its analysis of this aspect of French *seigneurie banale*, certainly served to misrepresent the situation in England.

---

[37] Bloch, 'Advent and triumph', pp. 159–60.

[38] P. Dockès, *Medieval Slavery and Liberation* (Chicago, 1982), pp. 24, 28, 178, 182–96.

[39] Ibid., p. 195.

What other evidence can be adduced to support Dockès' contention? Moving on from the celebrated disputes which we have considered, there are occasional indications of the peasants' attitudes to the mill, besides the numerous cases of evasion of suit to be found in court rolls. A possible irritant was the need to wait in turn whilst each man's corn was ground. It is easy to see how this could prove a burden, especially at busy times, and so we find references to people being 'hopper free', or having the right to jump the queue.[40] Not surprisingly, this was generally recorded as being reserved to lords and to their greater free tenants, but others paid for the privilege, so that we hear for instance of two people of the manor of East Brent, Somerset, in the 1330s paying threepence each so that when they turned up at the busy Rooks mill they could grind their corn 'next after the corn which is in the hopper'.[41] These payments were made to the lord, and so appear in the reeve's account, but if it was more usual to make agreements of this sort with the miller then they would have gone unrecorded. The practice, we may be sure, would have been a constant source of ill-feeling, and it is likely to have been an argument over priority that led to a quarrel between two men at Wakefield mill in 1313, which culminated in one of the men tipping the other's corn out of the hopper onto the mill floor.[42]

Crucial to any discussion of the peasants' attitudes to the mill was the rate of multure, the fee for grinding. Numerous references agree that this was always assessed not by weight but by volume, the miller using a dish or measure to take an agreed proportion of the corn before it was ground; however, in different parts of the country, and perhaps even from manor to manor, the rate at which multure was charged could vary enormously. The *Statutum de Pistoribus* or Statute Concerning Bakers, dating from about 1270, was also aimed at the activities of millers and stipulated that the rate of toll charged at a mill should be either one-twentieth or one twenty-fourth, depending both on local custom and on the strength of the water-course driving the mill; in reality rates of multure varied from the one-thirteenth that was almost universal in the northern counties of Durham and Northumber-

[40] *History of Corn Milling*, iii, pp. 66–8; *Feet of Fines, Northumberland and Durham*, ed. A. M. Oliver and C. Johnson (Newcastle upon Tyne Recs. Committee, 10, 1931), no. 21.

[41] Longleat MS 10,632, m. 12.

[42] *Wakefield Court Rolls*, iii, p. 3.

land to as low as one thirty-second and even less.[43] The rate of one-sixteenth which is most often quoted in secondary literature seems to have been less common than the rates laid down by law.[44] What makes it impossible to detect any more precise pattern in these variations is that the rate of multure is rarely given in manorial documentation, and is usually discovered only when it became the subject of dispute or litigation.

And these were the rates that were charged to customary tenants who owed suit of mill. Free tenants paid less, at rates which can also sometimes be ascertained, so that on the Durham Cathedral Priory manors in the 1370s there is evidence that the villeins paid one-thirteenth whilst the freeholders paid a twenty-fourth — a rate which nevertheless must still have given an acceptable return to the farmers of the mills.[45] Earlier, during the twelfth century, when the free tenants of several townships in county Durham purchased confirmation of their liberties from their lord, the bishop, including exemption from having to use his mills, the concessionary rate they would henceforth pay was still as high as one-sixteenth.[46] Lords, we may be sure, charged as much as they could, and therefore the tolls that free tenants paid reflected a market rate determined by a number of factors, not least of which would have been the proximity of other mills and the level of competition in the district.

In contrast, the rate of multure paid by suitors to the mill was presumably not affected by economic factors, being instead determined by what their lord felt he could exact without driving his villeins into open revolt. Thus at Wirksworth in Derbyshire in 1276 the lord thought he could increase the revenue from his mill by charging his customary tenants the one-fourteenth he claimed they had once paid, instead of the one-twentieth they had been paying; on this occasion, however, he had miscalculated the extent of his authority, because the aggrieved tenants took the matter to law.[47]

In essence, then, the freeholder paid a rate of multure that was by and large an economic one; the rate that a villein paid was extortionate.

---

[43] *Statutes of the Realm*, i (Record Commissioners, London, 1810), pp. 202–4.

[44] Bennett, *Life on the English Manor*, p. 133; For a fuller consideration of the variations in the rate at which multure was charged see chapter 5.

[45] *Halmota Prioratus Dunelmensis*, ed. W. H. Longstaffe and J. Booth (Surtees Soc., 82, Durham, 1889), pp. 106, 134.

[46] *Boldon Book*, p. 31.

[47] *Calendar of Inquisitions Miscellaneous, 1219–1307*, (London, 1916), no. 1055.

When a comparison of the two is possible, the degree of extortion is revealed in the extra amount of multure that was taken. So on the Durham manors where the two rates stood, apparently, at one-thirteenth and one twenty-fourth, the villein had to contribute some 3.5 per cent of what he ground over and above the economic charge. In Alrewas, Staffordshire, on the other hand, where a dispute over toll in 1329 indicates that the two rates were both lower, at one twenty-fourth and one thirty-third, the difference was such that the villeins had to give only an extra 1 per cent of the corn they ground.[48] This suggests that having to perform suit of mill, with all that it entailed, was a not inconsiderable burden in the north where multure was high; elsewhere it was more likely to have been irksome rather than genuinely onerous.

We must also be aware that many tenants may have had little or no need to mill corn. Simply to assume, as Dockès did, that all peasants ground their own flour to bake their own bread ignores the possibility that the cost of fuel or the fee for using a communal oven, where there was one, together with the time taken in preparation, led the small household usually to purchase bread. If the many landless labourers baked they must have done so with corn they had purchased or otherwise acquired, and on Ramsey Abbey manors at least suit of mill was owed only for corn the peasant had himself grown.[49] A smallholder, therefore, who grew wheat as a cash crop and bought cheaper grains for his own consumption should have been able to mill where he chose, at the lower rate charged to freeholders. Then there was the tendency, particularly during the later Middle Ages, for wages to be paid partly in food, which would have further reduced the dependence of poorer tenants on the mill.

It is unlikely that an illiterate population, however intelligent, would have made the sort of calculations that Dockès did. To cite a continued fondness amongst some of the peasantry for using handmills as proof of the essentially uneconomic nature of powered milling cannot, therefore, be justified. We need to look for other clues to peasant attitudes to the mill — such as, for instance, the question of whether or not free tenants regularly used local mills or whether they milled at home. No firm answer can be given, but the fact that there were indeed agreed rates of multure that applied to them shows that it was

---

[48] Staffordshire RO, DWO 312. I am grateful to Helena Graham, who supplied me with this reference.

[49] *Cartularium de Rameseia*, i, pp. 472–3.

not unusual for free tenants to use their lord's mill. And if they neglected to grind with the handmills they were at liberty to use, then it is clear that the advantages of the watermill and windmill were recognized at least by this section of rural society. The fact, too, that amongst the quantity of cases of evasion of suit of mill known to us from court roll evidence there is no obvious preference on the part of the villeins for the handmill is just as significant. Peasants accused of patronizing a mill outside the manor were making a deliberate choice in favour of mechanical milling, their objection being only to the unfair levels of multure claimed by their own lords. Fair tolls for grinding they could, in contrast, accept.

Bennett and Elton frequently referred to milling 'sokes', or areas within which the owner of a mill could claim suit. The essential flaw in their discussion of the whole problem of seigneurial control of the mill was the way in which they mixed, indiscriminately, evidence from both France and England.[50] Like Dockès, they seem to have been unaware that there is no indication that milling sokes in this continental form ever existed in medieval England. Norman aristocrats such as Cecily de Rumilly may have tried, during the decades following the Conquest, to extend their rights of private jurisdiction, but certainly by the thirteenth century suit of the lord's mill was occasioned only by a tenant's villein status.[51] Bloch, of course, with his incomparably greater knowledge of medieval society, realized that French rights of *seigneurie banale* were not transferred wholesale to England in the eleventh century; nevertheless, even he believed that all the rancour and bitterness that went with French milling disputes were to be encountered in England as well.

Suit of mill was undoubtedly of importance in the Middle Ages, but in England it was not the essential factor that has been suggested. It was not the *sine qua non* of powered milling, able to replace the handmill only by coercion. Without compulsory suit most English mills would have been less profitable, because they would have had to charge a lower fee for grinding, and many might have proved uneconomic if faced with legal competition; it is quite clear, on the other hand, that many peasants would have used watermills and windmills in preference to their own handmills. As it was, there were parts of England such as East Anglia where there were many free

---

[50] Bennett and Elton, *History of Corn Milling*, iii, *passim*.
[51] Bennett, *Life on the English Manor*, p. 130.

tenants, and where suit of mill can have been performed by only a minority of peasants.[52] Yet mills in this part of the country were scarcely less profitable than elsewhere, and everywhere we find the phenomenon that, according to Bloch and Dockès, could not have existed: the independent mill, only nominally under seigneurial control, and often without villeins owing suit to it. These independent mills were a highly significant feature, and so it is to them that we shall turn in the next chapter.

[52] For instance, in 1301 on the manor of Tilney in Norfolk belonging to the Abbot of Bury St Edmunds, the only two villeins each paid 6d a year in lieu of suit of mill; even so, the windmill was said to be worth £2: Brit. Lib., Harl. MS 230, fol 156v.

4
Independent Mills

The very quality of English manorial documentation can be said, paradoxically, to be its greatest drawback. It is all too easy to assume that the wealth of detail it provides amounts to a comprehensive picture of everyday rural life, and nothing illustrates this better than the way in which historians have received the information concerning mills. The regular pattern revealed in court rolls and reeves' accounts of the mills of each manor being able to depend on the custom of their owners' unfree tenants, and presumably competing only with the mills of neighbouring manors for the custom of the free, has never seriously been questioned. This is despite a considerable quantity of evidence from other sources indicating that the true situation was a good deal more confused. During the thirteenth century in particular there were a large number of mills not under the direct control of the manor, and whilst some nevertheless benefited from the suit of servile tenants, many apparently did not. These were indeed independent mills, and although they were not so common after 1300, a surprisingly large number were able to survive the less favourable conditions of the fourteenth and fifteenth centuries.

In order to get some indication of how many independent mills there were, a useful source is, again, the Hundred Rolls of 1279. There we find that the existence of mills is recorded in two quite distinct ways, with only a proportion included in the way that we might have expected, with the description of the demesne and its assets at the beginning of each survey. The others are listed together with the lands held in heredity by individual tenants. It is essential to establish the reliability of this source at the outset, as inevitably the evidence of the Hundred Rolls will be questioned, so contradictory is it of the accepted pattern of seigneurial ownership and control. For in eleven rural hundreds of Oxfordshire for which adequate surveys survive, of a total of 144 recorded mills there were only sixty-five, or less than half, that were demesne mills. Sixty-eight were held by tenants in hereditary free tenure, and a further eleven were held, remarkably, in customary tenure by villeins.[1] In the eleven surveyed hundreds of Cambridgeshire, where the windmill was now predominant, the situation was subtly different. All but six of the fifty windmills belonged to the lords of the manors where they stood, whilst the status of the watermills followed the Oxfordshire pattern with seventeen of the thirty-seven being held freely in heredity.[2]

Can these mills really have been held in hereditary tenure, and thus effectively outside seigneurial control? Would it not be safer to conclude that they were demesne mills that were recorded in this rather peculiar way in consequence of having been let at farm? The evidence is quite against that interpretation. Firstly, although six of the mills listed with the holdings of land were said to be at farm, being identified as held for fixed terms (and so have been included with the demesne mills), the rest, just as emphatically, were not.[3] Secondly, the rents that were paid for many of these mills were clearly not economic, being either just too low for the 1270s or even token rents of very little value that had most likely originated in acts of purchase. Sixpence was paid for a mill and 240 acres in *Selvirle*, Cambridgeshire; 1d for a mill, a messuage, and a meadow in Black Bourton, Oxfordshire; 6d for two mills and a virgate at Hampton Gay in the same county. Other mills were stated to be held in fee farm, at Sawston and Ickleton in Cambridgeshire, whilst a further number were held by church institutions for low rents or in free alms; that is, they were to be held in perpetuity in return for prayers for the donor. In Oxfordshire alone, twelve of the sixty-eight mills in free tenure were held in this way.[4] Thirdly, and most conclusively, the newly-arrived windmills of Cambridgeshire and Huntingdonshire (nearly all of them we may be certain built during the previous fifty years) were recorded in a markedly different way from the more ancient watermills, being practically all listed together with the other demesne assets. It was not thought necessary to record just how these windmills were operated, although we know that certainly several of those belonging to the Bishop of Ely and the Abbot of Ramsey in Cambridgeshire and

[1] *Rotuli Hundredorum*, ii, pp. 688–877.

[2] Ibid., pp. 356–590. The six independent windmills were at Shudy Camps, at Papworth St Agnes where there were two, at Fen Drayton, Over, and *Asle*: pp. 427, 473–4, 478, 590.

[3] Ibid., pp. 740, 741, 769.

[4] Ibid., pp. 698, 710, 777, 781, 788, 826, 828, 831, 842, 846.

Huntingdonshire were at farm.[5] The inescapable conclusion is that if the clerks compiling the Hundred Rolls entered so many watermills differently then their status was indeed different. The watermills listed with the demesne included, like the windmills, both mills that were at farm and those in hand; those listed with the holdings of hereditary land were indeed being held as we have concluded.

So contrary is this state of affairs to what has hitherto been accepted by medieval historians that we need to establish how it came about, if only to test the further veracity of the record. Manorial documentation from the twelfth and thirteenth centuries does confirm what we have seen, in spite of the general belief that any independent mills must have been rare exceptions. Specifically, what twelfth-century surveys show is that it was then nearly always the practice for mills to be let with peasant holdings, in return for a rent accompanied often by labour services. In the 1120s on the Peterborough Abbey manors of Alwalton in Huntingdonshire, and Warmington, Pytchley, Stanwick, Oundle, Cottingham and Ashton in Northamptonshire, mills were held together with virgates, as was Ramsey Abbey's mill at Elton in Huntingdonshire a few years later.[6] Not all mills were held in this way, though, as around 1120 at least four of the mills belonging to Burton Abbey (two in Burton itself, and two in Stretton) were leased for cash rents for fixed terms of years; for the other Burton Abbey mills no details of tenure are given, a cash rent simply being recorded in each case.[7] Detail is added to the picture by the survey made of Glastonbury Abbey's lands in 1189. Of the thirty-one recorded mills on twenty manors, only one, apparently, was held either on a short-term lease or was in direct management; the mill at East Brent in Somerset which was simply said to render forty shillings, in contrast with all the other mills of the estate which were held by named individuals for a specified

---

[5] Six of Ely's windmills in Cambridgeshire and Huntingdonshire had been described in 1251 as being at farm, at Ely, Littleport, Linden End, Fenton, and Little Gransden, and almost all were at farm in 1298: Brit. Lib. Cotton MS Claud. Cxi, fols 26, 39v, 54v, 98v, 139; PRO, SC 6/1132/10. Of Ramsey's windmills, certainly those of Ripton and Warboys were at farm around the time of the Hundred Rolls: PRO, SC6 875/6, SC6 885/30.

[6] Chronicon Petroburgense, ed. T. Stapleton (Camden Soc., old ser., 47, London, 1849), pp. 158−61, 166; Cartularium Monasterii de Rameseia, 3 vols, ed. W. H. Hart and P. A. Lyons (Rolls Series, London, 1884−93), iii, p. 258.

[7] The Burton Abbey Twelfth Century Surveys, ed. C. G. O. Bridgeman (Collections for a History of Staffordshire: William Salt Archaeol. Soc., 1916, Stafford, 1918), p. 214, 215, 218.

rent. The holdings of land that went with all but two of these mills varied in size from a croft at Damerham and two acres at Buckland Newton up to a whole hide at Christian Malford, with thirteen of them being of half a virgate, one virgate, or one and a half virgates. Seven others were substantial smallholdings of five acres or more, and in all there were fifteen of the twenty-eight holdings which owed labour services as well as cash rents.[8]

The twelfth century was also a time which saw lords alienating mills in perpetuity. We know that grants of mills to be held in heredity were being made around 1200 by Abbot Samson of Bury St Edmunds, and undoubtedly they were seen by contemporaries as proof of his capable management of affairs. His admiring, though not uncritical, biographer, the chronicler Jocelin of Brakelond, was most careful to contrast Samson's customary wisdom and prudence with the improvidence of his pious but unworldly predecessor.[9] Six mills that we know of were granted out in heredity by Samson between 1182 and 1211, and it is perhaps not difficult to appreciate why this was done. The rents to be paid for five of the mills ranged from 13s 4d a year up to 30s, although at Southwold, Suffolk, the mill was to render only a token rent of a shilling a year after an initial entry fine of £1 6s 8d.[10]

These rents — to be paid every year for ever — covered no outgoings. None of the grants made any mention of the question of maintenance of the property, but it is unthinkable that the abbey should have retained the heavy liability for repairing and rebuilding these mills. That, surely, was now the responsibility of the tenants, and from now on, therefore, the rents they paid could be viewed by the abbey purely as income. Adjustments to the rents were of course not possible, unless the tenancies fell in for want of heirs, and clearly Samson disregarded the implications of the inflationary tendencies of his own times. He obviously did not foresee the rise in mill values that would be so marked by the end of the thirteenth century.

What Samson probably did appreciate, however, was that a lapse into hereditary tenure of any valuable asset that was rented out was

---

[8] *Liber Henrici de Soliaco*, p. 76 and *passim*.

[9] *The Chronicle of Jocelin of Brakelond*, ed. H. E. Butler (London, 1949), pp. 1–7, 27, and *passim*.

[10] *The Kalendar of Abbot Samson of Bury St Edmunds*, ed. R. H. C. Davis (Camden 3rd ser., 84, London, 1954), 57, 58, 59, 95, 104, 128, 129, 136. The entry fine of £1 6s 8d for the Southwold mill seems very low, especially as the rent was to be only 1s; very possibly the consideration to be paid was much higher.

likely to happen anyway, whatever the terms of the formal agreement. Two of the abbey's mills at Stow were granted out during the decade after 1200 at a rent of £3 a year for the lifetime of the lessee, and the elaborate clauses inserted into the agreement to strengthen the abbey's hand in any litigation, should the mills not be surrendered upon the tenant's death, suggest that such an eventuality was foreseen.[11] Present-day historians have remarked upon the widespread tendency at this time for even the most temporary of leases to come to be regarded as conveying permanent rights of occupation.[12] Under these circumstances a shrewd lord such as Samson might have accepted that to grant an hereditary fee farm on his own terms was preferable to having a perpetual tenancy arise by default.

Meanwhile, a more important transformation in the nature of mill tenures was taking place, as the conditions under which customary tenancies were held were also gradually becoming accepted as fixed. This applied to mills as much as to villein holdings of land, and so we find that mill rents which had earlier responded to economic changes no longer did so in the thirteenth century. Just as custom decreed that the villein's heirs could inherit his land, so the heirs of the miller had a right to succeed to the mill, and at the accustomed rent. How far lords saw this as a serious problem is unclear, partly because they responded to it in different ways and at different times. Successive abbesses of Holy Trinity of Caen seem to have been content to allow the mills of their Cotswold manors of Minchinhampton and Avening to remain in hereditary villein tenure, whilst they considered it worth recovering by outright purchase two of their own mills in Norfolk and Essex that had lapsed into hereditary fee farm.[13] The great ecclesiastical estates which were the source of most surviving manorial documentation combatted the tendency most vigorously; the surveys of a variety of types of estate contained in the Hundred Rolls show that mills in free tenure (though no longer in 1279 the villein mills) remained very common indeed and were therefore probably tolerated by many lords.

Mills in customary tenure are at best elusive, and are rarely recorded

[11] Ibid., 74.

[12] See, for example, E. Miller, 'England in the twelfth and thirteenth centuries: an economic contrast?', *Econ. Hist. Rev.*, 2nd ser., 24 (1971), pp. 8–9.

[13] *Charters and Custumals of the Abbey of Holy Trinity, Caen*, ed. M. Chibnall (Brit. Acad. Records of Social and Econ. Hist., new ser., 5, London, 1982), pp. xlv, 20–4, 108, 112, 115, 121–2.

except in the full manorial surveys of the thirteenth century.[14] Subsequently there were far fewer of them, and of course there are no substantial references to them in any reeve's account. Whatever had been the situation earlier, by the time that the first accounts appeared in the thirteenth century, the demesne bore no responsibility for the villein mills, and their repair and maintenance had become the responsibility of their tenants. Their rents were never separately itemized, being included with the total of rents of assize, and so without a series of surveys or other fortuitous documentation these mills are seen only at single moments of time, their ultimate fates remaining hidden. It is, then, hardly surprising that a study of them must rely on evidence from no more than a handful of estates.

The best evidence for villein mills comes from the documentation for the manors of Glastonbury Abbey, which lay for the most part in Somerset, Wiltshire and Dorset. Excellent survey evidence from the twelfth, thirteenth and early fourteenth centuries, together with a miscellany of documents including the abbey's chronicle, demonstrates not just the extent of the phenomenon but also the chronology of recovery, as well as something of the ways in which this was achieved. To begin with, surveys of the manors made in the first years of the abbacy of Michael de Amesbury (1234–52) and in 1260 can be compared with those made in 1189 to which reference has already been made; by now the status of each of the mills was clarified – deliberately so, it would seem.[15] The three mills of Wrington, for instance, had simply been recorded in 1189 as being held for cash rents; half a century later one was described as being held freely, another, called the Beme mill, was held at the lord's will, and the third, Tosard's mill, was held in customary tenure. A fourth mill, unrecorded in 1189, was also in customary tenure.[16] One Stephen the chamberlain held the Beme mill, and when the abbey's chronicler Adam de Domerham came to tell how after many years of slack management

---

[14] In addition to the numerous examples quoted in this and other chapters, further examples may be found, for instance, in *The Domesday of St Paul's of the Year 1222*, ed. W. H. Hale (Camden Soc., old ser., 69, London, 1858), pp. 75–6; *Register of the Priory of St Mary, Worcester*, ed. W. H. Hale (Camden Soc., old ser., 91, London, 1865), 60a, 62b, 63a, 65a, 70a–b, 73b; *Select Documents of the English Lands of the Abbey of Bec*, ed. M. Chibnall (Camden 3rd ser., 73, London, 1951), pp. 48, 71–2.

[15] *Rentalia et Custumaria*, passim. For those surveys in the 1260 series omitted by Elton, see Brit. Lib. Add. MS 17, 450, fols 93, 106v, 112–41v, 151–7, 162–221v.

[16] *Liber Henrici de Soliaco*, pp. 90–1; *Rentalia et Custumaria*, p. 80.

Abbot Michael set out to restore Glastonbury's lost rights, amongst the victories he recorded was the recovery of this very mill from Stephen, the chamberlain of the Bishop of Wells.[17] Most likely the act of re-acquisition had pre-dated the survey, Michael having in fact negotiated a compromise with Stephen to sweeten the pressure he had put on him. This certainly happened in the case of the other recovery of a mill tenancy that Adam noted with approval: that of Batcombe mill, which he said that Abbot Michael retrieved from Henry Camel by means of litigation. The actual agreement made between Henry and the abbey in 1236 survives as a final concord, so that we know he acknowledged his mill to be really the abbey's property, a concession for which he was to be allowed a life tenancy at what appears to have been the accustomed cash rent of £1 0s 10½d.[18] When the time came in 1257 for the abbey to recover the third of the Wrington mills a similar agreement was reached. Its tenant, John Tosard, was made to concede that he had no hereditary rights in the mill, despite its having been held by Gilbert Tosard and Henry Tosard before him. Now he was to hold only at the lord's will.[19]

Tenancies in villeinage were thus vulnerable to legal, and doubtless also, financial pressure, and there was obvious advantage to lords in emphasizing that a mill was held in customary tenure. Not least, the entry fine for each new tenant could be set at such a level as to recover a proportion of the profits for the demesne. The three Damerham mills which in 1189 had paid only a cash rent (with in one case some light ploughing services in addition) were regarded as being in free tenure when Abbot Michael's survey was drawn up fifty years later, as they were entered with the other free tenements. Marginal amendments in a later hand, however, tersely revealed the subsequent assertion of seigneurial authority: the word *vilenagium* now appeared beside the entries, whilst *modo in dominico* — now in the demesne — against the third mill told of the perhaps inevitable conclusion to which it had come.[20]

[17] *Historia de Rebus Gestis Glastoniensibus Adami de Domerham*, ed. T. Hearne, 2 vols (Oxford, 1727), ii, pp. 502−4.

[18] *Pedes Finium, Commonly Called Feet of Fines, for the County of Somerset, 1196 to 1307*, ed. E. Green (Somerset Rec. Soc., 6, Taunton, 1892), p. 86.

[19] *The Great Chartulary of Glastonbury*, i, ed. A. Watkin (Somerset Rec. Soc., 59, Taunton, 1947), 1020.

[20] *Liber Henrici de Soliaco*, pp. 129, 131−2; *Rentalia et Custumaria*, pp. 112−13; Longleat MS 10,762, m. 31.

Adam de Domerham credited Abbot Michael with having recovered or built ten mills. The manorial documentation of the Glastonbury estates substantiates the figure but also shows that the six newly-built mills accounted for the greater part of the total.[21] It was Michael's successors from the 1250s onwards who brought his policy to fruition, taking further mills in customary tenure into demesne management. In the early years of the fourteenth century there were now, in addition to the thirteen windmills and one horsemill on the demesnes of twelve of the abbey's manors, at least fourteen demesne watermills on eleven manors.[22]

Once mills of questionable status, like the three at Damerham, had been brought under control, it was those that were indisputably in free tenure (and thus less susceptible to seigneurial pressure) that remained. The recovery of these mills was therefore a much more difficult matter altogether, and the 1279 Hundred Rolls demonstrate just how secure they were. In Cambridgeshire any villein mills were gone by that date, although nearly half the watermills were held freely. In Oxfordshire the 47 per cent of mills in hereditary free tenure had also clearly been able to withstand any attacks on their status, in contrast with those held in villeinage which now were a mere 8 per cent of the total. Under such conditions it was only with time and determination that even the most powerful of lords could resume control of milling on their manors.

Consider for instance the example of Fornham All Saints, a manor of the Abbey of Bury St Edmunds in Suffolk. In the 1270s there were in Fornham five watermills, all held freely, and unusually we know something about the origins of this situation.[23] The agreements survive

[21] The mills recovered for the demesne were at Batcombe, Wrington, Street and Damerham. New watermills had been built at Pilton and at Wrington, and windmills at Glastonbury, Westonzoyland, South Brent and Ashcot: *Historia de . . . Adami de Domerham*, p. 506; *Liber Henrici de Soliaco*, pp. 61, 132; *Rentalia et Custumaria*, pp. 5, 21, 80, 113; Longleat MS 10,762, mm. 4, 7, 8, 30.

[22] The windmills and horsemill were at Shapwick, Glastonbury, South Brent, Othery, Middle Zoy, Westonzoyland, Berrow, Ashcot, Walton, Grittleton, Meare, and Winterborne Monkton; the demesne watermills were at Uplyme, Pilton, Glastonbury, Damerham, Sturminster Newton, Longbridge Deverill, East Brent, Batcombe, East Pennard, Ditcheat, and Wrington: Brit. Lib. Egerton MS 3321, fols 2, 2v, 23v, 53, 82, 98, 123, 136v, 141, 155v, 183, 190v, 206v, 226v, 227, 251v, 282; Longleat MS 9623; 10,632, m. 12; 10,761, mm. 19, 26, 10,801; 11,272, mm. 84, 85.

[23] *The Pinchbeck Register*, ii, pp. 128–9.

by which two of the mills were granted out by Abbot Samson to be held in heredity, and so their independence from the demesne was guaranteed formally by charter; at least one of the others seems also to have been alienated in the same way.[24] As we have seen, however wise a policy this might have seemed in the 1190s, within a century the fixed rents that all the Fornham mills continued to pay were no longer appropriate to their market value. At most £1 11s, and going as low as 15s 10d, these were for quite substantial holdings of land as well, and no doubt by this time the abbey administration thoroughly regretted Samson's policy. Yet little could be done to challenge free tenures, and John de Northwold, abbot between 1279 and 1301, obviously felt he had no choice but to purchase one of these mills if he wanted a demesne mill in Fornham. Accordingly he paid an unspecified amount for Aylmer's mill — one of those alienated by Samson — and it was this mill that in a vacancy account made after John's death in 1301 was recorded as Fornham's only demesne mill.[25]

When the manor was next surveyed, in 1318, although there was still only one demesne mill two of the independent mills had disappeared. The abbey itself now held the tenement formerly of John de la Hill, one of the mill tenants of the 1270s, but if a working mill had been acquired with the tenement it must subsequently have been taken out of use. The mill of Adam de Creting too had gone, though as his holding was no longer recognizable in 1318 it is not clear what had happened to it.[26] And still the abbey had designs on the remaining mills. By the 1340s the mill that had been Rosa de Ponte's in the thirteenth century had come into the possession of Sir Thomas de Batesford; sometime between then and his own death, in 1361, Abbot William de Bernham recovered it by litigation in the royal courts, on the grounds that the original grant by Abbot Samson had been made without the assent of the abbey's chapter and had therefore been illegal.[27]

Thus of Fornham's five independent mills there was one that survived into the second half of the fourteenth century, Salmonford

---

[24] *Kalendar of Abbot Samson*, 57, 59. If, as seems likely, the second of the Fornham mills alienated by Samson, Salmonford mill, was one of those recovered by the abbey before 1318, then the mill recovered from Sir Thomas de Bateford (see below) was a third mill whose alienation by Samson is otherwise unrecorded.

[25] Brit. Lib., Add. MS 34689, fols 13, 16; Harl. MS 230, fol 147v.

[26] Brit. Lib., Add. MS 34689, fol. 13.

[27] Ibid., fol. 16.

mill, alienated by Abbot Samson, was by the 1370s in the possession of Sir Edmund Hemgrave, and then of his son Thomas; it existed still in 1442, owned now by Thomas Hethe, esquire.[28] If the abbey had tried to recover this mill employing the sort of strategy they had used against Sir Thomas de Batesford, they had obviously not met with success.

Amongst the significant features of this case is the indication that a proportion of the mills in free tenure, like the villein mills, fell victim to economic pressures which lords no doubt encouraged, but did not originate. The expenditure needed to keep a mill in operation could be considerable (as we shall see in chapter 5), and eventual decrepitude must have awaited many mills held by tenants without sufficient property holdings either to enable them to meet major repairs or to allow them to invest in improvements. Such no doubt was the fate of the two Fornham mills which had disappeared by 1318. Even so, there were mills in free tenure that were able to withstand not only economic adversity but even attacks from lords as powerful as the abbot of Bury St Edmunds to survive into the fourteenth century and beyond. The crucial factor, apparently, that enabled two Fornham mills still to be independent in the fourteenth century was that they had become the property of knightly families, able both to meet the costs of maintenance and to an extent to defend their ownership. The evidence of the Hundred Rolls is that already in 1279 mills in free tenure were often to be found as parts of large holdings, if not obviously aristocratic ones; given that such mills were an aberration, being valuable assets that paradoxically had come to be controlled by tenants from the lower reaches of feudal society, there is every reason to suppose that their ownership would continue to be concentrated increasingly in wealthier hands.[29]

Of the host of questions that surrounds mills in free or customary tenure, the most intriguing is whether they could depend on the suit

---

[28] Ibid., fols 7, 7v, 16v.

[29] For example, at Fordham, Cambridgeshire, a watermill was held with 100 acres for a rent of £1 4s, and at *Selvirle* the mill was held with 240 acres for 6d. In Oxfordshire mills were held with three virgates for £2 8s at Souldern, and with two virgates for £1 0s 6d at Sandford St Michael: *Rotuli Hundredorum*, ii, pp. 503, 589, 823, 844. Mills in free tenure were held by Sir Geoffrey de Langley at Brightwell and Chalgrove in Oxfordshire, most probably as part of a deliberate policy of investment. The Langley family had also acquired a number of independent mills in Warwickshire: *The Langley Cartulary*, ed. P. R. Coss (Dugdale Soc. Pubs., 32, Stratford-upon-Avon, 1980), *passim*.

of the unfree tenants of the manor. More accurately, how many could? And how far did the situation change with time? Such questions, of central importance to our understanding of the economics of medieval milling, simply cannot be avoided, despite the almost total lack of evidence with which to answer them. We can, though, be sure that as the independent mills we have considered were regarded as demesne assets during the twelfth century, their tenants could legally insist on grinding the corn of the local villeins. So how enthusiastically would lords have pursued their tenants who failed to perform suit of mill? Cecily de Rumilly, in alienating her mill in perpetuity to Embsay priory, threatened defaulters with confiscation not only of the corn illegally milled, but also of the horse that carried it — surely incentive enough for any lord to enforce the law.[30] In practice, however, we have seen that penalties as severe as this were inflicted only in exceptional circumstances, a fine of sixpence being more usual. No lord would have been quite so eager to collect such a relatively small fine, and particularly not during the thirteenth century when the consequent strengthening of the mill might act not to his own profit but to that of a tenant who now paid a fixed rent and was claiming an hereditary right.

For each of the independent mills, the turning point came when its lord began to attempt to reassert his control over it. So on the Glastonbury Abbey manors after 1234, for instance, a failure to enforce suit of mill would have been one of the more effective sanctions to be used against millers, to pressurize them into surrendering their tenancies. On a manor with several mills, once one had been recovered it is unthinkable that the remaining independent mills would have been able to claim the suit of any of the tenants. Examples are rare, but both of these suppositions can be observed in practice in the case of the manor of Bridgeham in Norfolk. The two mills that were there in 1086 were still in existence in 1222, by which date they were held on different terms: West mill was held at will for a rent of £1 4s, but Tun mill was described as being worth £1 10s — a sure sign that it had been taken into the demesne, and was in direct operation.[31] Thirty years later the differentiation had become much clearer, in keeping with the policy of the lord, the Bishop of Ely, of maximizing his revenue from milling. Tun mill was now worth £2, and said to have the suit of the tenants of the manor; West mill, still held at will,

---

[30] *Early Yorkshire Charters*, vii, pp. 55–6, no. 4.
[31] *Domesday Book*, ii, fol. 213b; Brit. Lib., Cotton MS Tib. Bii, fols 181–2.

was said to be without the suit of any tenants and its rent had actually fallen to £1.[32] There is no further survey for Bridgeham, but the vacancy account for the bishopric made in 1298 records a single demesne mill at farm for £5 4s, a figure which leaves no doubt that even if West mill was still working it no longer presented any serious competition to its demesne rival.[33]

Otherwise, the evidence for the enforcement of compulsory suit where there were independent mills is less precise. Of the seventy-nine mills known to have been held freely or in villein tenure in Oxfordshire in 1279, seven were on manors where the lord also possessed a demesne mill.[34] Certainly these seven would have had to compete with mills favoured with a legal monopoly: in Cuxham, one of the manors, we know that the manorial court acted to prevent bond tenants using other mills, including the mill that the Prior of Wallingford held in free alms there. In 1281 one Matilda Pitmore was in mercy for grinding corn and malt at a mill other than the lord's, though she was pardoned a fine because of her poverty, and in 1295 another woman was fined threepence for having neglected to use the mill.[35] There is no indication of how long the Prior's mill was able to continue under this disability, for whilst it was still there in 1297 there is no later document such as a survey that would record its existence.[36] And as for those manors where there was no demesne mill, the question of the imposition of suit remains unresolved. We have already seen, though, that the value of suit to a lord as a source of court fines was probably no more than marginal, and so the determining factor was the extent of his ultimate designs on the mill and its operating profits.

That was the position in the thirteenth century. Subsequent developments are far less clear, there being in the first place no later evidence of the quality of the Hundred Rolls, no surveys of whole localities which would enable all of the independent mills to be counted. The virtual disappearance, therefore, of detailed estate

[32] Brit. Lib., Cotton MS Claud. Cxi, fol. 241.

[33] PRO, SC 6/1132/10, m. 10.

[34] At Cuxford, Chalgrove, *Heyford ad Pontem*, Weston on the Green, and Stanton Harcourt: *Rotuli Hundredorum*, ii, pp. 758, 768–9, 826, 831, 856.

[35] *Manorial Records of Cuxham, Oxfordshire, c.1200–1359*, ed. P. D. A. Harvey (Historical Manuscripts Commission, JP23/Oxfordshire Rec. Soc., 50, London, 1976), pp. 609, 613.

[36] Ibid., p. 109.

surveys during the fourteenth century makes it impossible to establish just how many of these mills would eventually be taken into the demesne. The evidence of just the Glastonbury Abbey manors, though, is that the expansive phase of demesne milling did not continue long past 1300. The abbey's purchase in 1323 of the two mills held in villeinage in its manor of Sturminster Newton was apparently its last mill recovery: the remaining independent mills were then tolerated, with several still in existence at the beginning of the sixteenth century.[37]

If there was a failure to achieve a monopoly it was largely because Glastonbury's policy was not simply to recover all the mills it could. Instead, it was to acquire as great a proportion of the profits of milling as was feasible, and it was this that led to apparent inconsistencies in the abbey's attitude to independent mills. For instance, of the three mills of Damerham, reduced from free to customary tenure by the middle of the thirteenth century, one was to become the demesne mill by 1257 but another was to be sold off, and returned to free tenure. Described as lately having been held in villeinage, it was alienated in perpetuity for a consideration of £3 6s 8d and a rent of £1 8s, with an entry fine of 5s and heriot of the best beast to be paid on each change of tenant. It was carefully stipulated in the deed of sale that the villeins of Damerham were to use this mill only if the abbey's mills proved incapable of coping with demand.[38] Having thus reserved its monopoly over its own customary tenants, Glastonbury clearly felt that the immediate payment and the moderate rental income were preferable to any profits that might have been made by taking the mill into the demesne, when of course the abbey would still have been liable for repairs and maintenance. In other words, the policy of alienating mills to acquire a regular rental income that twelfth-century lords had pursued could still be seen as a valid one; the difference was that now this mill would pay a rent appropriate to thirteenth-century price levels rather than to those of a century before, and now also there was a demesne mill to receive the custom of the villeins.

It was also the case that some of the mills proved impossible to recover, for whatever reason. Most remarkably there were the three mills of Nettleton which in 1086 together paid £1 2s 6d rent, and 5s, 6s

[37] *The Great Chartulary of Glastonbury*, iii, ed. A. Watkin (Somerset Rec. Soc., 64, Taunton, 1956), 1129.
[38] Ibid., 1183.

and 15s respectively in 1189.[39] Despite being described in 1289 as being held for the lifetime of their tenants, when a terrier of a large part of the Glastonbury estate was made for Abbot Richard Beere between 1517 and 1520 the Nettleton mills were still held with their half-virgate or one and a half-virgate plots, and at rents little greater than those of the eleventh and twelfth centuries.[40] In all, of the thirty-three Glastonbury Abbey manors with mill histories that can be traced, there were ten more like Nettleton where demesne milling was not to be restored; nevertheless, for every one of them there is at least a suggestion that there were independent mills for the tenants to use. Direct references from fourteenth-century surveys provide evidence only for the two mills of Mells, Somerset, and that at Buckland Newton, Dorset, recorded as being in customary tenure in 1311 and 1325.[41] But although the two villein mills of Ashbury, Berkshire, noted in the surveys of 1189 and the 1230s, were, needless to say, not to be found in later manorial accounts, reference was made in the account for 1331 to land situated 'between the two mills'. As confirmation of their survival, the 1520 terrier recorded two watermills in the manor, both in hereditary tenure.[42] Mills in villeinage in the thirteenth century at Badbury, Wiltshire, and Marksbury, Somerset, thereupon disappeared from view; in 1517, however, each manor had a mill in the hands of a tenant.[43] Two more of the eleven manors were surveyed in 1517: at Idmiston, Wiltshire, there was only the site of the mill held in customary tenure in the thirteenth century, and the mill at Christian Malford described in 1289 as being at farm for two lives had disappeared.[44] Otherwise, there is no subsequent documentation that would directly record the King's mill of Marnhull, Dorset, which in 1260 had paid a rent of £1 5s and twenty sticks of eels, though in 1335 the receipt of the eels from one Atheldrida de Kyngesmulle appeared as a separate item in the reeve's account; from Kington St Michael nothing more is heard after Henry the miller paid 6s 8d in 1258 for a

[39] *Domesday Book* (London, 1783), fol. 66b; *Liber Henrici de Soliaco*, p. 104.

[40] Brit. Lib., Egerton MS 3321, fols 238v, 239; Harl. MS 3961, fols 31, 32, 33.

[41] Brit. Lib., Egerton MS 3321, fols 131, 132v, 271.

[42] *Liber Henrici de Soliaco*, p. 118; *Rentalia et Custumaria*, p. 53; Longleat MS 10,761, m. 2d; Brit. Lib., Harl. MS 3961, fols 124v, 132.

[43] *Rentalia et Custumaria*, pp. 60, 203; Brit. Lib., Harl. MS 3961, fol. 111; Egerton MS 3034, fol. 245v.

[44] Brit. Lib., Harl. MS 3961, fols 63v–85, 146.

place to erect a mill; and two mills at Doulting, held in villeinage, were last recorded in an undated survey made around 1300.[45]

The era of easy milling profits was coming to an end after 1350, and the number of demesne mills everywhere began to decline. It is, then, particularly significant that the independent mills that had demonstrated their ability to resist the pressures put on them by the abbey were also able to withstand the colder economic climate of the fifteenth century. For them the lack of a legal monopoly did not turn out to be the fatal disability that in logic it should have been, even where the abbot had his own mills. At Wrington, the existence of a demesne mill that had the advantage of the suit of the customary tenants did not prejudice the survival of the two villein mills, still working in 1517; moreover, the mill there held freely in 1189, 1260 and 1365 was also to see the sixteenth century, its ownership now shared by two gentry families who together paid the rent of 4s.[46] Shapwick's watermill, after its entry among the villein tenures in the survey of 1260, was ostensibly superseded by a windmill at some time between 1301 and 1325, yet in 1517 the manor had not only a demesne windmill but also a watermill in hereditary tenure.[47] Here, too, for all its privileges, the demesne mill had never been able to establish that local monopoly which would have put its competitor out of business.

In summary, we might say, then, that many of the independent mills owed their status to an inefficiency of lordship that had enabled tenancies-at-will to become seen as hereditary, paying immutable rents, and that others, even a majority, had been deliberately alienated by twelfth-century lords, apparently to shed any responsibility for the costs of repairs and replacement (and in the meantime ensuring a regular, predictable income). Perhaps a very few had never been the property of the lord of any manor, and whilst the rarity of these cases might well stem from the inability of practically everyone outside the aristocracy even to contemplate major capital investment, it must owe most to the overwhelming hostility of lords to the construction of mills

[45] Marnhull was alternatively known first as Kentlesworth and then as Burton, and was attached to Sturminster Newton: Brit. Lib., Add. MS 14,450, fol. 195v; Longleat MS 10,633 m. 4; 10,762, m. 21; Brit. Lib., Egerton MS 3321, fol. 84.

[46] *Liber Henrici de Soliaco*, p. 91; Brit. Lib., Add. MS 17,450, fol. 140v; PRO SC 11/621; Brit. Lib., Egerton MS 3034, fols 198, 221v, 222, 222v.

[47] Brit. Lib., Add. MS 17,450, fol. 106v; Longleat MS 11,272 mm. 15–17; Brit. Lib., Egerton MSS 3321, fol. 23v; 3134, fols 51v, 60.

by anyone but themselves. The phenomenon of the independent mill certainly did not come about by design. But whatever their origins, the ability of so many of these mills to survive must weaken the received image of a monolithic seigneurial monopoly, with all that that entails.

That historians have been mistaken in their view that illegal handmilling was the only alternative to the English manorial mill is important enough; far more important are the implications for the deeply-held suspicion that it was only by compulsion that peasants could be induced to use the detested mill. By this reasoning suit of mill was the prerequisite of powered milling during the Middle Ages — the factor without which the mill would not have made economic sense. Yet here were mills, without the benefit of suit, that, even in the face of opposition from a manorial mill, could attract enough custom to prosper.

5
The Profits of Milling

Throughout this discussion of the introduction of watermills and windmills, and the complexities of their ownership and operation, it has been assumed that milling was a profitable activity for those who controlled it. Already we have seen that it was regarded by contemporaries as a valuable contributor to seigneurial incomes, and one which, moreover, by means of careful management and judicious investment could be encouraged to grow. Now it is necessary to consider just what contribution mills did make, and how much lords felt it appropriate to invest in them. In the first place, we have to examine the ways in which these assets were managed at different times.

If we may suspect that earlier centuries had seen mills in the care of employees, or more likely of household slaves, then by the eleventh century they were held at will by tenants paying cash rents. Domesday Book, with very rare exceptions, valued mills precisely in money. With the possible exception of Glastonbury Abbey's mill at East Brent in 1189, all the rest of the mills in the twelfth-century surveys that have been looked at appear to have been rented out.[1] This was of course the period when these tenancies-at-will were coming to be seen as permanent, when lords were often willing to make grants of mills in free tenure or regarded them as suitable matter for pious gifts to religious institutions, the unavoidable inference being that mills were not then thought of as having any extraordinary merit as assets. It obviously did not occur to twelfth-century English lords, unlike their French counterparts, that they should preserve their mills and their monopoly of milling any more jealously than they did their other demesne properties and sources of rent.

By contrast, we now know that the thirteenth century saw lords make determined efforts to secure as great a proportion of milling

---

[1] *Liber Henrici de Soliaco*, p. 76 and *passim*.

profits as they could. It was a time of innovation and of investment in milling, and of high returns, as everywhere demesne mills began to be exploited in new ways designed to ensure that their aristocratic owners benefited from their increasing profitability. Having to recover so many of their mills, we may be sure, impressed upon lords and estate administrators the need for greater oversight if they were to remain safely as demesne assets. Accordingly, not only recently reclaimed mills but also new watermills, and the growing numbers of windmills, were in future to be more closely under seigneurial control than ever before, with many of them run as demesne enterprises by millers responsible to the manor. If mills were rented out it was by lease, for carefully stipulated terms. Both options were available, some lords preferring one and some the other; there was not necessarily any chronological order to them, as might be supposed. When farming, or leasing for a fixed term, in return for a cash rent, became virtually universal during the decades after 1350, this was a new development, related to the growing tendency of lords to withdraw from active participation in agricultural activities in favour of drawing rents. Before 1350, the obvious failure on the part of lords to come to any conclusion as to the superiority of either method strongly suggests that although each had advantages and disadvantages there was very little to choose between them; many lords, it appears, changed from one system to the other as if to gain the benefit of some temporary change in circumstances.

Like other lords, the bishops of Ely were faced with the problem of how best to exploit the mills lately in customary tenure. Uncertainty of their value, rather than a firm faith in the efficacy of direct management, was the most likely reason that led them at first to employ their own millers. After 1222, when only three of Ely's mills had a value assigned to them, the situation began to change quite rapidly, and by 1251, with its impressive windmill-building programme now virtually complete, the bishopric controlled forty-nine mills of which only twelve were at farm.[2] The supposition that this was intended to be a temporary situation is borne out by evidence of a complete reversal of the policy within a relatively short space of time. The vacancy account of 1298 shows that of the bishopric's fifty-three demesne mills, all but three were now at farm for cash rents, and it is not even certain that those three were in hand as they were simply

[2] Brit. Lib., Cotton MS Tib. Bii, fols 86–233v; Cotton MS Claud, Cxi, fols 25–312.

recorded in the account as rendering grain.[3] One of the windmills in 1251 had been described as being at farm at the lord's will for thirteen quarters of grain a year, and there is abundant evidence that farms of this kind were common.[4] The less complete vacancy account for the estate made in 1316, for instance, shows grain farms for five of the windmills.[5]

Against the various disadvantages of rents in kind, their supreme advantage must have been as obvious in the famine year of 1316 as it ever was: that the value of the rent increased as the price of grain rose.[6] The three windmills of Somersham were together at farm for sixty-one quarters in 1316, and during the nine and a half-week period of the account eleven quarters, one bushel and three pecks of mixed grains were handed over to the reeve by the farmer. Half — five quarters and five bushels — was promptly sold for £2 10s 7d, at prices ranging from 8s a quarter up to 13s 4d.[7] And although the Ely documentation practically ceases at this point, it is known that in 1341 two of the Somersham mills were at farm for grain and one for a cash rent, an indication that this lord at any rate continued to favour rents in kind.[8]

The situation was not dissimilar on the nearby estates of Ramsey Abbey, though the annual accounts that exist in considerably greater profusion for these manors provide so much bewildering detail of apparently conflicting trends as to dispose of any idea of there having been a conscious abbey policy on the whole matter.[9] Perhaps the best

[3] Of the three, two were in Norfolk, at Shipdham, and the third was at Doddington, in Cambridgeshire: PRO, SC 6/1132/10, mm. 4, 11, and passim.

[4] The mill at Somersham, in Huntingdonshire: Brit. Lib., Cotton MS Claud. Cxi, fol. 98v.

[5] Three were at Somersham, and the others at Kelshall and Little Hadham in Hertfordshire: PRO, SC 6/1132/13.

[6] H. S. Lucas, 'The Great European Famine of 1315, 1316, and 1317' in E. M. Carus-Wilson (ed.), Essays in Economic History, ii (London, 1962), pp. 49–72, repr. from Speculum, 5 (1930); I. Kershaw, 'The Great Famine and Agrarian Crisis in England 1315–1322' in R. H. Hilton (ed.), Peasants, Knights, and Heretics (Cambridge, 1976), pp. 57–132, repr. from Past and Present, 59 (1973).

[7] PRO, SC 6/1132/13. These prices were at least double those of previous years: J. Z. Titow, English Rural Society 1200–1350 (London, 1969), p. 98; D. L. Farmer, 'Some grain price movements in thirteenth-century England', Econ. Hist. Rev., 2nd ser., 10 (1957), p. 212.

[8] PRO, SC 6/1135/8, m. 1.

[9] In the years before 1300, Ramsey's mills at Weston, Broughton, Elton, Bythorn, Abbot's Ripton, Houghton, Wistow, and Popinho were recorded as being in hand, or at

that can be said is that the advantages of both cash and grain rents were kept constantly under review, mill by mill, and that after 1300 it was the advantages of the latter that were preferred.

The Earl of Norfolk's estates, too, began to show a preference for rents in kind, although here the shift in emphasis was detectable well before 1300; again this was a shift that came about not as a deliberate change in overall estate policy, but simply through managing each mill in what seemed the most profitable way in the short-term. On twenty-three of the earl's manors in Norfolk and Suffolk, there were around 1270 twenty-eight mills paying a cash rent, and ten rendering grain.[10] By 1300 there were only seventeen paying cash, whilst those either in hand or at farm for a grain rent totalled twenty-three.[11] Fortunately, despite the uneven survival of accounts making it difficult most of the time to be absolutely precise as to just when the change occurred, there are sufficient cases to demonstrate the unevenness of the process. So we find on the one hand the two windmills of Stonham, Suffolk, which in 1287 had been at farm for cash were by 1289 — and still in 1306 — in hand and producing a render of tollcorn.[12] The windmill at Cratfield, too, changed from a cash rent at about the same time, between 1283 and 1288.[13] And then on the other hand there was the windmill at Hollesley, which was at farm for grain in 1272, paid a cash

---

least rendering a grain rent, whilst those of Warboys, Lawshall and Chatteris were at farm for a cash rent: PRO, SC 6/765/6, 17; 874/2; 875/16; 878/14, mm. 1, 6; 885/19, m. 2d, /30, mm. 2, 4, 7d; 942/12; 1001/7. The early fourteenth century saw the mills of Holywell, Weston, and Bythorn at farm for grain, with Warboys, and now Wistow, Broughton and Abbot's Ripton as well let for cash rents: PRO, SC 6/875/10, /19; 877/17; 882/13; 882/18; 885/18, 20, 22, 31. By 1325, however, the mill at Chatteris was farmed for grain, as was the mill of Lawshall by 1335: SC 6/765/20; 1001/8. The mills of Burwell were in hand in 1307 and farmed for grain seven years later: 765/6, 7. At Cranfield and Therfield grain farms were paid in 1307, and the mill at Popinho remained at farm for grain in 1338: SC 6/740/10; 872/17; 942/16.

[10] The twenty-three manors were Attleborough, Caistor, Ditchingham, Earsham, Forncett, Framingham, Halvergate, Hanworth, Loddon, Lopham, Suffield and Walsham, all in Norfolk: Bungay, Cratfield, Dunningworth, Hollesley, Hoo, Kelsale, Peasenhall, Soham, Staverton, Stonham and Walton, all in Suffolk: PRO, SC 6/929/14; 932/11; 933/20; 934/12; 935/2, 20; 936/2, 18; 937/22, 27; 944/1, 21; 991/6; 994/28; 995/15; 996/6; 998/18; 1000/8; 1003/10; 1004/1; 1005/8, 24; 1007/4.

[11] PRO, SC 6/929/21; 932/26; 934/9, 39; 935/17, 37; 936/17; 937/9, 26; 938/11; 944/9, 31.

[12] PRO, SC 6/1005/27, 29; 1006/7.

[13] PRO, SC 6/995/2, 3.

rent in 1275, and was in hand in 1279. Rented again for cash in 1287 and 1291, by 1293 it was once more in the lord's hand.[14] After several years of the lowest grain prices in decades, this last change may of course have been brought about by nothing more profound than an inability to find a farmer.[15] Other examples can be quoted, further confirming the pragmatic management of each of this estate's mills.

It is logical to conclude that this open-minded policy of constant trial and error, observed both on the Earl of Norfolk's manors and on those of Ramsey Abbey, ought to have led to broadly correct judgements being made: the overall move towards mills being at farm, therefore — though for a grain rent rather than cash — really was in the best interests of the lords who owned mills. Regional differences may have been important, as the diversity of arrangements on other large estates gives warning that the advantages of a grain rent were far from universally recognized. In East Anglia they apparently were, so that on the manors of the Bishop of Norwich situated mainly in Norfolk during the period of the vacancy 1324 to 1326 there were seventeen mills returning grain and only ten rented for cash.[16] The mills on the East Midlands estates of Peterborough Abbey seem also to have paid in grain, for although they were all assigned a value in 1321, only four of the twenty-two were unmistakeably producing a cash rent.[17] But in the other regions of England during the early decades of the fourteenth century, cash rents on balance predominated.

In the north, the mills of the bishopric of Durham were recorded as returning cash rents both in a valor of about 1300 and in a vacancy account of the see made in 1310; two surviving accounts show that on the manors of Henry de Lacy in Lancashire and Cheshire there were in 1296 some eighteen mills, all paying cash rents, and that there was an identical situation nine years later.[18] On a group of Yorkshire manors belonging to Thomas, Earl of Lancaster, there were in 1322 twenty-one corn mills, of which fifteen were at farm for a cash rent.[19]

---

[14] PRO, SC 6/998/19, 20, 21, 24, 25, 26.

[15] Titow, *English Rural Society*, p. 98; Farmer, 'Some grain price movements in thirteenth-century England', p. 212.

[16] PRO, SC 6/1141/1.

[17] Brit. Lib., Add. MS 39758, fols 116—128v.

[18] PRO, SC 11/1012; SC 6/1144/17; *Two Compoti of the Lancashire and Cheshire Manors of Henry de Lacy*, pp. 4—54, 57—111.

[19] PRO, SC 6/1145/21. I am grateful to J. L. Langdon for providing me with a transcript of this document.

Cash rents were favoured in the West Midlands, too, though here the preference was less marked. The mills of three of Westminster Abbey's manors in Worcestershire, Gloucestershire and Warwickshire were at farm for cash in the period after 1300, whilst two more returned grain and the status of a sixth is unclear.[20] On seven Beauchamp manors in Warwickshire in 1315 five mills were in hand and three were at farm.[21] Like East Anglia, this region saw apparently abrupt changes of emphasis, so whilst all but one of the mills of the bishopric of Worcester were at farm in 1269, by 1299 there were twenty demesne mills in hand out of a total of thirty-one.[22] Only three years later rents were recorded for all the estate's mills, except those of Ripple.[23] Arguably this last change had nothing to do with estate policy, but had come about by very reason of the vacancy which also produced the minister's account for 1302; an absentee Crown official might, after all, have himself opted to draw cash rents for his own convenience. There is, though, no need to postulate such a course of events. The mills of Alvechurch, said to have been worth £3 10s in 1299 were, according to a marginal note, leased out a year later for a term of five years at a rent of £4: the bishop's administration saw the advantage of this farm, and the situation during the vacancy could well have been nothing more than the result of a change that was already under way.[24] Interestingly, on the fifteen manors for which a mill value is available for both years, the six farms and the estimates of value in 1299 totalled £49 0s 10d, and the farms in 1302 were only slightly less at £47 4s 7d.[25] The evidence of reeves' accounts is that whereas farmers generally bore all but the cost of structural repairs, the lord who kept his mill in hand had to meet even the smallest cost of maintenance; without even any millers' wages to pay, there was

[20] Westminster Abbey Muniments Room, 8424, 21047, 22093, 22092; Gloucestershire RO, 1099 M 31/40. I am grateful to J. L. Langdon for providing me with these references.

[21] The manors were Berkswell, Brailes, Sutton Coldfield, Tanworth, Haseley, Beausale and Lighthorne: PRO, Inquisitions Post Mortem, 9 Edw. II, file 49, mm. 17, 18, 20, 21, 22. I am grateful to J. L. Langdon for providing me with this reference.

[22] Red Book of Worcester, pp. 459–64 and passim.

[23] Ibid., pp. 498–540.

[24] Ibid., p. 237.

[25] The fifteen manors were Henbury/Stoke, Bibury, Withington, Cleeve, Bredon, Kempsey, Fladbury, Wick, Northwick, Hartlebury, Alvechurch, Stratford, Tredington, Paxford and Blockley.

considerable advantage to the estate in putting these mills at farm which far outweighed the small reduction in income.

Further to the south-west, cash farms were usual at the beginning of the fourteenth century on the mainly Somerset manors of the Bishop of Bath and Wells. The situation during the vacancy of 1302 of there being eighteen mills at farm for cash rents and two in hand was confirmed six years later in 1308 when twenty mills were at farm and two in hand.[26] Incidentally, the accounts that contain these figures both illustrate that we should not be too ready to assume that such cash rents were particularly to be found during a vacancy when the whole estate was administered by an official looking for quick returns. The first covered a vacancy of only fourteen weeks and consequently must show existing arrangements; the second, running from December 1308 to the following May, includes two quarterly payments of the mill rents made at Christmas and Easter, and then until Whitsun for all but three of the mills a value for their issues – though it is not made clear whether this was paid in tollcorn or in cash. What seems to have happened is that the temporary administrator realized at Easter 1309 that before the mill rents were due on the next quarter day the vacancy would have been filled, and thus it would be in his interest to cancel the existing arrangements and either to collect a weekly rent or even to take the operation of the mills into his own hand – if that were possible – for the remaining seven weeks of his office. That cash rents were normal on this estate is further borne out by the account made at the time of the next vacancy from May to July 1329, when all of the bishopric's twenty-one mills were at farm.[27]

Elsewhere in the south-west, the Duchy (previously the Earldom) of Cornwall also customarily rented out its mills. All but two were at farm in 1296 and were still so in 1337.[28] The detailed rental of the latter year, the *Caption of Seisin*, lists a minimum of twenty-three demesne mills in Cornwall, all paying cash rents to the Duchy. However, in the county of Devon, the mills of the Earl of Devon were all in hand during the thirteenth century, except for one at Tiverton which was farmed out after 1286. The mills of Tiverton were paying

[26] PRO, SC 6/1131/3, 4.

[27] PRO, SC 6/1131/6.

[28] The two were the mills of Trematon, of which it was noted that they were to be put at farm in future: *Ministers' Accounts of the Earldom of Cornwall*, ii, pp. 237–8, 253 and *passim*; *Caption of Seisin*, ed. P. L. Hull (Devon and Cornwall Record Soc., NS 17, 1971), *passim*.

cash rents in 1309, but it is not clear what was happening on the Earl's other manors.[29] The Bishop of Exeter's manor of Bishop's Clyst was in hand in 1308, and the two mills of Syon Abbey's manor of Yarcombe were in hand in the 1320s and 1330s.[30] Tavistock Abbey, though, had its mills at farm before the Black Death, and Glastonbury Abbey's mill at Uplyme returned what looks like a farm of grain in 1335.[31]

How far should we attempt to see in this diverse pattern genuine regional variations? Or how significant were underlying factors which might be expected to have affected much larger areas of the country, and which we have merely seen operating at different times? Fluctuations in the prevailing price of grain, already suggested as a likely reason for shifts between cash rents and rents in kind, could sometimes have been localized but at other times were felt throughout the country. Finally, to complicate further this discussion of the methods that lords used to exploit their mills, it needs to be pointed out that in considering the potential income from a farm, very few lords would have been able to put a precise value on their tollcorn. It was very unusual for lords to sell more than a small proportion of the grain they received in multure from a mill in hand. The wheat was sold, and frequently the malt as well; the much greater quantities of what was usually referred to simply as tollcorn or multure was as a matter of course used to feed the *famuli* or full-time demesne employees. This was the mixed corn, or often in East Anglia the barley, that the peasants of the manor had had ground for their own consumption, and which we may guess was of as low a quality as any of the grain to be found on the market – and thus from the lord's point of view ideal for issuing to his servants.

If lords took care to exploit their mills in the most effective way they could, it was because the income at stake was so great. The windmills of Glastonbury Abbey brought in rents only rarely as low as £1 5s; most frequently they were rented for £2 and occasionally for as much as £3.[32] Watermills, whether at farm or in hand, were often worth more as a result of their greater potential size and the greater

[29] K. Ugawa, 'The economic development of some Devon manors in the thirteenth century', *Trans. of the Devonshire Assoc.*, 94 (1962), pp. 657–8; Devon CRO, CR 490.

[30] N. W. Alcock, 'An East Devon manor in the later Middle Ages', *Trans. of the Devonshire Assoc.*, 102 (1970), p. 146; Devon CRO, CR 1431, mm. 3–7.

[31] H. P. R. Finberg, *Tavistock Abbey* (Cambridge, 1951), p. 195.

[32] For instance at Grittleton, Othery, South Brent, Middle Zoy and Walton: Longleat MSS 11,272; 11,244; 10,632; 10,801.

consistency and strength of their power source, though not all were so valuable. The mill at Pilton, for instance, was at farm for only £1 6s 8d in 1301, at the same time as Rooks mill at East Brent had an annual value of £12. Ditcheat mill was rented for £3, and in the 1330s the mills of Damerham, Sturminster Newton and Wrington brought in £6 13s 4d, £6 12s 8d and £8.[33]

On the dry lands of East Anglia mills paid rents comparable with those received by Glastonbury Abbey. The Bishop of Norwich had a windmill at Battisford in Norfolk farmed for £1 6s a year in the 1320s, and another at Thornham for £2, with watermills farmed for £1 6s and £2 12s a year at Thornage, and £4 6s 8d at Homersfield in Suffolk.[34] The Earl of Norfolk's windmills, returning rents of between £1 6s 8d and £2 10s or even £3 in the thirteenth century, were producing farms of grain by 1300; by then his watermills had shown some increase in value and were most often at farm for £6 each, as at Bungay, Ditchingham and Earsham on the river Waveney.[35] In the Midlands, too, similar levels of rent prevailed, with Peterborough Abbey's windmills worth in 1321 between 13s 4d and £2 13s 4d and its watermills £2 6s 8d or £3.[36] The abbey's double mill at Warmington in Northamptonshire was rented for £5, and the similar mill at Alvechurch belonging to the bishopric of Worcester was at farm for £4 in 1300.[37] Others of the bishop's watermills in Gloucestershire, Warwickshire and Worcestershire were in 1299 rented for £2 3s 4d, £1 16s and £1 6s 8d, and the most valuable, the complex of three mills in one building at Stratford-upon-Avon, was worth £9.[38]

A region where rents were undoubtedly higher was the richer lands around the Fens. The vacancy account of the bishopric of Ely for 1316 shows a windmill at farm for as much as £11 6s 8d, at Linden End, Cambridgeshire, and the lowest windmill farm by far that year was the £2 16s 8d, paid at Downham, in the Isle of Ely.[39] Contrary to what one

[33] Longleat MSS 11,272; Brit. Lib., Egerton MS 3321, fol. 206v; Longleat MSS 10,632; 10,761.

[34] PRO, SC 6/1141/1.

[35] For instance, the windmills of Ditchingham, Halvergate, Senges and Bungay: PRO, SC 6/933/20; 936/2; 943/10; 991/16; 991/28; 934/9; 934/39.

[36] Brit. Lib., Add. MS 39,758, fols 116–128v.

[37] Ibid., fol. 121v; in 1393 these two mills at Warmington were described as being under one roof — *sub uno tecto*: Brit. Lib., Cotton MS Nero Cvii, fol. 89. *Red Book of Worcester*, p. 237.

[38] *Red Book of Worcester*, pp. 368, 263, 61, 244.

[39] PRO, SC 6/1132/13.

might suspect, these rents had not been inflated to unusually high levels by the famine conditions of 1316, as comparison with the vacancy account for 1298 confirms that mill rents had risen only slightly between the two dates.[40]

But it was in the north that mills produced most revenue. Rents of £12 16s, £12, £10 and £8 were paid in 1296 for the mills of Colne, Clitheroe, Burnley and Congleton belonging to Henry de Lacy, whilst across the Pennines in Yorkshire the mills of Thomas, Earl of Lancaster, were in the 1320s rented for more modest amounts: the windmills nearly all for between £1 and £1 10s, and the watermills for between £4 13s 4d and £9.[41] The mills of the nearby manor of Wakefield were generally at farm for substantially more. In 1316 Raistrick mill was farmed for £21 6s 8d, and Cartworth and Holmfirth mills together for £27 6s 8d, although in this case the high grain prices consequent on the famine conditions of that year had apparently forced these rents up to exceptional levels.[42] Probably the farms of £13 6s 8d and £17 6s 8d paid for Raistrick and Cartworth mills three years previously, in 1313, had been more usual: even so, they still seem very high when compared with mill rents in the southern counties.[43]

Highest of all were the mill rents paid in the counties of Durham and Northumberland, for which evidence from around 1300 comes only in the form of a severely mutilated vacancy account for the bishopric of Durham. The first half of this document is missing, though it evidently dates from the reign of Edward I; fortunately the rents of the bishop's properties, including mills, were itemized for each of the quarters, so that annual totals can be calculated.[44] Thirty-one manors and townships belonging to the bishopric produced an annual mill rent of £554 9s 4d, or on average nearly £18 each — a massive amount. No clue is given to exactly how many mills contributed to this

[40] PRO, SC 6/1132/10.

[41] *Two Compoti of the Lancashire and Cheshire Manors of Henry de Lacy*, pp. 4, 8, 13, 55; PRO, SC 6/1145/21. I am grateful to J. L. Langdon for providing me with a transcript of this document.

[42] *Court Rolls of the Manor of Wakefield, iv, 1315–17*, ed. J. Lister (Yorks. Archaeol. Soc. Record Ser., 78, 1930), p. 153.

[43] *Court Rolls of the Manor of Wakefield, iii, 1313–16, 1286*, ed. J. Lister (Yorks. Archaeol. Soc. Record Ser., 57, 1917), pp. 9, 14.

[44] PRO, SC 11/1012. Obviously there may have been some rents that were not paid at every quarter, but as the mill rents for the two surviving quarters were identical there can be little doubt that mills paid their rents regularly.

total, but by using the detailed survey of the bishop's manors made around 1380 it can be shown that many of the manors in fact had only one mill.[45]

Of the factors that no doubt contributed to such high rents, by far the most important was the level of toll or multure that was charged at the mills. As we have already seen, the rate of toll was often higher than those laid down in the *Statutum de Pistoribus*, with the highest rates occurring precisely in those parts of the north where mills were most profitable. The mills of Norton, in county Durham, were farmed for £26 13s 4d at the end of the thirteenth century; in 1380, still returning the same rent, they were revealed as three named mills to which all customary tenants of the manor owed suit at a rate of toll stipulated to be one-thirteenth.[46] This was also the toll levied in Durham Cathedral Priory's manor of Aycliffe at about the same time, and which was indeed long-established in the region.[47] Amongst all the final concords for the counties of Durham and Northumberland between 1196 and 1272, four specified the rate of multure owed by customary tenants at mills that were being conveyed, and in each case it was one-thirteenth.[48]

It was also the rate to be taken from free tenants, if possible. John le Marescallus was to do suit of mill and pay multure of one-thirteenth for the twelve bovates of land he took in 1246 at Calverdon, even though he was to hold freely (and of course must have been legally free to have been a party to a final concord); Wymarc de Hethewi, however, refused in 1227 to acknowledge that a similar rate was due to her lord from whom she held one-eighth of a knight's fee, and was

---

[45] At Chester-le-Street and at Gateshead rents of £26 13s 4d were clearly for more than one mill, as around 1380 rents of £22 had formerly been paid on both manors for two watermills and two watermills and a windmill respectively: *Bishop Hatfield's Survey*, pp. 80, 89. At Easington, however, a single windmill was said in 1380 to have been formerly worth £13 6s 8d, and therefore had probably accounted for the whole of the farm of £15 13s 4d at the beginning of the century; similarly, the single mill of Cornforth had formerly paid a rent of £20 and so presumably had paid, on its own, the rent recorded at that level c.1300: ibid., pp. 131, 186.

[46] PRO, SC 6/11/1012; *Bishop Hatfield's Survey*, pp. 175–6.

[47] *Halmota Prioratus Dunelmensis: Extracts from the Halmote Court or Manor Rolls of the Prior and Convent of Durham 1296–1384*, ed. W. H. Longstaffe and J. Booth (Surtees Soc., 82, 1889), p. 134.

[48] *Feet of Fines, Northumberland and Durham*, ed. A. M. Oliver and C. Johnson (Newcastle upon Tyne Records Committee, 10, 1931), 21, 60, 65, 66.

able to reach an agreement with him that she and her heirs might grind at his mill at one-seventeenth.[49] In the twelfth century the tenants of the Bishop of Durham living in three townships between the Rivers Wansbeck and Blyth in Northumberland paid £4 annually to purchase release from a range of obligations and labour services; for a further £4 they acquired exemption from suit of the bishop's mills, and were now to be able to grind at the concessionary rate of one-sixteenth.[50] No previous rate of multure was specified, but it can hardly have been less than one-thirteenth.

The ability of lords in the far north of England to impose suit of mill so widely, and to extract such a high rate of multure, was not to be encountered in the rest of the country. One-sixteenth is the rate said by Bennett and Elton and by H. S. Bennett to have been the most common, although it was settled on as an average of the rates they found; H. S. Bennett, in particular, included a disproportionate number of northern examples amongst the sample he cited.[51] Instances of one-sixteenth being paid are recorded, for example at both Lockington and Birdsall in Yorkshire, and in Cheshire, at Chester and at Stockport; at Altrincham, however, it was one-eighteenth, and one-twentieth at Congleton, Knutsford and Macclesfield.[52] Rates as high as one-sixteenth may have been a feature only in parts of the north, although in truth there are too few statements of multure for a regional pattern to be established with any confidence. One-twentieth was stated in 1331 to be the rate to be paid at the mills of Warley and Soyland in Yorkshire, and the same rate, it was agreed in 1245, should be paid by the villeins of Normanby in Lincolnshire; as we saw in chapter 3, the tenants of Wirksworth, Derbyshire, were paying one-twentieth before their lord attempted to increase the rate to one-fourteenth in 1275.[53] In 1298 Ramsey Abbey paid one twenty-fourth

[49] Ibid., 180, 73.

[50] Boldon Book, pp. 31–3.

[51] Bennett and Elton, History of Corn Milling, iii, p. 154; H. S. Bennett, Life on the English Manor (Cambridge, 1937), p. 133.

[52] Chronica Monasterii de Melsa, 3 vols, ed. E. A. Bond (Rolls Series, London, 1866–8), ii, pp. 59–61; H. J. Hewitt, Medieval Cheshire (Chetham Soc., New Ser., 88, 1929), p. 36.

[53] Court Rolls of the Manor of Wakefield, v, 1322–31, ed. J. W. Walker (Yorks. Archaeol. Soc. Record Ser., 109, 1944), p. 163; Final Concords of the County of Lincoln 1244–1272, ed. C. W. Foster (Lincoln Record Soc., 17, 1920), p. 25; Cal. Inq. Misc. 1219–1307, 1055.

when its own grain was ground at its own mill at Wistow, Huntingdon-shire, so the customary tenants of the manor must surely have paid more than that; however, the same toll when levied by Simon the miller of Holiwell in Hertfordshire was declared in 1374 to be excessive.[54] He should have taken one thirty-second, the court affirmed, though whether from free or customary tenants is unclear. Perhaps on many manors the rate of multure really was as low as one thirty-second for villein tenants: certainly it was so at Plympton, Devon, in 1287.[55]

It comes as no surprise that it was in the north that mills made their greatest contribution to aristocratic incomes. E. A. Kosminsky, working mainly from inquisitions *post mortem* of the latter part of the thirteenth century, was able to demonstrate that the revenue derived from monopolies was huge throughout Northumberland and Westmoreland. Of far greater value than the proceeds of demesne arable cultivation, it provided those secular lords whose estates had been surveyed after their deaths with over one-third of their rental income. In fact, practically all of this revenue must have come from mill rents, as the rents from other monopolies such as communal ovens and forges were in comparison very small.[56]

The situation on ecclesiastical estates was very similar, and the £554 9s 4d, received each year from its mills by the bishopric of Durham in the latter part of the thirteenth century, was a quarter of its rental income of £2,107 10s 4½d, or practically 10 per cent of its total revenues of £5,695 0s ¾d.[57] During the eleven-week vacancy that occurred in 1311 the total receipts of the bishopric were £1,536 8s 9½d, and £170 14s of this, or some 11 per cent, came from mill farms.[58] These totals were, it seems, a cash value of all the revenues of the bishopric, from which expenses, amounting to £403 0s 8½d around 1300, were to be deducted. Mill expenses, including the cost of building two new mills, came to £28 8s 11½d, so the contribution that

---

[54] PRO, SC 6/885/30, m. 5; Guildhall Lib. MS 10, J12/162. I am grateful to C. C. Dyer for providing me with this latter reference.

[55] Ugawa, 'The economic development of some Devon manors in the thirteenth century', p. 657.

[56] E. A. Kosminsky, *Studies in the Agrarian History of England in the Thirteenth Century* (Oxford, 1956), p. 182; *Bishop Hatfield's Survey*, pp. 8, 10, 32 and *passim*.

[57] PRO, SC 11/1012.

[58] The vacancy lasted from 3 March 1311 until temporalities were restored on 20 May: PRO, SC 6/1144/17.

the mills made to the net revenues from the estate was £526 0s 4½d out of £5,291 19s 4¼d, or still 10 per cent.[59] This was appreciably more than a similar estate further south received. It has been calculated that the mills of the bishops of Worcester during the same period produced 6 per cent of the total of the rents and services due to them, and so obviously considerably less than that as a proportion of total income.[60]

Mills provided a much larger proportion than this of the income of the Earl of Norfolk in the latter part of the thirteenth century, whilst not of course being so valuable as those in the north. The revenues of thirteen manors in Norfolk, Suffolk and Essex belonging to the earldom were analysed by Kosminsky, who calculated that mills produced £58 9s 9¼d annually out of a total of rents, services and related payments of £380 1s 7¾d.[61] At over 15 per cent of the earl's rental income, the contrast with the Bishop of Worcester's mill revenues is obvious. Are we justified in seeing this as another regional variation, or was it perhaps that mills may have contributed more substantially to the rents received by lay estates? There seems no reason why the latter should have been so, though the former is equally unlikely, judging by the revenues received from the mills of the nearby manors of Norwich Cathedral Priory. An examination of the income of this particular estate is all the more interesting for the attempts made by the priory administration themselves during the thirteenth and fourteenth centuries to calculate the profits from their manors. Perfectly understandable as this may now appear, it was nevertheless unusual: a medieval account was intended not to show profits, but was designed as a means of preventing the reeve and other manorial servants from cheating. It was as difficult for contemporaries as it is for present-day historians to discover the real level of surplus from this record of all the activities which entailed cash or goods passing through the reeve's hands. The assessments that the monks of the priory made between 1293 and 1340, therefore, and which were entered into the surviving volume known as the *Proficuum Maneriorum*, are particularly valuable in that we can be sure that any conclusion we may come to concerning

[59] PRO, SC 11/1012.

[60] C. C. Dyer, *Lords and Peasants in a Changing Society: The Estates of the Bishopric of Worcester, 680–1540* (Cambridge, 1980), pp. 73–4.

[61] Kosminsky, *Studies in the Agrarian History of England*, p. 166. These figures differ slightly from Kosminsky's, as probably through a typographical error he gave the rent of the Hanworth mills as 6s 8d, rather than as £5 6s 8d. He also made a trifling mistake in totalling the mill rents.

the value of the estate's mills was known also to their medieval lord. Some of the priory's accounting techniques may now appear strange, but this will not have led to any great distortion of the results obtained. During the seven accounting years between 1293 and 1300, nine of the priory's sixteen listed manors had mills, and the income they produced was 4.3 per cent of the total profit. From just those manors with mills it was 5.7 per cent, and it is this figure that must be compared with the 15 per cent of the revenues of the Earl of Norfolk, as only manors that had mills were chosen by Kosminsky for his sample.[62]

When mill rents, as we have seen, could vary so much from manor to manor, it is not remarkable that two large estates in the same part of the country should derive such differing amounts from milling. What remains certain, nevertheless, is that by 1300 aristocratic incomes everywhere could depend heavily on mill profits, and that this was of course a relatively recent situation. The intensive exploitation of demesne mills had begun only a generation or so before, and the extent of its success is impressive. The mills of Glastonbury Abbey, for example, had shown a rapid rise in value since the middle of the thirteenth century. Thirty-two of the manors surveyed in 1189 then possessed between them twenty-nine mills which returned £19 1s 2d in rent with a further £2 by estimation from Rooks mill at East Brent.[63] Actually, the value of these mills to the abbey was appreciably less than £20 annually, as holdings of land — some quite large — went with most of them. By the early years of the fourteenth century the same thirty-two manors now had forty mills, twenty-six being watermills and thirteen windmills, with one horsemill. There had been a four-fold increase in revenue, to more than £80, which had come about entirely since 1235 and in the main within the previous quarter-century.[64]

[62] E. Stone, 'Profit-and-Loss Accountancy at Norwich Cathedral Priory', *Trans. Royal Hist. Soc.*, 4th. ser., 12 (1962), pp. 25–48; Norfolk CRO, DCN 40/13, fols 1–37v.

[63] *Liber Henrici de Soliaco*, p. 76 and *passim*. The thirty-two manors were Glastonbury, Meare, Pilton, Batcombe, Ditcheat, East Pennard, Butleigh, High Ham, Westonzoyland, Middle Zoy, Othery, Ashcot, Shapwick, Walton, Street, Berrow, East Brent, South Brent/Brent Marsh, Lympsham, Wrington, Nettleton, Grittleton, Kington St Michael, Christian Malford, Ashbury, Badbury, Winterborne Monkton, Idmiston, Damerham, Sturminster Newton, Kentleworth/Marnhull, Buckland Newton.

[64] Brit. Lib., Egerton MS 3321, fols 2, 2v, 23v, 53v, 82v, 98, 123, 136v, 141, 142, 143v, 155v, 157, 166v, 183v, 190v, 206v, 226v, 227, 238v, 239, 248, 251v, 258, 271, 282, 289;

Yet had the abbey not pursued its policy of building new mills and taking existing mills into demesne operation its income from milling would have remained static, despite inflationary pressures, as the cash rents of customary holdings were by the thirteenth century largely immune to seigneurial attempts to raise them. A closer examination of the situation on the Glastonbury manors shows that clearly. Even after 1300, there were some sixteen of these watermills that remained in free or customary tenure, and still only ten in the abbey's demesne: it was this latter group, though, that were producing around £40 annually in the 1320s, whilst the fixed rents of the sixteen independent mills totalled only some £13 17s.[65] Of all the mills on the thirty-two manors, there were 40 per cent independent of the demesne, and which contributed only 17 per cent of the total revenue.

As we should expect, it was where the newly-introduced windmill made most impact that there was the greatest increase in the contribution made by milling revenues to seigneurial incomes. In 1222 the Bishop of Ely received £37 3s 4d from his mills; in 1251, after the building of a large number of windmills, only thirty-three of his fifty-four mills were valued but even so were said to be worth £83 3s 4d.[66] The vacancy account of 1298 recorded rents from forty-seven of the fifty-three mills, and together they added up to £192 2s 10d.[67] This, representing probably a six-fold increase since the 1220s, was nearly 6 per cent of the bishopric's estimated gross income of £3,500.[68] At a time when the estate's revenues were rising generally – the result of a variety of factors including the reclamation of land from the Fens and enhanced proceeds from courts and markets – the rise in mill rents was in line with the prevailing pattern of increasing seigneurial exploitation.[69] And given the number of windmills erected in all parts

---

Longleat MSS 10,761; 10,632; 10,801. This was not all of Glastonbury's income from milling. Manors that were not surveyed in 1189, such as Longbridge Deverill, Monkton Deverill, Doulting, Uplyme, Marksbury and Mells also had mills in the early fourteenth century, bringing the total annual value of the abbey's mills to over £90: Brit. Lib., Add. MS 17450, fols 84, 105v, 131, 132v, 133, 215; Longleat MSS 9,623; 10,705; 10,632.

[65] The independent mills were at Pilton (4), Wrington (3), Nettleton (3), Christian Malford, Marnhull, Buckland Newton, Sturminster Newton and Ashbury (2): Brit. Lib., Egerton MS 3321, fols 142, 143v, 157, 166v, 238v, 239, 248, 258, 271, 289; Longleat MS 10,761.

[66] Brit. Lib., Cotton MS Tib. Bii, fols 86–233v; Cotton MS Claud. Cxi, fols 25–312.

[67] PRO, SC 6/1132/10.

[68] E. Miller, The Abbey and Bishopric of Ely (Cambridge, 1951), p. 81.

[69] Ibid., pp. 93–7.

of eastern England during the thirteenth century, there were similar benefits for all those magnates and minor lords of the region who were willing to make the necessary investment.

The matter of investment was of course crucial to the increased profitability of milling at this time. A lord aspiring to a greater share of the profits of grinding the corn of his tenants had first to expend quite considerable sums of money either on building new mills or on recovering any mills in customary tenure. The scale of seigneurial investment in regaining control of independent mills can now only be guessed at, but we can make a more informed estimate of the amount of cash that some lords saw fit to spend on new mills, especially where the new mills were windmills — which were built at a fairly standard cost. Enough building accounts have been identified to make it certain that during the latter decades of the thirteenth century a new windmill in East Anglia usually cost around £10.[70] The thirty-two windmills that the bishops of Ely had built by 1251 thus had cost in the order of £320; by 1298 twelve more had been built, for an investment of perhaps a further £120.[71]

It would be misleading, though, to set just their initial building costs against the high rents that these valuable assets could fetch. It was precisely because windmills, like other mills, were such attractive investments that there was a constant commitment to keep them in good repair, and this frequently proved to be expensive. The Earl of Norfolk's mill of Kelsale, for instance, having been constructed in 1294 at a real cost of £8 or £9 was, in its first year of operation, at farm for £3 4s — a rent recorded also for 1301, 1303 and 1306. The cost of repairs borne by the manor were nothing in the first year, £2 8s 3½d in 1301, 6s 6d in 1303, and £2 1s 10d in 1306, the major items of expenditure being new millstones.[72] Taking these four random years together, maintenance costs totalled £4 16s 7½d or 38 per cent of the £12 16s paid in rent. Soham mill, also in Suffolk, was at farm for £3 6s 8d in 1296, the year after it was built, and for £2 13s 4d in 1301 and 1304. Repairs in these three years came to 4s 3d, 10s 4d and £2 6s 8d, a maintenance bill that at 35 per cent of the rental income was comparable with that at Kelsale.[73] In the circumstances, the Abbey of Bury St Edmunds appears not to have been unduly pessimistic when

---

[70] For the cost of building a windmill around 1300 see Appendix 2.
[71] Brit. Lib., Cotton MS Claud. Cxi, fols 25–312; PRO, SC 6/1132/10.
[72] PRO, SC 6/1000/19, 20, 22, 23.
[73] PRO, SC 6/1004/11, 12, 14.

it concluded in the 1280s that one-third of the income from each of the four windmills of nearby Redgrave should be assigned for repairs.[74]

This highlights one of the disadvantages of the windmill, for at least some watermills were cheaper to keep in good repair. At the Bishop of Ely's well-documented watermill at Great Shelford maintenance costs were considerably lower, at £14 16s for the seventeen years between 1320 and 1348 for which accounts survive, or just over 12 per cent of the rental income of £119 6s 8d.[75] But just as watermills were less uniform than windmills, as shown by the wider range both of their rents and their construction costs, so it would be unwise to assume a uniform level of repair costs. Unlike the similarly-designed windmills which all faced into the same wind, each watermill differed from its neighbour because their sources of power were dissimilar. Swift mountain streams or slow but powerful lowland rivers: the individual problems they presented could be endless, and every mill demanded different provision in the way of pools, sluices and leats.

In this respect at least it is unfortunate that the English medieval watermill should have already had such a long history, as the construction of new watermills on new sites had virtually ceased before the first manorial account was drawn up. Consequently it is very rare to find evidence of the expense of excavating and constructing a completely new water-control system. In nearly every case the account covering the building of a new watermill makes it clear that an already existing site was being used. At Hollesley, Suffolk, for example, the new mill built in 1294 required an outlay of only 9s 2d on the millpool, work that was described as repairs. This was evidently the pool of an earlier mill that had gone out of use between 1269 and 1272, and which was being brought back into service to supplement the windmill.[76] Otherwise the work of constructing dams and leats would doubtless have cost far more, judging by what had to be spent elsewhere. At Standon, in Hertfordshire, when it was found necessary in 1336 to move and renovate a pair of mills at a total cost of £47 8s 11½d, £14 was the millwright's fee and £10 7s 8d was paid out for the work of dismantling the old sites. The cost of constructing the new pools and sluices came to £18 3s, but the need to spend money on repairs began again almost at once when in the following year one of

---

[74] The mills were let either for £2 13s 4d or for £2, and their repair costs were estimated at 17s or 13s 4d: Brit. Lib., Add. MS 14,850, fol. 66v.

[75] See Appendix 3.

[76] PRO, SC 6/998/27, 28; C 132/38/17.

the dams was damaged by flood. On this occasion the damage was made good at a cost of £1 8s.[77] Probably this was not an unusual level of expenditure, as repairs done to the dam of Rook's mill at East Brent took fourteen weeks to complete in the summer and autumn of 1335, costing £5 3s 2d.[78]

When mills were rewarding their owners with high rents or renders in kind, spending on new mills and on maintenance represented excellent value for money. But the unpredictability of the cost of watermills in particular meant that there were limits beyond which even the mills of the thirteenth and early fourteenth centuries were incapable of justifying investment. Interestingly, these were limits which otherwise shrewd men of affairs were sometimes unable to recognize, being as they were so used to high returns from milling. Accordingly, we find cases such as that of Henry of Eastry, Prior of Christ Church, Canterbury (1285–1331). Prior Henry, like other lords of his time, pursued a policy of investment not just in agriculture but also in urban land and in mills. At the time of his death he had acquired or built eight and a half mills which he reckoned were bringing in an extra £20 rent annually. One of these mills was the new windmill at Milton Hall, Essex; another was at Lydden on the Isle of Thanet in Kent.[79] The mill there had been destroyed in the 1290s, and Henry replaced it at a cost of £143 13s. Perhaps before undertaking the work he had failed to realize how much the rebuilding might cost, because to yield a good return on such a large sum the rent paid by the mill would have had to have been higher than any other yet discovered. This was evidently a tide mill, and he would clearly have been far better off building a much cheaper windmill as he did at Milton Hall, and as the Earl of Norfolk did to replace both of his tide mills at Walton when they succumbed to the ravages of the sea.[80] There was not even enough water to work the mill properly, and so when it was damaged by floods in 1316 it was moved to a better position. For this the priory had to pay out a further £74 13s 4d — a

---

[77] PRO, SC 6/868/22, 23.

[78] Longleat MS 10,632, m. 12.

[79] J. F. Nicholls, 'Milton Hall: the compotus of 1299', Trans. Southend-on-Sea and District Antiquarian and Hist. Soc., 2 (1932), p. 136 and passim; M. Mate, 'Property investment by Canterbury Cathedral Priory 1250–1400', Journal of British Studies, 33 (1984), pp. 8–9 and passim.

[80] For the circumstances surrounding the replacement of the Walton tide mills see chapter 8.

wholly disproportionate amount just to acquire a rent of twenty-five quarters of wheat. But again in 1326 the mill was ruined by high tides, and so finally it was decided to move it to another site altogether, this time at a much more realistic cost of £12 19s.[81] Whatever had possessed Henry of Eastry to rebuild a mill on such an unsatisfactory site in the first place, the enterprise was at last recognized to have been an expensive error and was, in effect, abandoned.

[81] Mate, 'Property investment by Canterbury Cathedral Priory', pp. 8–9.

6

The Millers

Brawny and thickset, his snub-nosed face crowned with a shiny bald pate and fringed beneath by a bristling red beard, the miller of Chaucer's *Canterbury Tales* inevitably thrusts himself forward as the archetype of his dusty calling. Most vigorously depicted of all the pilgrims, Robin the miller of the *Prologue* is the model for Simkin of *The Reeve's Tale*: physically similar, they share characteristics of drunkenness and aggression. Above all they are incorrigible rogues, shamelessly stealing the corn they grind. Robin entertains with bagpipes and lewd songs, and to give greater point to his coarse manners, the bright clothes he wears and the sword and buckler he affects suggest wealth and social pretensions. Simkin, likewise, is over-conscious of his yeoman status. As befits a man set apart by prosperity from the mass of the rural poor he has made a good marriage, to the bastard daughter of the local parson: their own daughter will inherit her grandfather's wealth and Simkin is determined that she, too, will marry well. With a hot temper to match his physical strength, other men are understandably wary of the sword he wears and the little Sheffield dagger concealed in his hose; so cunning is he that, try as they might, the two young clerks cannot prevent the theft of their corn.

During the night they seize their chance to get their revenge by seducing Simkin's wife and daughter and beating him into the bargain, and then fleeing with the bread made from their stolen corn. The expressions of pleasure at the humiliation of this swaggering villain reveal the odium felt by the medieval audience for the miller: after all, this is social parody, which is humorous only when it contains enough barbs of truth to be effective. Medieval millers were reputed thieves, and doubtless they were unpopular. Consequently it is all the more important to realize that there are other elements of Chaucer's story that do not ring true, that Robin and Simkin are unlikely to have been drawn from life: in short that *The Reeve's Tale* is not necessarily a truthful portrait of a fourteenth-century miller.[1]

The story's plot, with so many of its details, came from Boccaccio's *Decameron*.[2] Chaucer's own contribution was the adroit provision of a justification for the seductions, presenting them as the humiliation of a detested member of society who deserved all he got. By substituting a miller for Boccaccio's harmless innkeeper, he was able to introduce material to enliven the narrative and give it the humorous drive that the limp and drearily anecdotal original so notably lacks. This was not written as a story about a miller, therefore, but was a traditional story in which the central character was turned into a miller as a more satisfactory butt for malicious humour. Other details, meanwhile, had to remain as they were, being essential to the plot. Thus everyone must share the same pitch-dark bedchamber, or the story does not work; to deduce that it was customary for the family of an English miller all to sleep together in a single room would be as mistaken as to assume that Italian rural inns had just one room for all their guests. Both may well have been so, but we cannot cite either Chaucer or Boccaccio as authorities. Simkin's comfortable lifestyle and trappings of wealth, too, become suspect immediately we realize that greed is an essential facet of his character, and so the story demands that he cannot be depicted as a poor man. Chaucer's audience might not have been nearly so amused by the further humiliation of a hard-working wretch who stole only to make a meagre living.

Unfortunately, in complete contrast with Chaucer's persuasive portrait, the medieval miller is in reality a very shadowy figure. Because of his tendency to come to our attention usually as a defendant in the manorial court, his misdeeds are perhaps exaggerated in the historical record, and for that very reason we must do rather more than simply string a few anecdotes together, confirm him to have been no more than a worthless thief, and so pass on.[3] To accept Simkin without

---

[1] Geoffrey Chaucer, *The Canterbury Tales*, ed. W. W. Skeat (Oxford, 1912), ll, 545–66, 3855–920. For a similarly hostile attitude to millers, see 'Against Millers and Bakers', in *The Minor Poems of John Lydgate*, ed. H. N. MacCracken (Early English Text Soc., London, 1934), ii, pp. 448–9. This is not to deny that there are many details of *The Reeve's Tale* that are drawn from life: J. A. W. Bennett, *Chaucer at Oxford and Cambridge* (Oxford, 1974), pp. 87–116.

[2] Giovanni Boccaccio, *The Decameron*, trans. M. Musa and P. Bondanella (New York, 1977), ix, 6, pp. 581–5.

[3] As, for instance, H. S. Bennett did: *Life on the English Manor*, p. 135.

further ado as the typical medieval miller is not good enough. If we are to understand the place of the mill in English rural life, we can hardly neglect to consider in as balanced a way as possible the evidence for the man who was responsible for its operation.

To begin with, it is quite obvious that the miller's social position could be far more varied than his superficial reputation would suggest. As we have seen, between the twelfth and the fourteenth centuries the ways in which lords received income from their mills were liable to major changes; so if by removing control of their mills from the tenant millers they greatly increased their rental income, this was a matter that concerned the millers as closely as it did themselves. And when a mill, previously in hand, was put out to farm, again the miller could not but be affected, perhaps to his detriment. Clearly his status and prosperity might depend very much on the efficiency with which the mill he worked was exploited by the lord who owned it.

The miller appears in manorial accounts when his mill was directly managed, because then he was a demesne employee and his wages were recorded. Most such cases date from the thirteenth century, and show that the miller was not then well-paid: on the Bishop of Winchester's manors in the 1280s his pay averaged 6s a year or less, with an allowance of around five quarters of grain.[4] The mill belonging to Glastonbury Abbey's parsonage at Middle Zoy was tended by a miller earning 6s and four quarters and one bushel in 1275, though the miller at the abbey's mill at Longbridge Deverill received only four shillings and four and one-third quarters in 1335.[5] In eastern England, the miller at Cranfield, Bedfordshire, received four shillings in 1246, whilst at Walton, Suffolk, the wage was 3s 4d in 1283, but had fallen to 3s by 1291; at Forncett, Norfolk, the miller was paid only 2s.[6] In none of these instances was a livery of grain specified, but at Forncett there certainly was an issue of grain — perhaps a fixed proportion — to augment the miller's miserable two shillings. In 1272 the issue of the mill there was stated to be twenty-eight quarters of barley after the

---

[4] At Bitterne, Hampshire, the miller's wage was 10s and 6½ quarters; at Downton, Wiltshire, 8s and 6½ quarters; at Burghclere, Hampshire, 6s and 5⅛ quarters; at Rimpton, Somerset, 5s and 4⅛; at Havant, Hampshire, 4s and 4⅓; and at Overton, Hampshire, two millers each received 3s and 4 quarters: Hampshire RO, Winchester Pipe Roll 1283–4, Eccl. II, 159306.

[5] Longleat MSS 11,244, m. 34; 10,603.

[6] PRO, SC 6/740/7; 1007/11, 15; 935/4, 5.

Plate 2 Customers bringing sacks of grain to a fourteenth-century windmill (British Library Add. Ms. 42130 fo. 158). Reproduced by kind permission of the British Library.

deduction of tithes and the miller's allowance.[7] This must have been the arrangement at the other mills, as the cash wages alone would have been quite inadequate at a time when a casual labourer expected to earn a penny a day, and might earn twopence.[8]

What is remarkable about these levels of pay is how little account they seem to take of the miller's undoubted skill, and the responsibility he carried for the valuable machine he tended. His wages were often no different from those of the other demesne servants such as the ploughmen and the carters. Most remarkably, at Burwell in Cambridgeshire in 1307 the millers of the two mills each received 4s 6d and four quarters of grain, whilst the ploughmen were given 5s and apparently the same grain ration.[9] At Ripton, Huntingdonshire, all of the *famuli*, including the miller, were paid 4s in 1243; at Weston in 1298, however, the miller earned 6s — twice as much as the others.[10]

Working a mill single-handed would have been at best difficult, and millers often — perhaps always — had a boy to help them. One quarter of grain every twenty-four weeks was the stipend paid to the boy at Cranfield in 1351, though the two servants at the Bishop of Winchester's mill at Southwark in 1211 were much better paid, sharing 8s to the miller's 6s.[11] But it is very rare indeed for these servants to appear in manorial accounts, and their existence has to be deduced from a miscellany of incidental references. Their pay can only have come out of the miller's already inadequate remuneration, as we are told was the case when a new windmill was brought into operation at Newborough, Anglesey, in 1303, and the miller was paid a fee to cover both his own services and those of his boy.[12] In a very real way the almost unknown figure of the miller's boy is as important as the miller himself, not only for his duties at the mill but because it must have been in a boyhood passed as a mill-servant to his father or another man that each miller learnt his craft.

---

[7] PRO, SC 6/935/3.

[8] J. E. Thorold Rogers, *Six Centuries of Work and Wages* (London, 1884), p. 170.

[9] PRO, SC 6/765/6.

[10] PRO, SC 6/875/6; 885/19.

[11] PRO, SC 6/740/16; *The Pipe Roll of the Bishopric of Winchester 1210–1211*, ed. N. R. Holt (Manchester, 1964), p. 155.

[12] PRO, SC 6/1170/3, translated by J. Salmon, 'Erection of a Windmill at Newborough (Anglesey) in 1303', *Archaeologia Cambrensis*, 95 (Cardiff, 1940), pp. 250–2. Thirteenth-century references to a *sub-molendinarius* at Sugwas, Herefordshire, and to the miller's boys at Hemingford, Huntingdonshire, are to be found in *Cal. Inq. Misc. 1219–1307*, 2069; *Ramsey Abbey Court Rolls*, p. 220.

Even when a miller was a demesne servant he did not necessarily receive a fixed wage, but instead may have taken a proportion of the tollcorn. Direct references to this practice in manorial documentation are rare, though it was done in 1279 at Staverton, Suffolk, where the miller received one-third of the tollcorn, and at Farleigh Hungerford, Somerset, where the miller in 1413 received one-fifth.[13] What amounts to the same practice is referred to in the thirteenth-century *Statutum de Pistoribus*, which recognized that there were millers who were paid no wages, but who levied an additional toll for themselves.[14] This would always go unrecorded in the reeve's account, except in a negative way: it is presumably a sign that an arrangement of this sort was working when, as sometimes happens, the account records an issue of tollcorn from the mill but makes no mention of any miller.

At other times the reeve's account may record a suspiciously rounded total of tollcorn, or even more suspiciously the total may have been the same in successive years. These are the indications, if the account itself does not make it clear, that the mill was at farm for a render of grain. As we saw in the previous chapter, this arrangement was extremely common in the years around 1300, and as far as the miller was concerned it entailed entirely different conditions of employment. Rather than a fixed wage or a commission, he would now be entitled to whatever surplus he might be able to make over and above the fixed render he had agreed to pay for his tenancy. The advantage to the lord is transparent, for although an agreement of this sort held out the prospect of the miller's being able to acquire a greater share of the proceeds of the mill, it also transferred to him all of the uncertainty. A poor year left the lord unaffected, while the miller struggled by whatever means he knew to meet his commitment.

Conditions during the thirteenth century enabled English lords to intensify steadily the demands they made on their tenants, and we have already seen how their mills, like their other assets, were made to yield higher revenues. What is now clear is that the greater profits that came from milling by the end of the century were won not just from the peasant users of the mill. The millers, too, were vulnerable, and it is all too likely that they found themselves increasingly impoverished at a time when their mills were prospering.

Had there ever been a time when millers enjoyed a higher status? If the mills of Domesday Book generally paid economic rents, as it

[13] PRO, SC 6/1005/10; 971/1.
[14] *Statutes of the Realm*, i, p. 203.

appears they did, then we should not look to the eleventh-century miller as being particularly wealthy beyond his fellow-villagers. The Glastonbury Abbey surveys show millers faced with rising rents after 1086, but they also show that they had become fixed by 1189.[15] There would be no more rent increases after that date beyond very minor adjustments, so that it was only by breaking the hold of the peasant millers and taking its mills again into its own hand that Glastonbury Abbey was again able to draw a realistic income from them. Here, undoubtedly, was a period, during the late twelfth century and the thirteenth — on some manors extending into the fourteenth — when often the miller could be at least moderately wealthy, the master of his own mill. If the prosperous Simkin had any basis in reality, it was during the conditions of a century and more before Chaucer's day that his *persona* had entered the popular canon of stock characters.

Certainly among the tenants of Glastonbury Abbey's mills in the early thirteenth century there were such men, who despite their villein status were far from being poor, exploited menials. Leuric the miller, for example, who held a mill at Sturminster Newton, Dorset, in the 1230s, paid a rent of 16s and twenty sticks of eels, as well as 5s for a normal peasant holding of half a virgate of land.[16] His successor as tenant in 1259 paid the same rent, which had not altered since at least 1189.[17] When this mill was recovered by the abbey, by purchase in 1323, it was not rented out but operated by a demesne employee: we know, therefore, that in the accounting year 1331 it took over forty-five quarters of tollcorn, nearly all of which was sold for £6 12s 8d.[18] As no mention was made of the miller's stipend he had presumably been working for a proportion of the tollcorn, and so the mill had actually taken a further five quarters or so. Eighty years before, if the mill had worked at the same capacity, the lower grain prices then prevailing would have given Leuric a gross revenue of about half that figure or as much as four times his rent, thus providing him with an income well beyond the wages paid to any miller.[19] And although manorial documentation represents the social position of tenants only

[15] See table 2, chapter 1.

[16] *Rentalia et Custumaria*, p. 87.

[17] Brit. Lib., Add. MS 17,450, fol. 197; *Liber Henrici de Soliaco*, p. 134.

[18] *The Great Chartulary of Glastonbury*, 3 vols, ed. A. Watkin (Somerset Record Soc., 59, 1947; 63, 1952; 64, 1956), iii, 1129; Longleat MS 10,761, m. 15.

[19] Titow, *English Rural Society*, pp. 97–8; Farmer, 'Some grain price movements in thirteenth-century England', p. 212.

poorly, in Leuric's case there is some confirmation of his prosperity. By the custom of the manor he was entitled, like the other villeins, to various perquisites, which were carefully enumerated. At Christmas there was free firewood, and then the lord's feast for the tenants and their households: not only Leuric and his wife, but his miller as well.[20] The manorial official who drew up the survey simply assumed that the tenant of a holding such as Leuric's might normally be expected to employ a full-time employee to work his mill.

The point is also made, incidentally, that the term 'miller' needs to be used advisedly. In this document, *molendinarius* is used both of Leuric and of his employee, of both the mill-tenant and the mill-servant. It was not only when the mill was in the lord's hand that the actual work of milling might be performed by an employee. Indeed, when labour was so cheap, it would be naive to think it could have been otherwise. The most unreal element in *The Reeve's Tale* is that, prosperous as he is, Simkin works his mill on his own; but again, this is a detail demanded by the plot. The presence of working sons or of servants would have complicated the bedroom farce beyond belief, or else they would have slept in another room — in which event there would have been no need for John and Aleyn to have shared a room with Simkin, his wife and his daughter.

By the 1380s, when Chaucer came to write *The Canterbury Tales*, demesne mills were most often at farm for cash rents. May we perhaps see elements of the prosperous, independent Simkin in the men who took these tenancies at fixed rents for a period of years, and who must have felt that despite the risks they took there was the chance of a good profit? It is possible, although the farmer was more than just a miller. There are persistent indications that mills were farmed frequently by men who were not millers at all, and who could not have operated their mill without hired help. The *Statutum de Pistoribus* assumed not only that all mills would be farmed, but also that the farmers would employ millers.[21] The farmer of the mill at Alrewas, Staffordshire, around 1330, although frequently accused of malpractice seems rather to have been an absentee who was guilty of tolerating his servants' dishonest behaviour.[22] Tenancies were held by men identified as goldsmiths at Stapenhill in Derbyshire in the decade

---

[20] *Rentalia et Custumaria*, p. 87.

[21] *Statutes of the Realm*, i, p. 203.

[22] Staffordshire CRO, DWO 316, 319, 320, 321, 322. I am grateful to Helena Graham for providing me with these references.

before 1120 and at Hereford a century later, whilst the new mill that Glastonbury Abbey built at Walton, Somerset, in 1342 was farmed by a rising villein called William Pyntel.[23] Like his father, William had served as reeve of the manor for long periods, and would continue to be reeve for three years after taking the lease: both men had previously augmented the family holding with leases of demesne land. It is not impossible that William had learnt the miller's craft at some time or other, but it is unlikely. The first tenant of a combined cornmill and fulling mill built in 1387 at Great Shelford, Cambridgeshire, showed a similar lack of specific experience, being neither miller nor fuller but a carpenter, and a carpenter farmed two mills in the manor of Wakefield in 1307 for a low rent on agreeing to put them back into working order.[24]

These were men with spare capital who were taking tenancies of mills as investments. From the lord's point of view the suitability or otherwise of a man to farm a mill was not determined by his knowledge of the craft, but by his ability to pay the rent at the appointed terms, and to see that the repairs for which he was responsible were done. Mill rents, like other rents, were paid quarterly or half-yearly in advance, whilst tollcorn was taken regularly week by week, and it is difficult to see how a farmer could have got by without some reserves of cash. It is not uncommon, therefore, to come across cases such as that of the windmill at Brancaster, Norfolk, in hand during 1352 for want of a farmer and so operated by a miller for a wage of a bushel a week.[25] There was no difficulty in finding an employee to do the work, only in finding someone who was prepared to take over the responsibilities of the farmer at an uncertain time. In the same year, too, at Biggin, Huntingdonshire, there was no one willing to pay the accustomed farm of £3 13s 4d, and the miller's annual wage of 7s was being paid by the lord.[26] Perhaps these millers were reluctant to become farmers; perhaps, though, they found it impossible to make

---

[23] Leving the goldsmith, and William the goldsmith who received a grant of a mill from Hereford Cathedral Chapter: *Burton Abbey Twelfth-Century Surveys*, p. 239; Hereford Cathedral Lib., Dean and Chapter Muniments, 1,111. I am grateful to Julia Barrow for providing me with this reference. I. Keil, 'Building a Post Windmill in 1342', *Trans. Newcomen Soc.*, 34 (1962), pp. 151–4.

[24] PRO, SC 6/1134/1, 2, 3; *Court Rolls of the Manor of Wakefield, ii, 1297–1309*, ed. W. P. Baildon (Yorks. Archaeol. Soc. Record Ser., 36, 1906), p. 124.

[25] That is, 6½ quarters a year: PRO, SC 6/931/4.

[26] PRO, SC 6/875/1.

the transition from mill-servant to mill-tenant. The remuneration that millers normally received can rarely have enabled them to accumulate the sort of capital necessary to rise above the level of the hired hand.

The farmer's obligation to meet essential running costs was a further factor ensuring that only a man of some means could contemplate leasing a mill. When the Abbot of Ramsey agreed to let his windmill at Chatteris, Huntingdonshire, to Walter of Horseth in 1285, ten shillings of the £2 rent was to be paid straight away, and the tenant's responsibilities in maintaining the mill were specified. Whilst the abbot was to be liable for the post, sails and ironwork, Walter was to maintain everything else. On quitting the mill after the expiry of seven years he agreed to leave everything as he had found it: even the millstones had been carefully measured to ensure that they were replaced with an equivalent pair.[27] This was a considerable burden for any farmer, and especially so in eastern England where it was customary to use expensive, imported millstones. As a consequence, on several of the Earl of Norfolk's manors the farmer paid in instalments: literally by inches, for every year his stones were measured and he had to pay a shilling for each inch he had used. The estate then purchased new stones when they were deemed to be necessary.[28] But this was exceptional, and making the farmer pay for millstones seems to have been a practice confined to the eastern counties during the thirteenth century. At other times, and elsewhere, millstones were the lord's responsibility.

Detailed mill leases are perhaps not trustworthy as far as the farmer's responsibilities are concerned, it being perfectly possible that the terms of the agreement entered into were unrealistic. The different costs that in practice were met by lord and farmer are best discovered through manorial accounts, by comparing the expenditure on mills in hand and those at farm. Major timbers, for example, were always supplied by the lord, and the farmer was exempt from the costs of felling and dressing which also are always to be found paid for by the manor. It was also generally not the farmer's responsibility to renew

---

[27] *Ramsey Abbey Court Rolls*, pp. 271–2.

[28] Usually the reason for the supplement to the rent of the mill is not made so clear as it was at Lopham, Norfolk, where in 1269 4s 6d was added because 4½ inches of millstone had been used that year: PRO, SC 6/937/27. In at least one case the payment has been erroneously interpreted as a licence for handmills: *Medieval Framlingham: Select Documents 1270–1524*, ed. J. Ridgard (Suffolk Records Soc., 27, Woodbridge, 1985), pp. 12–13.

the ironwork of the mill. Sometimes, though, the account is quite specific as to how the expenses should be shared. At Hanworth in Norfolk in 1306 the reeve made an error in his account, and charged up all the expenses on three watermills and one windmill, together at farm for £9 6s 8d. The accountant added a marginal note to the effect that repairs should be done by the farmers, and struck out everything except a new millstone for the windmill, bought for £1 11s 5d, and repairs to one of the mill houses costing 5s 7d. The expenses that the accountant had refused to allow totalled 17s 11d and covered a quantity of small repairs to the ironwork of the mills and to the waterwheels, as well as the cost of fitting the new stone.[29]

Certain expenses must always have been regarded as the farmer's: oil and tallow for lubrication and lighting, for instance, or dressing the millstones, and steeling and sharpening the mill bills that were used in this task. The mill at Eye in Suffolk was in the lord's hand during the latter part of 1316 because a farmer could not be found, and it was for this reason, the reeve stated, that the account contained expenditure of 2s 6d on canvas bought for the sails of the mill, 4d on tallow and oil, and 2d on sharpening the bills. The account for the previous year, when the mill had been at farm, recorded expenditure of 6s 1d, mainly on the ironwork of the mill, and £2 on a new millstone, although 1s expended on installing the stone was disallowed as being the responsibility of the tenant. Not that we should look for consistency of practice from manor to manor, or even from year to year, however. The year before that, the reeve of Eye had included in his account the cost of fitting a new millstone and the accountant had passed it.[30]

Even when the farmer was a moderately prosperous tenant he bore little resemblance to the most famous of fictional millers, as it seems that the actual work of the mill was usually done by an employee. The status of the working miller, we may suspect, was always low, although, as has already been suggested, his job required considerable expertise. It was in his ability to handle the variety of regular duties that needed to be performed to keep the mill working, as well as to grind the corn brought to him in such a way that the flour was not spoilt or burnt, that the working miller demonstrated the skills of his craft. Most laborious must have been dressing his own stones. Not only was this the job of the farmer, or more correctly his employee; even when the

[29] PRO, SC 6/937/9.
[30] PRO, SC 6/996/14, mm. 8, 7, 6.

mill was in the lord's hand, and mill bills were steeled and sharpened at the lord's expense, there was never any payment made to anyone for the regular and difficult task of levering off the top millstone, turning it upside down and re-cutting the pattern of grooves on both grinding surfaces.[31] Being able to accomplish this in such a way as to ensure that the grain was properly cut by the stones rather than crushed was, like the miller's other skills, something to be learnt only from experience, in the years spent in service to another miller. But as wage rates were hardly excessive, there must have been no shortage of men who were expert in the craft and who were looking for employment, making it quite feasible for a man without a background in milling to become a mill-tenant. If ever there was a shortage of millers it was during the windmill's early years, when there can have been very few men confident of handling the new device with its inconsistent and unpredictable power source. Contributing to the windmill's initially cautious adoption, then, there might have been a manpower shortage, with the observed process of steady diffusion across the country being in part the slow diffusion of the windmiller's craft.

Millers were not generally expected to repair the mill machinery. Replacement cogs and rungs, and a labour charge for fitting them, are items that are frequently to be found among the mill expenses in the reeve's account. It is easy to see how, when a mill was put out to farm, a carpenter might make an appropriate tenant, and those instances that have been cited were probably far from isolated. The frequency with which carpenters took the tenancies of mills in the Paris region during the eighteenth century has likewise been remarked upon.[32] There was more, though, to running a mill than just keeping the machinery going. The traditional view, that in the Middle Ages each mill had its own clientele, bound to use it by law, does, as we have seen, need to be modified. Free tenants — who in many places were a substantial minority of the population, and formed the majority in several of the eastern counties — were not obliged to use their lord's mill, and on the many smaller manors where there was no mill presumably even the villein tenants could take their corn where they pleased. We have seen that there were mills that were independent of

[31] For a description of dressing millstones see J. Russell, 'Millstones in wind and water mills', Trans. Newcomen Soc., 24 (1943–5), pp. 55–64.
[32] S. L. Kaplan, Provisioning Paris: Merchants and Millers in the Grain and Flour Trade during the Eighteenth Century (Ithaca and London, 1984), pp. 249–50.

their lord's authority, and some were specifically stated to have no right to claim suit from the tenants of the manor. And then there were the many villeins willing to risk being fined for evading suit, or perhaps rather, as the fine was often the same, who were prepared to pay for permission to use another mill.

In short, we have to be aware that the miller's occupation was one in which market forces, in the shape of at least an element of competition, loomed larger than historians have generally supposed. On occasion a mill's dependence on voluntary custom, over and above the suit of the villein tenants, might lead to its being severely damaged by a successful rival, if not put out of business altogether. So the miller at Attleborough in Norfolk discovered, when a neighbouring lord in 1295 erected his own mill no more than a furlong away. The fact that his windmill had for a while been without a millstone cannot have helped the miller in his attempts to keep his customers in the face of this unwelcome opposition, and as a result his takings were considerably down.[33]

And if documented examples of this sort are rare, it is on the other hand common to find evidence that millers were not content to wait at the mill for custom to come to them, but instead sought it out — or were expected to do so by their employers, whether lords or farmers. In 1294 Richard the miller of Hemingford, Huntingdonshire, was presented in the manorial court for a string of misdemeanours and shortcomings including his failure to send out the mill boat to search for custom.[34] Its position on the Great Ouse, close to the riverside towns of Huntingdon, Godmanchester and St Ives, meant that Hemingford mill would have depended in large measure on water-borne trade: elsewhere, in the case of windmills and of watermills that were not driven by navigable rivers, horses provided a more appropriate means of fetching and carrying. In an attempt made during the 1350s to enforce greater use of the lord's mills at Lostwithiel in Cornwall, it was expressly forbidden for strange millers to carry corn belonging to the burgesses out of the town, which implies a regular horse-drawn traffic; meanwhile a scatter of references to the cost of feeding and shoeing horses entered amongst the mill expenses listed in manorial accounts shows that they were often felt to be worth their keep.[35] At Uplyme, in Devon, one horse was kept in the 1330s; two horses, though, were thought necessary at Eaton, Norfolk, and at

[33] PRO, SC 6/929/21.
[34] *Ramsey Abbey Court Rolls*, p. 220.
[35] *Register of Edward the Black Prince*, 4 vols (HMSO, 1930–3), ii, 25.

the Bishop of Winchester's mills at Southwark.[36] As one might expect, they must always have been regarded as the responsibility of the farmer, and as a rule are to be found only in the accounts of mills in hand. Otherwise they have to be sought through casual references, such as that to the mill horse of Wood Hall, Suffolk, for which a shillingsworth of pasture was rented by the farmer of the mill in 1348.[37] Confirmation of the existence of mill horses in the fifteenth century, when mills were seldom in hand, is therefore rare.[38]

When there was competition between mills for at least part of their trade, perhaps we may be forgiven for wondering how it was that notorious thieves could continue to attract custom to their mills. This is not to suggest that millers did not steal: the modest rewards received by most men employed to tend the mill, and the temptation constantly placed before them, made it inevitable that many took more in multure than they should have done. Those with a substantial number of suitors to their mill, and perhaps no competition nearby, would have been most tempted. But it was one thing for the miller to take an amount of grain that was so small as to be virtually undetectable, especially when the customer was convinced he did so anyway; to stoop to the sort of blatant theft that was Simkin's speciality was another matter altogether. Taking so much corn that he was certain to be discovered would only bring the miller before his lord's court, as John Bundeleg, the miller of Holywell-cum-Needingworth in Huntingdonshire, found in 1288. Accused of having stolen one bushel of the three brought by the reeve's son to be milled, he was ordered to make restitution and fined sixpence — a considerable portion of his stipend. Thereafter he was more careful. Six years later he was still stealing, but now by means of a false toll-dish, with which he was taking a larger proportion of his customer's grain than he was entitled to, and again he was fined sixpence.[39]

---

[36] Longleat MS 10,633, m. 13; Norfolk RO, DCN 60/81; DCN 40/13, fols 22, 29v, etc.; *Pipe Roll of the Bishopric of Winchester 1210–1211*, p. 155.

[37] PRO, SC 6/1008/13.

[38] There were mill horses at Catesby, Northamptonshire, in 1415, and there were two kept at Havant, Hampshire, to seek out corn for the mill: G. Baker, *The History and Antiquities of the County of Northampton*, 2 vols (London, 1822–41), i, p. 281; Hampshire RO, Winchester Pipe Roll 1465–6, Eccl. II, 155833. Several more instances of the use of horses, and a useful discussion of this aspect of the miller's responsibilities, are to be found in Bennett and Elton, *History of Corn Milling*, iii, pp. 133–8. See also J. L. Langdon, *Horses, Oxen and Technological Innovation* (Cambridge, 1986), p. 117.

[39] *Ramsey Abbey Court Rolls*, pp. 189, 225.

Millers must have frequently been tempted to use this deceit, as it was far from easy to detect; even when their customers suspected how they were being cheated it might have been difficult to obtain proof. Adam Cosin and his neighbours found this to be so in 1286, when they attempted to put an end to the malpractices of their local miller. Believing that Robert Styrk, one of the servants at Cartworth mill in the West Riding of Yorkshire, had for eleven weeks past been using a measure that took not one-seventeenth, as was customary, but as much as one part in thirteen and a half, Adam removed the offending dish, helpfully giving Robert a correct one to replace it. Robert was not beaten yet, however, and demanded an examination of what he claimed were the two vessels, whereupon the inquest, on finding that his own was in fact sound and the replacement too small, fined Adam 6s 8d. Three weeks later justice was at last done when it was concluded in court that Robert had substituted a different pair of measures, an offence for which he was fined 4s. This was quite beyond his means, and so he fled, accompanied by his two fellow-servants.[40]

More inventive, and much more in keeping with the traditional image of the artful miller, was William Scutard, the miller of nearby Thornes, who was discovered in 1275 to have contrived a hidden compartment under his millstones into which some of the flour he ground would fall undetected.[41] But it would be mistaken to believe that by means of such tricks a dishonest miller necessarily made himself conspicuous within the honest community that sheltered him. Theft was as much a feature of everyday life in the Middle Ages as it has ever been, if the care taken to protect mills and their contents from burglars is any guide. It was not a mere fancy of the illustrator that the Luttrell Psalter watermill should have been depicted with a door hung on stout hinges, and bearing a prominent keyhole: judging by the frequency of references in manorial accounts the doors of mills, like other buildings, were invariably fitted with locks. Locks, too, were fitted to the toll-hutches or arks, the chests in which the tollcorn was stored, and whilst this was no doubt a precaution against pilfering by the mill servants, the general concern with securing the mill indicates that the threat not just to the miller's own property but more

[40] *Court Rolls of the Manor of Wakefield*, iii, *1313–16, 1286*, ed. J. Lister (Yorks. Archaeol. Soc. Record Ser., 57, 1917), pp. 169, 175, 178; i, *1274–97*, ed. W. P. Baildon (Yorks. Archaeol. Soc. Record Ser., 29, 1900), p. 235.

[41] *Wakefield Court Rolls*, i, p. 51.

importantly to grain that had been left overnight came from others in the village.[42]

Nevertheless, it is the image of the miller as being unusually dishonest that has come down to us, and it is all the more regrettable that serious historians have done little to expose its superficiality. It has effectively overshadowed the honest miller of folklore, whose deeds were apparently once recounted without any hint of irony. When, according to legend, King James V of Scotland was entertained incognito by the miller of Doune and his family, he was so impressed by their virtue and piety that he arranged for them to stay in their mill when the owner would in effect have turned them out by doubling their rent.[43] The circumstances of the tale give an aura of realism to an improbable plot; how different it all is from *The Reeve's Tale*, with its quite commonplace events unfolding in a world with no lords, where millers need give no thought to how their rent will be paid. Here was a story received and passed on by simple people who saw nothing amiss in the concept of an honest miller: neither did they consider it strange that a miller, like any man with a precarious tenancy, was likely to find that any prosperity he might attain would eventually be transferred to his lord through an increase in his rent.[44] Displaying the same sensitivity to the realities of contemporary society, the fourteenth-century Swiss, Conrad of Ammenhausen, commented on the miller's reputation for dishonesty and gave it as his opinion that a few rogues gave the many honest men a bad name. And if millers did steal, he went on, they could hardly be blamed, because their rents were set too high.[45]

Chaucer wrote to entertain an aristocratic audience, and his cast of pilgrims was not intended to be representative of the 1380s, being instead an ideal social group of personalities that was determined by artistic convention. Accordingly, whilst we may catch echoes in Simkin of the independent millers of a century and more before, amplified it may be by the status of some of the mill farmers of the late fourteenth

---

[42] For instance, locks were bought for the doors and toll chests of the windmills at Walton, Suffolk, in 1291: PRO, SC 6/1007/15. Many more such examples can be given.

[43] K. M. Briggs, *A Dictionary of British Folk-Tales*, Part B, vol. 2 (London, 1971), pp. 99–101.

[44] See also the story of the miller whose quick-witted servant saved him from summary eviction: Briggs, *Dictionary of British Folk-Tales*, A, ii (London, 1970), pp. 485–7.

[45] G. F. Jones, 'Chaucer and the medieval miller', *Modern Languages Quarterly*, 16 (1955), p. 10.

century, his character and features stem from traditional imagery. Robin of the *Prologue* has a red beard because red-headed millers were a literary commonplace, the colour denoting deceit and treachery, whilst his coarse features were the outward sign of his low tastes and behaviour. The wart on his nose, far from being a realistic flourish on Chaucer's part, was a conventional symbol of lechery. Robin and Simkin were strong, truculent and generally the worse for drink because that was how the audience expected them to be portrayed.[46]

Characterization of this sort expresses a view of the world, albeit a stylized one. In *The Canterbury Tales* the members of the aristocracy and their dependants are sympathetically represented through Chaucer's expressions of conventional admiration for their ideal virtues: the prowess in war of the knight, the dainty good manners of the prioress, the piety and good sense of the parson. The lower social orders, by contrast, are treated less kindly, their characteristic skills and social functions being not so readily acceptable as conventional qualities. The ploughman appears as a virtuous paragon, the solid foundation of the social pyramid, but there is no recognition that it was on his labours that the whole feudal economy was based. It is particularly significant that the miller and the reeve should have been depicted so vividly, as they must have been two members of the village community that an aristocratic audience could distinguish from the rest of the grey mass of the peasantry. On the efforts of the reeve, whether loyally or grudgingly given, the income of the aristocracy in part depended, for he was in charge of the day-to-day administration of the manor; the skills of the miller, too, were exercised more to the benefit of his lord than to himself. For both to be stereotyped in such an unattractive way demonstrates an indifference to the human qualities of their real-life counterparts; it implies, too, a contempt amongst the aristocracy for the very servants on whom their economic power rested.

[46] Ibid., p. 4; J. Mann, *Chaucer and Medieval Estates Satire* (Cambridge, 1973), pp. 160–2.

7

1086 – 1350:
A Growing Number of Mills

The precision and completeness of Domesday Book, which allowed Sir Henry Darby to calculate that there were 6,082 mills in England in 1086, demand that it should be the starting point of any attempt to estimate how the number of corn mills in medieval England changed. It is not completely correct, of course: Yorkshire and Lancashire are poorly recorded whilst the other counties of what is now northern England – Durham, Northumberland, Westmoreland and Cumberland – were not included at all, as they lay outside the jurisdiction of the Crown. London and Winchester, too, the leading cities of the realm, are missing from the survey. The total also includes many examples of that distinctive feature of Domesday Book – the fraction of a mill. A matter of ownership rather than of physical reality, halves of a mill belonging to neighbouring manors are explicable as one mill; it is the isolated fractions of as little as one-sixth which present a problem of enumeration. Is each to be counted as a single mill, on the assumption that the other fragments of ownership have not been recorded? Or are they to be discounted, as fragments of mills already recorded as being held in their entirety? Despite difficulties of this sort, Darby's is as good a figure as any that is likely to be produced.[1]

Darby assumed too that details of mills entered into Domesday Book are accurate, that the royal commissioners (who after all completed their work in a matter of months) did not miscount. Although for practical purposes we have little choice but to treat Domesday Book as if it were accurate in every respect, the likelihood of some degree of error has to be admitted. It was possible for settlements to be omitted, and for any particular manor an incorrect

[1] Darby, *Domesday England*, pp. 270–5, 361.

number of mills could have been recorded. However, the many instances of low-value mills, or mills that paid no rent at all, or of those that served their owners' households, make it unlikely that there were many watermills that the commissioners ignored.

The ability to extract from Domesday Book mill statistics for each manor or vill, each county or region, invites comparison with later evidence. But whilst comparing the details from the Domesday survey with details taken from manorial documentation is worthwhile, it is a most hazardous exercise, full of snags and delusions ready to perplex and deceive the unwary. The principal reason arises from the nature of manorial documentation itself. As the English manor did not usually coincide with the village, very few surveys of manors can be relied upon to list all of the mills serving the whole village community; from Domesday Book, on the other hand, with its scrupulous recording of every manor and sub-manor of the vill, comes a complete list. Thus only where we can identify a later manor with its eleventh-century forebear is a comparison between them valid. Still there are pitfalls, though, of which the most obvious is that a mill quietly acquired from a neighbouring manor, or through the absorption of another manor, will appear to be a new mill when in truth it represents no increase in milling capacity at all.

The ideal comparison with Domesday Book, it goes without saying, would therefore be a later survey taken on similar lines: that is, compiled on a territorial basis, village by village. The Hundred Rolls of 1279 alone meet the specification, and if that survey was ever finished it survives only as a collection of fragments. As we saw in chapter 2, only the rolls for Oxfordshire, Cambridgeshire and Huntingdonshire are reasonably complete; nevertheless, that any such document should be available is fortunate. Again, before we use the Hundred Rolls, it would be as well to enquire as to their accuracy. E. A. Kosminsky, whose work on this and other contemporary sources was as extensive as it was thorough, identified few serious errors or omissions and was confident that the Hundred Rolls were a reliable historical record.[2] He was, though, analysing details of land-holding and tenurial relationships: can we be sure that the hundredal juries were as careful when it came to reporting the number of mills in each village? The valuation of manorial assets was not, after all, the primary purpose of the survey.

Already in chapter 2 we have seen what the Hundred Rolls have to

[2] Kosminsky, *Studies in the Agrarian History of England in the Thirteenth Century*, pp. 40–1.

tell of the spread of the windmill during its first century. Now the recorded numbers of mills need to be looked at again, to compare them with the totals for the eleventh century. Huntingdonshire in 1086 had thirty-six mills (not thirty-seven, as Darby calculated): by 1279 forty-eight windmills had been built, most if not all of them in the thirteenth century.[3] As for the total of watermills, this had reportedly fallen to twenty-six, plus the indeterminate number of mills at Godmanchester (where the Domesday commissioners had counted three).[4] Actually, this is an underestimate. Four mills at Huntingdon, Hartford and Buckden, each with a high value of £1 10s or £2 in 1086, would surely have been included in the 1279 total if the surveys of these vills had survived; the loss from Hemingford of two mills worth as much as £6 yearly in 1086 seems more probably to have been an error than a genuine disappearance.[5] Supporting this supposition is the obvious change by 1279 in the way that waterpower was exploited in the county, for undoubtedly watermills had disappeared, but from minor rivers and streams. In 1086 there had been seven low-value mills of which Kimbolton, at 5s, had been worth most. The others – Leighton, Spaldwick, Broughton, Wistow, Upton and Catworth – had been worth 2s or 3s, and all seven had gone by 1279 to be replaced by windmills.[6]

All of the other Domesday mills had been situated on the Great Ouse and Nene. The twenty-six watermills (excluding Godmanchester) recorded for Huntingdonshire in 1279 occupied sites which had carried only twenty mills in 1086: by avoiding a crude comparison between the two surveys, therefore, it can be shown that greater use was being made of the county's two major watercourses, with the evidence pointing towards an increase in their milling capacity of the order of 30 per cent. So at the same time as mills on the lesser watercourses had been taken out of use, to be replaced by the windmills which were more suited to this low-lying region, where there was adequate waterpower the number of watermills was continuing to rise.

The Hundred Rolls for neighbouring Cambridgeshire present a picture that is not dissimilar, after allowance has been made for their

[3] *Domesday Book*, fols 203–207b; *Rotuli Hundredorum*, ii, pp. 591–687.

[4] *Domesday Book*, fol. 203b; *Rotuli Hundredorum*, ii, p. 597.

[5] *Domesday Book*, fols 203, 203b, 204, 207; *Rotuli Hundredorum*, ii, p. 680.

[6] *Domesday Book*, fols 203b, 204, 205b, 206; *Rotuli Hundredorum*, ii, pp. 600, 602, 615, 616, 620, 622, 625. The Wistow windmill was recorded in Ramsey Abbey's version of the 1279 surveys: *Cartularium de Rameseia*, i, p. 271.

shortcomings which fortunately are readily identifiable. Villages in eleven of Cambridgeshire's hundreds were surveyed in 1279, and so their situation may be compared with that in 1086. In the eleventh century these vills were served by ninety-nine watermills, whereas two centuries later the recorded figure was thirty-seven, there being now in addition over fifty windmills.[7] In fact there had been no overall decline in mill numbers in Cambridgeshire, the problem being a degree of under-recording in 1279 which can easily be detected by the way it varied from hundred to hundred. The apparent rejection of the watermill is seen particularly in Staploe, Wetherley and Flendish hundreds. In Staploe, the vills surveyed in 1279 had possessed eighteen mills in 1086, but now seemingly had no more than four, and had no windmills either.[8] The decline in numbers recorded for Wetherley and Flendish — from fourteen and one-sixth down to two, and from six to none at all — is similarly quite preposterous.[9] What condemns these figures is that whilst it is likely that low-value mills had indeed disappeared, as they had done in Huntingdonshire, these Hundred' Rolls do not show their replacement by windmills. Such a circumstance is simply not to be believed, given the windmill's popularity in the region.

For the remaining eight hundreds of Thriplow, Chilford, Whittlesford, Staine, Chesterton, Papworth, Northstow and Longstow (Armingford, Radfield and the two hundreds of the Isle of Ely not being included in the surviving Hundred Rolls), the 1279 surveys are clearly more reliable. In 1086 these hundreds had been served by fifty-three watermills, and in 1279 thirty-one were recorded, as well as fifty windmills, an increase in the total of mills of over 50 per cent. The overall decline in the total of watermills is probably genuine, as again low-value mills were recorded as having disappeared, and in such a way as to preclude the likelihood that they had simply been omitted. At Swaffham Prior there had been four mills in 1086, and all had gone by 1279, to be replaced by two windmills.[10] At Lolworth, the single

[7] *Domesday Book*, fols 189—203b; *Rotuli Hundredorum*, ii, pp. 356—590.

[8] *Rotuli Hundredorum*, ii, pp. 499—506. No mill was listed for Soham, although a manorial account made seven years previously referred to a watermill and a windmill there; neither were there any mills recorded for Burwell, a manor which according to a contemporary survey of the Ramsey Abbey estate had two watermills and one windmill: PRO, SC 6/770/1; *Cartularium de Rameseia*, i, p. 275.

[9] *Rotuli Hundredorum*, ii, pp. 432—45; 554—66.

[10] *Domesday Book*, fols 195, 199b; *Rotuli Hundredorum*, ii, pp. 484—5.

mill in Northstow hundred in 1086, and worth precisely nothing, would give way to a windmill; and although Radfield hundred is not included in the Hundred Rolls, it is known that there too the single mill in 1086 — at Balsham and worth only 4s — was to disappear before 1222, after which date a windmill would be built.[11]

In Oxfordshire, where in 1279 the windmill was still a curiosity, the Hundred Rolls at first sight show an overall contraction in milling capacity since 1086. Once more, a detectable degree of under-recording is concealing what was at the least a moderate increase. In the twelve Oxfordshire hundreds for which surveys survive, 141 watermills and four windmills were recorded where previously there had been 175 mills; on this occasion, however, the returns for two of the hundreds — Pyrton and Chadlington — do not stand up to close scrutiny, and for the present purpose are best disregarded.[12] Other identifiable discrepancies can be corrected. The Hundred Rolls entry for Witney in Bampton hundred omits any mention of mills, but four corn and malt mills were in use; in addition, in the ten hundreds that now constitute our sample there were six vills possessing a total of twelve mills in 1086, but for which there are no published surveys made in 1279.[13] When these are omitted from the reckoning, then a new total of 119 mills in 1086 can be seen not to have subsequently diminished, but to have grown to 130 watermills. So, unlike the situation in the

[11] *Domesday Book*, fols 201; 190b; *Rotuli Hundredorum*, ii, pp. 446 – 63; Brit. Lib., Cotton MS Tib. Bii, fols 126v – 29; Claud. Cxi, fol. 121v.

[12] *Domesday Book*, fols 148b; 154 – 61; *Rotuli Hundredorum*, ii, pp. 688 – 877. Pyrton hundred which had four mills in 1086 was recorded as having none at all in 1279, although an oblique reference to one in the survey of Watlington suggests that here, and probably at the other vills of the hundred, the jury had ignored all of the mills. In the hundred of Chadlington (called Shipton hundred in Domesday Book) a suspiciously large drop between the two dates, from thirty-seven mills down to fourteen, is accounted for only in part by the omission of certain of the vills from the surviving 1279 surveys. Even when these vills are excluded from the sample, the recorded reduction from twenty-nine mills to fourteen still seems improbable, particularly as nine vills had lost their mills altogether. It is not credible that the two mills at Taynton on the Windrush worth £4 15s in 1086, or the mill at Fulbrook, also on the Windrush, or that at Lyneham on the Evenlode, should all have vanished: *Domesday Book*, fols 156b – 8b; *Rotuli Hundredorum*, ii, pp. 812 – 9; 725 – 47.

[13] P. Hyde, 'The Borough of Witney', *Oxfordshire Rec. Soc.*, 46 (1968), pp. 89 – 107; Hampshire CRO, Winchester Pipe Roll 1283 – 4, Eccl. ii, 159306. The six vills were Banbury, Deddington, Burford, Hempton, Water Eaton and Shipton-on-Cherwell: *Domesday Book*, fols 155, 155b, 156, 157b, 158, 224b.

eastern counties, in Oxfordshire the number of mills grew during the twelfth and thirteenth centuries as a result, not of the introduction of the windmill, but of the more intensive exploitation of the county's many miles of streams and rivers.

The evidence of the Hundred Rolls, therefore, shows the effects of three separate but nevertheless related tendencies. Firstly, on water-courses that were powerful and reliable, the number of watermills increased between 1086 and 1279. Secondly, where water resources were poor, windmills had been built during the thirteenth century in the quantities that were detailed in chapter 2. Lastly, in apparent contrast, many of the least profitable watermills had disappeared, as the Huntingdonshire evidence most clearly demonstrates. So not only were there more mills in 1279 than there had been, it is clear that the average mill was now larger and more efficient than had been the case in the eleventh century. We have seen already how the impact of the windmill was so different from county to county; the Hundred Rolls emphasize also the extent to which this was only part of a general movement of expansion and rationalization of milling capacity, with development occurring in the way most appropriate to each district.

To learn more of the increase in the number of watermills, we have to turn to the records of individual manors and of the large estates. A suitable estate with which to begin is that of the bishops of Worcester, consisting of eighteen manors in Worcestershire, Warwickshire and Gloucestershire. The total of thirty-two mills belonging to the bishopric in the eleventh century owes much to the twelve mills recorded for Blockley, but there is no reason why we should disbelieve this entry for what was after all a vast upland manor with several small centres of settlement.[14] When the estate was surveyed around 1170, the numbers of mills recorded for the different manors corresponded closely with Domesday Book entries. The valuation for Blockley was said to include mills, although none were listed in the survey, and Bibury was not surveyed in 1170; leaving these aside, the remaining manors had eighteen mills in 1086 and sixteen a century later, and on eight of the manors the number of mills was the same in both surveys.[15]

A further comparison with the position at the end of the thirteenth century demonstrates a modest rise from thirty-two mills in 1086 to thirty-eight in 1299.[16] Fortunately the Worcester material is unusually

[14] Ibid., fols 164b, 165, 172b–4, 238b.
[15] Red Book of Worcester, p. 314 and passim.
[16] Ibid., passim.

helpful, and at the same time illustrates just how misleading such simple comparisons can be. In the first place, behind the increase lay several contrasting movements. Five windmills had been built, bringing adequate milling facilities to settlements without sufficient waterpower, and there were new watermills to serve new centres of demand. At Stratford, it was the foundation of the successful new town in the 1190s that caused the replacement of the single mill at Shottery by the complex of two corn mills and one malt mill which was bringing in £9 a year in the 1290s. There were multiple mills, too, at Fladbury, Alvechurch and Henbury, constructed to make the most of good sites on steady rivers.[17] Meanwhile other mills had disappeared, most spectacularly at Blockley, where from twelve the total had by 1299 fallen to three.[18] This was not a poor manor, and there can have been no sign as yet of the depopulation which would begin to affect this part of the Cotswolds in the latter half of the fourteenth century.[19] The principal reason for the change was evidently the rationalization of milling resources that the Hundred Rolls show had occurred elsewhere, although in this case the mills that had been taken out of use were not on lowland streams that had never been satisfactory. The purpose of the rationalization, we may be sure, had been to concentrate milling at three centres. Whilst this was undoubtedly less convenient for the tenants of the outlying hamlets, the suit that most of them owed to the bishop's mills ensured their continued custom; from the estate's point of view the move would have brought considerable savings, even allowing for redevelopment of the chosen sites.

So once again we have seen evidence of watermills going out of use in the twelfth or thirteenth centuries in what seems to be a reorganization of resources, and one moreover that is firmly attributable to seigneurial initiative. It is virtually certain that it was a widespread phenomenon, as lords closed small mills to concentrate on establishments that could be more profitable. In most instances, of course, this would have involved development of the existing site, and so an increase in capacity would go unnoticed in a comparison of numbers.

The Worcester documentation illustrates a further hazard which needs to be taken into account in any attempt to calculate the number

---

[17] Ibid., pp. 62, 125, 151, 172, 210, 244, 327, 380.

[18] Ibid., pp. 296, 317. The third of these mills was at Paxford, which had been part of Blockley in 1086.

[19] R. H. Hilton and P. A. Rahtz, 'Upton, Gloucestershire, 1959 – 1964', *Trans. Bristol and Glos. Archaeol. Soc.*, 85 (1966), pp. 70 – 146.

of medieval mills. Of the thirty-three watermills recorded in 1299, twenty-five were demesne mills, and the remaining eight were described in such a way as to show that they were independent mills.[20] Their presence is recorded because this was intended to be a thorough survey of all the lands and assets of each manor; the briefer survey of the Worcester estate made around 1290 ignored all but one of them, that at Bredon. The vacancy account of the bishopric made in 1303 after the death of Bishop Godfrey Giffard again ignored the independent mills, with the exception this time of the mill at Wick that was held in villeinage.[21] As we saw in chapter 4, it is the nature of the document that determines whether independent mills are included or not: demesne extents and accounts record the income only from demesne mills, whereas a complete survey of a manor should list all of the mills in the lordship. In other words, if documents other than full surveys are used, the exercise of counting mills will succeed only in totalling demesne mills. And whilst the results of such an exercise might prove useful, they would not convey the extent to which new mills continued to appear for more than two centuries after Domesday Book.

A reliable picture of changes in mill numbers in the south-west is provided by the excellent Glastonbury Abbey documentation. Like the Worcester surveys, the Glastonbury evidence demonstrates the extent to which the failure of most documentation to list independent mills is likely to lead to an under-estimate of watermill totals during the fourteenth century. Of the thirty-five manors surveyed in 1189 there were thirty-two that remained in Glastonbury's possession, and for which there is later evidence.[22] For all but one — Damerham — there is firm evidence for the number of mills during the early decades of the fourteenth century: if Damerham is excluded, therefore, it is possible to be certain of mill numbers between 1086 and 1350. This large sample of thirty-one manors had twenty-one mills in 1086, twenty-six in 1189, and forty in the early fourteenth century.[23] Of this

[20] *Red Book of Worcester*, pp. 5, 53, 105, 192, 193, 212, 370, 395.

[21] Ibid., pp. 107, 521.

[22] Blackford, Winscombe and Pucklechurch later became the property of the bishopric of Wells.

[23] *Domesday Book*, fols 59b, 66b, 72b, 77b, 90, 90b; *Liber Henrici de Soliaco, passim*; Brit. Lib., Egerton MS 3321, fols 1–2v, 23v, 53v, 82v, 98, 123, 136v, 141, 142, 143v, 155v, 157, 166v, 183v, 190v, 206v, 226v, 227, 238v, 239, 248, 251v, 258, 271, 282, 289; Add. MS 17450, fol. 186; Longleat MSS 10,761; 11,215; 10,801; *Rentalia et Custumaria*, p. 166.

last total, twenty-seven were watermills, so here too there had been the modest increase in watermill numbers that has already been observed elsewhere. What is also important is that we can be sure that only thirteen, or fewer than half, of these watermills were demesne mills, even after 1300: if we had only Glastonbury Abbey accounts to work from, we should be led to believe that watermill numbers on the estate had fallen since 1086, from twenty-one to thirteen.[24]

For a large part of Suffolk, the Itinerary of Solomon of Rochester provides a massive sample of whole vills rather than of manors, following the pattern of its relative, the Hundred Rolls. The spectacular evidence it provides for the flurry of windmill-building in East Anglia during the thirteenth century has already been examined in chapter 2; the survey also notes that in addition to the sixty-five new windmills there were thirty-four watermills. Here was a small but unmistakeable increase in this, amongst the driest of English counties, over the twenty-eight mills recorded for the same villages in Domesday Book.[25]

But the greatest increases came, not surprisingly, in the extreme south-west where there had been so little need of powered milling in the eleventh century. In Cornwall there were no more than six mills in 1086; by 1300 the mill was as common a feature as it was elsewhere. The estates of the Duchy of Cornwall possessed by the fourteenth century twenty-seven or twenty-eight mills, where previously there had been three, and a very damaged account of the temporalities of the bishopric of Exeter made in 1291 shows mills in every one of six named Cornish manors.[26] In Devon, too, where there had been only ninety-six mills in 1086, a sample of six manors belonging to the Earl of Devon, the Bishop of Exeter and Syon Abbey had had no mills at all but acquired twelve by 1300.[27]

Out of all this, certain trends become abundantly clear. Once unsatisfactory data from manorial accounts have been discounted, once the shortcomings of the Hundred Rolls have been identified and

---

[24] There were, in addition, twelve windmills and one horsemill.

[25] *The Pinchbeck Register*, ii, pp. 30 – 281; *Domesday Book*, ii, fols 120b, 288b, 289, 357 – 359b, 361b, 362, 364, 365, 366, 366b, 367b, 368b, 369, 403b, 416, 434, 448b.

[26] Darby and Finn, *The Domesday Geography of South-West England*, p. 334; *Ministers' Accounts of the Earldom of Cornwall*, ii, *passim*; PRO, SC 6/1138/1.

[27] Darby and Finn, *The Domesday Geography of South-West England*, pp. 276 – 8; Ugawa, 'The economic development of some Devon manors in the thirteenth century', p. 657; Devon CRO, CR 1431, 1436; CR 1131; Alcock, 'An East Devon manor in the later Middle Ages', pp. 141 – 87.

allowance made for them, everywhere a growth in mill numbers between 1086 and 1300 is confirmed. As well as the appearance of the windmill which met a long-felt need of the eastern counties, the steady rise in the number of watermills observed in the Midlands, the Home Counties, the West Country and even in East Anglia was a most important development. No very firm estimate of the total number of mills in early fourteenth-century England can be advanced as the rate of growth differed from region to region: the Glastonbury estates saw an increase of 80 per cent; those of the bishopric of Worcester 19 per cent. In percentage terms the most impressive growth must have come in the south-west, whereas the greatest overall growth came in the eastern counties. In Norfolk, Suffolk, Cambridgeshire and Huntingdon-shire, where the windmill's impact was most obvious, there had been 953 mills in 1086, and whilst the fourfold increase in mill numbers in the manors of west Suffolk may not have been experienced everywhere in these four counties, we have seen that the evidence supports a widespread threefold increase. And these, furthermore, were not the only counties where the windmill would be well-established by the fourteenth century. All in all, a total of 10,000 English mills by 1300 seems a cautious estimate. It may even be that the total was greater than that, having doubled since the eleventh century, and that there were now as many as 12,000 windmills and watermills grinding England's corn and malt.

Medieval England would never have so many corn mills again. The second half of the fourteenth century would see a precipitate fall in the total of demesne mills, which would usher in a long period during which the profitability of milling would decline, and the number of mills continue to fall. The circumstances surrounding this collapse in milling activity, and the reasons for it, will be considered in chapter 10.

8

Mill Technology and Innovation

One of the most satisfying aspects of the English medieval mill is that it is possible to know so much about how it was constructed. The details entered into reeves' accounts of repairs and occasional rebuildings, and even rarer new buildings, provide a composite picture of a simple yet sturdy device made almost entirely of wood. There were a few parts which were invariably of iron, and stone and brass were also used. Even though the accounts give no description of precisely how the timberwork was put together, it is clear that the construction was similar to that of early modern mills, of which several survive and have been described.[1]

As the purpose was to make the upper of a single pair of millstones revolve quickly enough to grind corn poured into the hole at its centre, and expel the meal at its edges, the motion of the water-wheel, mounted vertically on a horizontal axle, needed to be transferred through ninety degrees. Gearing was thus required, and a wooden cog-wheel or trundle-wheel was mounted at the inner end of the axle to intermesh with a lantern-pinion wheel on the vertical spindle that turned the stone. When the windmill made its entrance during the twelfth century it employed the same mechanism: it was not a new machine, therefore, but an adaptation of an existing machine to a new power source.

Rather disappointingly, this wealth of documentary evidence is not matched by any great quantity of identified physical remains. Archaeological excavations of the sites of medieval mills have been relatively rare, and with few exceptions have provided information about the channelling of the water supply into the mill, or about the windmill's foundations, whilst adding little or nothing to our knowledge of their mechanisms or superstructure. Yet there are

---

[1] See, for instance, W. A. McCutcheon, 'Water power in the North of Ireland', *Trans. Newcomen Soc.* 39 (1966–7), pp. 70–1.

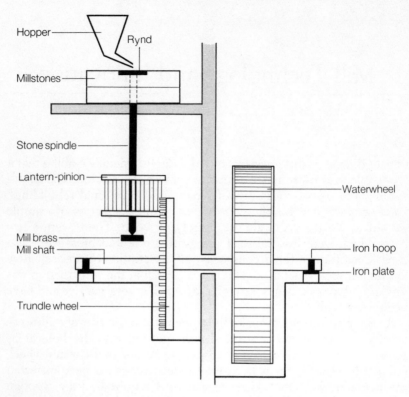

Figure 5 Internal arrangements of a medieval vertical water mill.

problems concerning the watermill that can never be solved by documentary research, the most important by far being that of the replacement of the horizontal mill by the vertical mill. We have seen that there is good reason to believe that the horizontal mill was at one time as ubiquitous in England as it was across the Irish Sea. But when, and why, did it disappear from the English countryside? For disappear it certainly did, and by the thirteenth century, according to manorial documentation. The reeves' accounts that begin to survive in large numbers after that date make mention only of vertical mills, or at any rate they abound with terminology that can only have been applied to vertical mills. Inner wheels and outer wheels, the cogs and rungs of the gear wheels, the provision of bearings on which a horizontally-laid axle could run, show conclusively that by this time all the mills being described had vertical wheels.

We can be certain that both types of mill coexisted in England before the tenth century.[2] Had the horizontal mill already disappeared by the time of the Conquest, or were there still many to be found amongst the 6000 mills of Domesday Book? The difficulty of producing any satisfactory answer matches the importance of the question, for modern studies of the survival of horizontal mills in peasant communities demonstrate the machine's relatively inefficient use of the available waterpower, but also its ease of construction and low repair costs.[3] A major replacement of horizontal mills by vertical mills would thus have entailed an appreciable increase in the total volume of milling power, but could have been achieved only by means of a large initial outlay, and by a greater commitment to maintenance.

If there were still horizontal mills in 1086 then were they perhaps amongst the mills that paid low rents, and which in some cases can be seen to have gone out of use during the century or so following? In several counties there were 'winter mills' which presumably were unable to work in the dry summer months, and other mills paying no rent at all. There is, though, nothing to link these marginal enterprises with any particular design of mill, and accordingly we have to pursue a more fruitful line of enquiry, by examining the horizontal mill itself, and its distinctive role. For Cecil Curwen was surely correct when he identified it as being 'characteristic of peasant cultures', observing that horizontal mills were often owned in common by peasants for their own use.[4] Sometimes a group of them would be found together on a single stream, all serving the needs of one community. Studies of the horizontal mills of the Shetlands and elsewhere have confirmed the pattern, with some mills built by their peasant owners to be operated

[2] See chapter 1.

[3] E. Gauldie, *The Scottish Country Miller 1700 – 1900* (Edinburgh, 1981), pp. 115 – 19; D. W. Gade, 'Grist milling with the horizontal waterwheel in the Central Andes', *Technology and Culture*, 12 (1971), pp. 43 – 51; J. K. G. Boucher, 'Watermill research and development in Nepal', *Wind and Water Mills*, 5 (1984), pp. 43 – 8; S. Maxwell, 'A horizontal water mill paddle from Dalswinton, and some notes on the occurrence of this type of mill in Scotland', *Trans. Dumfriesshire and Galloway Nat. Hist. and Antiquarian Soc.*, 3rd ser., 33 (1954 – 5), pp. 185 – 96; G. Goudie, 'On the horizontal water mills of Shetland', *Procs. of the Soc. of Antiquaries of Scotland*, new ser., 8 (1885 – 6), pp. 257 – 97; F. F. Strauss, '"Mills without wheels" in the sixteenth-century Alps', *Technology and Culture*, 12 (1971), pp. 23 – 42.

[4] E. C. Curwen, 'The problem of early water-mills', *Antiquity*, 18 (1944), p. 130.

for profit, and others owned and maintained by groups of families to be used communally.[5]

All too often, however, horizontal mills have been considered in isolation from the cultures which produced and used them. Two notable recent exceptions have been works by Philip Rahtz and Anthony Bryer, describing the horizontal mills of, respectively, Crete and the Pontos region of Turkey.[6] Having drawn attention to their straightforward design, Bryer suggested that this might have had consequences for the way in which society had developed in the Pontos in the medieval period, for in contrast with the situation in the West there was a complete absence of any seigneurial monopoly of milling or compulsion to use watermills. Low installation costs and easy maintenance could thus have been the factors that kept milling as a peasant activity, with the great estates operating mills only for their own use. Attractive as this might appear to anyone wishing to see social change as a product of developments in technology, what Bryer was unable to explain was the absence of the vertical water-wheel from the whole of the Byzantine East. The Greeks were making use of it until the fifth and sixth centuries, but thereafter it is not recorded; and whilst the horizontal mill may be the logical design for the Pontos where valleys are narrow and rushing streams abound, the same is not true of other regions where the more efficient vertical wheel would have been more appropriate. He could only suggest that there had been a widespread process of technical regression.

In fact, having correctly identified the link between the horizontal mill and the absence of a seigneurial monopoly, Bryer drew the wrong conclusion. The situation throughout the Byzantine Empire becomes explicable if his argument is inverted, if we see the ubiquity of the horizontal mill as a consequence of the very lack of seigneurial compulsion he described. The horizontal mill flourished everywhere that peasants were able legally to operate their own mills, being the least expensive design; the vertical mill, on the other hand, with its far greater costs of construction and maintenance, was everywhere

[5] J. and R. Bedington, 'The "Norse" watermills of Shetland', *Wind and Water Mills*, 5 (1984), p. 33; Strauss, '"Mills without wheels"', pp. 32—4.

[6] P. A. Rahtz, 'Medieval Milling', in D. W. Crossley (ed.), *Medieval Industry* (Council for British Archaeology, Research Report 40, London, 1981), Appendix A, 'Horizontal-wheeled Watermills on Crete', pp. 8—13; A. A. M. Bryer, *The Empire of Trebizond and the Pontos* (London, 1980), pp. 405—11 of Section vii, 'The Estates of the Empire of Trebizond'.

associated with large-scale milling. Whether milling was carried on as a major capitalist enterprise competing for custom, or as a feudal one maximizing its profits through legal compulsion, the vertical mill with its greater overall efficiency and much greater potential power was likely to be preferred.

If we accept that the medieval horizontal mill was a product not of an unexplained process of technical regression, and particularly not of cultural or ethnic differences, but instead was associated with the very different ways in which European lords exploited their estates, then its disappearance in the highly feudalized parts of the West — in northern France, of course, but also in England and Germany — becomes less mysterious. There the striving of lords for monopoly powers favoured the more powerful vertical mill; conversely, where the nature of local lordship was rather different — in Italy, Spain, southern France, Ireland, Scandinavia, and highland societies everywhere — horizontal mills predominated until modern times. In Spain they were often built by groups of peasants and even by individuals, and the vertical mill was hardly used despite its having been known there since at least the tenth century.[7] The *contado* of Florence, too, which few would dare describe as a backward region, was in the early fifteenth century served by enormous numbers of mainly horizontal mills — 711 in all — of which half were owned by individuals and the other half by syndicates, families, rural communes and the Church.[8]

Accordingly, if we are to search for signs of the horizontal mill's existence in eleventh-century England, or to postulate a chronology for its demise, the most fruitful course first of all may be to examine the tenurial status of the mills recorded in Domesday Book. Potential examples would thus be the five mills at Leeds in Kent which belonged to the villeins of the manor, or the mills to be found in several counties that paid no rent to any lord.[9] The eight mills in Somerset that were

[7] T. Glick, *Islamic and Christian Spain in the Early Middle Ages*, (Princeton, 1979), pp. 147–8, 230–3.

[8] J. Muendel, 'The Distribution of Mills in the Florentine Countryside during the Late Middle Ages', in J. A. Raftis, (ed.), *Pathways to Medieval Peasants* (Toronto, 1981), pp. 87, 97–9 and *passim*. See also Muendel, 'The horizontal mills of Pistoia', *Technology and Culture*, 15 (1974), pp. 194–225; G. Sicard, *Les Moulins de Toulouse au Moyen Age* (Paris, 1953), p. 46; H. Amouric, 'De la roue horizontale à la roue verticale dans les moulins à eau', *Provence Historique*, 33 (1983), pp. 157–69.

[9] *Domesday Book*, fol. 7b. Mills that paid no rent are recorded, for example, for Kent, Sussex and Worcestershire: fols 5, 10, 17b, 28, 173b.

said to pay no rent were described in the Exeter Domesday as grinding their own grain — *qui molit annonam suam* — a statement that leaves it unclear as to whether they worked just for the lord's household or were co-operative ventures built and owned by groups of villein families.[10] It is also possible that among the mills paying low rents may have been many that did so because they had been built by their tenants.

We have already seen that the triumph of the seigneurial mill in England was not nearly so complete as it was in France. Again, among the mills in free and customary tenure might there not have been many that continued to employ the simpler technology of the horizontal mill? It seems plausible enough, considering that their tenants had to maintain them. The period following on the assertion of demesne control would, by this reasoning, have been the time when an expensive conversion of the mill and its water control systems took place, to allow operation by the more powerful vertical wheel.

There is just a possibility that the horizontal mill is occasionally identified, albeit imprecisely, in some of the earliest manorial documentation. References are sometimes made to 'small mills' in such a way as to raise the suspicion that the *parvum molendinum* under discussion is not being distinguished merely by size, but is an identifiable type of mill. The term was used of a mill belonging to Burton Abbey at Stapenhill in Derbyshire that Leving the goldsmith held with four bovates of land for 8s in the years before 1120, and of another at Winhill in the same county rented for only 4s 6d; of the various mills granted out by Abbot Samson of Bury St Edmunds in the years around 1200 only one was described as a small mill; and at Bitterne, Hampshire, soon after 1200, a small mill was rented for 5s, when oddly there was no other mill in the manor which would require its being identified by any qualifying term, so that the adjective would seem to be superfluous.[11]

We must now turn to consider the vertical mill, and its construction. The initial building costs of demesne watermills were examined in chapter 5, and were shown to be at a level that was quite beyond the means of peasants. The constant expenditure on repairs, too, was justifiable only if the mill was doing sufficient work to ensure a

---

[10] Ibid., fols 91b, 92, 92b, 96, 99; Darby and Finn, *Domesday Geography of South-West England*, pp. 190–1.

[11] *Burton Abbey Surveys*, pp. 239, 243; *Kalendar of Abbot Samson*, 95; *Pipe Roll of the Bishopric of Winchester 1210–11*, p. 5.

comfortable level of profit. Repair costs were high partly because, as we saw in the previous chapter, however skilled the miller might have been, professional craftsmen were always employed for a range of tasks. The regular services of the smith, for instance, were called upon, as it was generally considered essential for certain parts of the mill to be made of iron. Principally these were the spindle, usually called the *fusillum*, and the rynd or *ynkum* which was the iron fitting that held the upper millstone or runner, so that it rested on and moved with the spindle. Not surprisingly, the spindle needed to be strong to support the constant weight of a millstone running perhaps at over a hundred revolutions a minute; it is also not surprising that this was one of the parts of the mechanism that required most frequent attention. Sixty pounds of iron were bought for a new spindle and rynd for Great Shelford mill in 1368 at a cost of 5s, and the wages of the smith making the parts was 2s 6d. Only a year later, when a new millstone was fitted, the spindle had to be lengthened with thirteen pounds of iron, at a total cost of 2s 4d. In 1372 a new spindle was made with twenty-two pounds of iron for 3s 4d, and in 1376 twenty-eight pounds of iron was bought for a spindle, one or two bearings and strengthening bands for the cogwheel. Two years later yet another spindle was needed, this time made by the smith with twenty pounds of new iron for 2s 7d. The next year thirty-four pounds of iron were bought for the spindle, and when the year after that a new spindle was again needed it was made with eighteen pounds of iron.[12]

All lists of mill repairs entered into reeves' accounts tell the same story of the constant failure of the spindle — though few, it must be said, do so with quite the same monotony as the Great Shelford accounts which are an unusually complete series. The constant twisting stress to which the spindle was subjected, being driven at one end to turn at the other a millstone weighing perhaps half a ton, led inevitably to irreparable fracture. The purchase of new iron for spindles is recorded so frequently as to indicate a regular practice, although it is far from clear whether the new spindle was always to be made entirely of new iron, or whether any of the previous spindle could be re-used. A new windmill built at Saxtead in Suffolk in 1286 was fitted with a spindle and a rynd made of an unspecified quantity of new iron; the eventual fate of some old spindles and an old rynd is somewhat unclear, but they seem to have been used by the smith, possibly

[12] PRO, SC 6/1134/4; 1133/5, 7.

together with new iron, to make bearings and strengthening bands.[13]

With the whole weight of the upper millstone carried on the lower end of the spindle, it would as it spun round have set up considerable friction with the bearing on which it stood. The rate of wear was probably compensated for as the grinding surfaces of the millstones also wore away, and so over a long period the upper end of the spindle and the rynd literally sank lower and lower. It was when a new stone was to be fitted that the spindle would be found to be now too short, and if it was not to be replaced altogether it had to be lengthened. This is again so frequently encountered when a new stone was installed as to indicate a routine necessity, although the connection between the two operations is seldom made so plain as it was in 1334 in the account for Longbridge Deverill, Wiltshire. There it was stated that the spindle had been lengthened with six pounds of iron because of the new millstone – *propter novum molarem.*[14] Sometimes a detachable section was fitted to the lower end of the spindle, judging by occasional references to the foot being replaced or mended, and a harder material might be used – steel at Overton and Burghclere, Hampshire, and brass at Cheriton.[15]

Metal was also commonly used for bearings, although it was not essential. Bearings of some sort are necessary in every machine with moving parts at points where they come into contact, and a vertical watermill needed them where the weight of the turning water-wheel and axle were supported, and at the base of the spindle. In windmills they were at essentially the same points: below the spindle, at the inner end of the windshaft and at its neck where it entered the mill. At least so much can be detected from the profusion of brief references to bearings, and amid the confusion of a multitude of different terms. The most important was the bearing that carried the spindle, and which was very often of brass. At Barton, Bedfordshire, 2s 8d was paid for sixteen pounds of brass for a *pilwe* to be positioned beneath the spindle; at Great Shelford *buldyr* was the term recorded most often, though *milbras*, used here in 1455, perhaps had wider currency.[16] A piece of brass called *le bras* was purchased for the new mill at Standon, Hertfordshire, in 1329; eight years later a new *melnebras* weighing

[13] *Medieval Framlingham*, p. 27.
[14] Longleat MS 10,603.
[15] Hampshire CRO, Winchester Pipe Roll 1283–4, Eccl. ii, 159306.
[16] PRO, SC 6/740/15; 1134/1, 3, 5; 1135/1.

eight pounds was bought.[17] But we should be wary of assigning too specific a meaning to these names: in 1352 a *pylwe* of brass was bought for the windshaft of the windmill at Biggin, Huntingdonshire.[18] Anyway, many mills must have had a bearing of iron, and so 'mill brass' as a general term would be inappropriate. The *sole* — commonly recorded in the eastern counties, and always of iron — may have gone under the spindle, although in no document has this connection been made.[19] The use of the term in the singular is the only indication of its purpose.

The bearings of the axles of both windmils and watermills are recorded as being of iron, and were almost invariably named as *pannae* and *patellae*, which in other contexts would mean 'pans' or 'bowls'. The terms were interchangeable, for at Acle, Norfolk, two *pannes* were made in 1269 for the axle of one of the windmills; at Hacheston, Suffolk, a *patella* was fitted as the neck bearing of a windmill in 1301.[20] At Caistor-cum-Markshall and Earsham, Norfolk, in 1300 and 1306, *patellae* were fitted beneath the outer and inner ends respectively of the axles of the watermills there.[21] Variations of terminology are to be found, however, such as the *plata* or plates of the mill at Weston, Huntingdonshire, renewed with iron in 1325, and the new *clutum* or clout made to go under the axle of the mill at Haughley in Suffolk in 1315.[22] The iron *dagshoes* found in the lists of repairs of Suffolk mills were also probably bearings.[23] Unless the wooden axles and windshafts themselves ran directly on these bearings, contact was with the iron hoops or collars that the accounts frequently record as having been fitted. As the reason for these hoops is never made clear they may have been intended for strengthening, though it is much more likely that their primary purpose was to provide a suitably hard surface.

What is uncertain is how many mills had bearings of metal, and how many used less expensive substances. Archaeological evidence suggests

[17] PRO, SC 6/868/20, 22.

[18] PRO, SC 6/875/1.

[19] The term was used, for example, at Elsworth in Cambridgeshire, Biggin, Huntingdonshire, and Wood Hall, Suffolk: PRO, SC 6/776/23; 875/2; 1008/4.

[20] PRO, SC 6/929/1; 998/11.

[21] PRO, SC 6/932/26; 934/39.

[22] PRO, SC 6/885/19; 996/14, m. 11.

[23] For instance at Hollesley, Staverton, and Stonham: PRO, SC 6/999/3; 1005/21; 1006/7.

that many mills used bearings of stone. In the course of the excavation of the mill at the site of Bordesley Abbey in Worcestershire, for example, pebbles that had been used as bearings were found in 1984, and a similar bearing of slate was found during the excavation of the site of two late medieval post mills at Bridlington.[24] When the nineteenth-century archaeologist J. R. Mortimer unwittingly excavated several other post-mill sites in the East Riding of Yorkshire, he found at one mound what he described as the broken corner of a small trough of hard sandstone, and in another of the mill mounds that he took to be a prehistoric barrow a similar object made of chalk.[25] These sound as if they were bearings, with an indentation caused by wear. Stone bearings have been found in modern windmills, both marble and flint having been used, as well as blocks of glass.[26] It is not impossible that the fused and heat-twisted pieces of glass mixed with burnt wood uncovered by Mortimer at one of his sites were the remains of a glass bearing that had been in a windmill destroyed by fire.[27] Even bearings of hard woods have proved serviceable in modern times, and so it is perfectly possible that there were medieval mills with axle or windshaft turning on nothing more than wooden pads attached to the surface of the supporting timbers.[28]

We know so little about how common it was to use these substitutes for metal because unfortunately this is the sort of information that the documentation never directly provides. No expenditure was entailed in picking up a large pebble from the river bed, or a slab of sandstone, chalk or flint from the fields, and so the reeve had no reason to mention it in his account, which included details only to justify payments and liveries he had made. It is therefore important to be aware of any features that are missing from lists of repairs in a long series of accounts. Great Shelford illustrates the point well, for it is exceptionally well-documented in this respect, there being surviving accounts for forty-two separate years between the earliest, for 1319–20, and the replacement of the mill by a new one in 1387.[29] As we know,

[24] 'Medieval Britain and Ireland in 1984', *Medieval Archaeology*, 29 (1985), p. 186; Earnshaw, 'The site of a medieval post mill at Bridlington', pp. 31–2.

[25] J. R. Mortimer, *Forty Years' Researches in British and Saxon Burial Mounds of East Yorkshire* (London, 1905), p. 338.

[26] R. Wailes, *The English Windmill* (London, 1954), p. 120.

[27] Mortimer, *Forty Years' Researches in British and Saxon Burial Mounds*, p. 206.

[28] Wailes, *The English Windmill*, p. 120.

[29] PRO, SC 6/1132/14, 15; 1133/1–7.

there are copious references to the spindle being lengthened or replaced, and the iron hoops at both ends of the mill axle were replaced in ten of the forty-two documented years — although, interestingly, eight of these occasions were recorded in the latter fifteen of the accounts, dating from 1367 onwards. It is all the more noticeable, then, that none of the accounts makes any mention of metal bearings being repaired or replaced, and obviously the mill worked without them. In 1380 two carpenters worked for six days for a total of 4s 6d, making cogs and rungs and also repairing the water-wheel and the bolsters and pillows for it — bolstres et pelwes ad idem.[30] But these bearings were not necessarily of timber, as it might appear, for inserting stone bearings into timberwork would also be a job for carpenters: moreover, the frequent replacements of the iron collars on the mill axle after 1367 indicate that by then it was running on something much harder than pads of timber. Then, when the mill was completely rebuilt in 1386–87 a metal spindle-bearing at least was fitted, for by 1393 the buldyr of the mill needed re-founding with brass worth 3s 4d, and from that date the bulder, bolster, or milbras was replaced or repaired with brass or iron at regular intervals.[31] Still, however, there are no references to bearings beneath the iron-bound axle, and so presumably it continued to run on wood and stone throughout the fifteenth century.

As so many mills had metal bearings, it can only be presumed that they were generally deemed superior; the reason for not using them was their expense. The mill brasses bought for Great Shelford cost 3s 4d in 1393, 3s 4d in 1401, 4s 3d in 1414 and 6s 8d in 1440, and no doubt others had been purchased in years for which no account survives.[32] An iron collar around the axle cost 1s 8d to renew in 1393, which was about average.[33] Had iron bearings been used beneath the axle, these too would have needed regular renewal: one at Lawshull, Suffolk, cost 2s to replace in 1336 which again was a typical amount. Repairs to the bearings at Lawshall cost the greater part of 4s 1d in 1385.[34]

The extent to which the vertical and the horizontal mill needed to make use of metal is an important factor in any comparison of their

[30] PRO, SC 6/1133/7.
[31] PRO, SC 6/1134/1, 3, 5, 8; 1135/1.
[32] PRO, SC 6/1134/1, 3, 5, 8.
[33] PRO, SC 6/1134/1.
[34] PRO, SC 6/1001/9; 1002/3.

relative merits. It is quite obvious in the case of the former that although the use of iron for some of the bearings was optional, nevertheless there were components for which no other material would do. Given the strain on parts such as the spindle, frequent recourse to the professional services of the smith was inevitable. The owner of the horizontal mill, however, could choose to avoid this expense altogether, for his mill could be constructed entirely without the use of metal. It needed only one bearing, at the base of the shaft on which was mounted both the water-wheel and the runner stone; in the Tamworth mill a steel plate was used, and the base of the shaft that ran on it was tipped probably with a steel gudgeon, but this was a special mill, associated with the Mercian royal palace nearby. In less exalted contexts such sophistication was judged quite unnecessary, and the wooden shaft of the near-contemporary Moycraig mill in Ireland was fitted with a pebble at its foot which would have turned upon another stone.[35] The more primitive at least of the modern horizontal mills have similarly relied for their construction on wood and stone, and so it is plain that the attractiveness of this simple machine to its owner did not lie just in its avoidance of gearing.[36]

Apart from the rynd, spindle and bearings, the rest of the mechanism of the vertical watermill was always of wood, as indeed was that of its offspring, the windmill. Iron was used everywhere in the form of nails, and as bands and even chains to strengthen the water-wheel, trundle-wheel and the cog-wheel; until the development of cheap smelting and cast iron in the eighteenth century, however, it was not feasible to make such components entirely of iron. Oak, though rarely specified, was undoubtedly the preferred wood for most of the mechanism; boards of black poplar were also on occasion purchased for a variety of purposes, from making a new door or a new hopper to general repairs on the mill and the water-wheel.[37] When a sailyard had to be replaced on a windmill the type of timber chosen was of less importance than the qualities of length and straightness that the young tree possessed: oak, elm, ash and alder were all recorded.[38] The crab apple tree purchased for Layham mill, Suffolk, however, was deliberately chosen

[35] Rahtz and Bullough, 'The parts of an Anglo-Saxon mill', pp. 17–18.

[36] R. Wailes, 'The "Greek" and "Norse" waterwheels', p. 163.

[37] At Great Shelford, and at Hanworth, Norfolk: PRO, SC 6/1134/5, 6; 937/12.

[38] At Weston, Hertfordshire; Halvergate, Norfolk; Walton, Somerset; Tanshelf, Yorkshire: PRO, SC 6/873/25; 936/2; Longleat MS 10,801, 10,807; PRO, SC 6/1145/21.

for the strength and resilience of the cogs for which it was intended.[39]

Again, such apparently detailed source material nevertheless has its shortcomings. It may be specified that a water-wheel was put together by carpenters and sawyers with 200 nails bought for 4d, at a cost of 6s in labour, but we are given no clue as to how it was constructed, or as to what type of wheel it was.[40] The fourteenth-century Luttrell Psalter shows an overshot wheel at work, and the contemporary mill at Batsford in Sussex was driven by an overshot wheel nearly nine feet in diameter, and a foot wide, made entirely of oak and held together by iron nails and wooden dowels.[41] It had four radial spokes to the Luttrell Psalter mill's five, but otherwise was similar. The Bordesley Abbey mill-wheel was undershot, and the eleventh-century mill at Castle Donington was said by its excavator to have had a breast-shot wheel.[42] All three types of vertical water-wheel were thus available to the medieval millwright.

It is worth noting that the Luttrell Psalter mill is in every respect an accurate representation. The roof is clearly thatched, like that of Great Shelford mill, where the straw thatch was completely renewed in 1377 at a cost of 9s 2d.[43] The mill at Tiverton, Devon, was thatched with straw in 1425, and that at Houghton in Huntingdonshire with rushes in 1408.[44] Not all mills were thatched: the Malt mill at Standon, Hertfordshire, was tiled in 1337 with 5,000 ceramic tiles and 165 ridge-tiles costing 16s 7d.[45] This was much more than was usually spent on roofing, and so whilst the actual material used is seldom specified there can be little doubt that it was nearly always thatch. The structure of the mill, too, is accurate, being timber-framed with wattle-and-daub infill like most English medieval secular buildings. At Standon, the renovation of the Malt mill included work on the walls, for which 1,000 lath-nails were purchased, and 1s 6d was paid to a dauber; the mill at Great Shelford similarly required the attentions of

[39] PRO, SC 6/1002/12.

[40] At Standon, Hertfordshire, in 1274: PRO, SC 6/868/19.

[41] O. Bedwin, 'The excavation of Batsford mill, Warbleton, East Sussex, 1978', *Medieval Archaeology*, 24 (1980), p. 194.

[42] Personal communication from the director of the excavation Dr G. G. Astill; P. Clay, 'Castle Donington', *Current Archaeology*, 102 (1986), p. 210.

[43] PRO, SC 6/1133/5.

[44] Devon CRO, CR 498; PRO, SC 6/878/23.

[45] PRO, SC 6/868/22.

Plate 3 A fourteenth-century watermill from the Luttrell Psalter (British Library Add. Ms. 42130 fo. 181). The mill-pool contains traps for eels and other fish. Reproduced by kind permission of the British Library.

a dauber from time to time.[46] Many mills, though, may have been weatherboarded, judging by the frequency of payments for quantities of planks and boards. Often they were for repairs to sluices or wheel-pits, but just as often no reason was given for their purchase. At Walton, work done in 1269 on the walls of the watermill required thirty-six boards costing 3s with 300 nails at 7½d, and at Wood Hall, also in Suffolk, sawyers prepared 1,760 feet of boarding for works on both the building of the mill and the water-wheel.[47]

Whereas in the modern period watermills and even windmills invariably had several sets of millstones, the mechanism of the medieval mill was never adapted to drive more than one. Every reeve's account recording the provision of stones for a new mill, or the replacement of stones that were old or broken, confirms that. Rather than this being the result of an inability on the part of the millwrights and the lords who employed them to appreciate how the mill might be improved to achieve a greater output, it seems to have been a genuine limitation of the mechanism. On occasion there were more complex mills constructed, but far from helping to resolve the matter, the existence of the rather peculiar device that has been dubbed the 'multiple mill' serves only to confuse it.[48] For where there was a demand for extra milling capacity, it was sometimes decided to build what was in effect a pair of mills, each with its own mechanism and its own water-wheel, but housed side by side in the same millhouse. Contemporaries always recognized the arrangement as being two mills, and references in manorial documentation to 'two mills under one roof' or 'in one building' are not uncommon. But how far are we justified in treating it as a significant arrangement? Or, to put it another way: were mutiple mills really so different from the many pairs of mills which shared a site but were in separate buildings?

The question demands our attention because of its implications for our understanding of medieval attitudes to technical innovation, and in particular because extravagant claims have been made for the multiple mill. Not least is the assertion that the early Middle Ages had seen improvements in the gearing of corn mills enabling several sets of

---

[46] Ibid.; PRO, SC 6/1132/14; 1133/4.

[47] PRO, SC 6/1007/4; 1008/2. Unplastered weatherboarding may have been often judged the most practical construction for buildings which were subject to a high level of vibration.

[48] J. Tann, 'Multiple mills', *Medieval Archaeology*, 11 (1967), pp. 233–5.

stones to be worked by one water-wheel.[49] The absence of any evidence
for such a development has already been remarked upon, and during
the course of the present study only once has a multiple mill with a
single mechanism been identified. This was a combined corn mill and
fulling mill at Layham, Suffolk, where in the latter part of the
fourteenth century the same water-wheel worked a pair of millstones
and a set of fulling stocks.[50] Combined mills of this kind were to be
found elsewhere, for example there was the new mill built at Great
Shelford in 1387, but always the millstones and the fulling stocks had
separate water-wheels.[51] Fortunately much light has been shed on the
probable internal arrangement of such mills by Alan Graham's
excavation of a multiple mill at Abbotsbury in Dorset. The positioning
of the two water-wheels next to each other, making use of the same
leat but driving mills on opposite sides of the stream, was a sensible
one, and illustrates how the mill at Layham could have worked.[52] If
instead of a pair of wheels just one had been used, its axle extending
into both halves of the millhouse, the arrangement of driving two
mechanisms with one wheel could have been contrived without
recourse to extra gearing.

It is at least arguable, however, that this would have offered no
advantages over using two wheels: indeed, that it was a disadvantage,
and one, moreover, that was recognized at the time. Mills that were
entirely separate worked independently, and either could be stopped,
for whatever reason, without affecting the output of the other. This
was impossible in a single mechanism without using a disconnecting
device, unknown to medieval millwrights. Layham mill's obvious lack
of imitators is the surest indicator that it was not a success, and it is no
surprise that medieval people preferred not to build multiple mills
with only one wheel if the need to cease both operations to do any
repair work led to their standing idle more often than other mills. In
full knowledge of the patent limitations of the materials that were
available, medieval man did not strive for more complicated machinery
than he already possessed, and wisely sought efficiency in simplicity of
design.

[49] Ibid.

[50] PRO, SC 6/1002/10, 11, 12, 13.

[51] PRO, SC 6/1134/1.

[52] A. H. Graham, 'The Old Malthouse, Abbotsbury, Dorset: the medieval watermill
of the Benedictine Abbey', *Procs. of the Dorset Nat. Hist. and Archaeol. Soc.*, 108
(1986), pp. 103—25.

This is not the only example of a medieval 'innovation' in milling which under closer examination turns out to be not quite what it seems. Several technological historians have also lovingly described the supposed steady growth in the number of tide mills: that is, watermills driven not by running streams but by the twice-daily ebb of the tide in estuaries and creeks. Little progress, unfortunately, has ever been made in discovering the antiquity of these mills or more importantly in assessing their significance during the Middle Ages, owing in large part to an apparent reluctance to look beyond two dubious references to tide mills from the eleventh century — one to their use in the Venetian lagoon before 1050, and the other to a mill at Dover mentioned in Domesday Book.[53] Whether or not tide mills could have been a viable proposition in the Adriatic with its insignificant tidal range is a matter that no amount of argument will resolve; similarly the question of the mill at Dover, of which all that is known is that its outflow adversely affected shipping, might as well be laid to rest if no more evidence is forthcoming.[54] Earlier than either of these doubtful cases is a charter dated from 949 referring to the mouth of the mill creek or estuary at Reculver, Kent, the *mylenfleotes mupan*; and although only circumstantial evidence of a tide mill it is still a more worthy candidate for the earliest documentary reference than either of the foregoing, and is contemporary with the tenth- or eleventh-century record of tide mills at Basra on the Persian Gulf.[55] Far older, however, were the two tide mills excavated on Little Island, in county Cork, of which the first, a horizontal mill, was dated by dendrochronology to 630, and the second, a vertical mill, was built a little later.[56]

A string of references from the twelfth and thirteenth centuries to tide mills confirms that they were certainly no novelty around the

[53] W. E. Minchinton, 'Early tide mills: some problems', *Technology and Culture*, 20 (1979), pp. 777–86. Lynn White saw the invention of the tide mill as 'the symptom of a new attitude which was to alter the whole pattern of human life', and for Jean Gimpel the tide mill was 'typical of the medieval urge to discover new sources of energy' — views apparently shared by most other historians of technology: White, *Medieval Technology and Social Change*, p. 85; Gimpel, *the Medieval Machine: The Industrial Revolution of the Middle Ages* (London, 1977), p. 23.

[54] *Domesday Book*, fol. 1.

[55] Rahtz and Bullough, 'The parts of an Anglo-Saxon mill', p. 24; Minchinton, 'Early tide mills', p. 778.

[56] Wikander, 'Archaeological evidence for early water-mills', p. 155.

The Abbey Mill, Abbotsbury

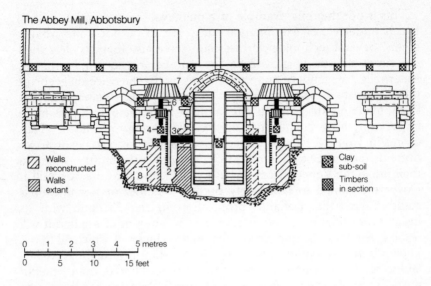

Figure 6 The Old Malthouse Abbotsbury: The Abbey Mill reconstructed. 1. The wheel chamber and water-wheels; 2. The pit-wheel pit and pit-wheel; 3. The main shaft; 4. Horizontal beam, adjustable for height, supporting the vertical shaft upon which the upper mill-stone turns; 5. The lantern pinion; 6. Vertical shaft upon which the upper mill-stone turns; 7. The mill-stones; 8. The spill-way.
Reproduced from the *Proceedings of the Dorset Natural History and Archaeological Society,* 1986, **108** by kind permission of the excavator Alan Graham.

English coast. Walter Minchinton has noted some thirty-seven from before 1300 in a list that shows their numbers increasing century by century.[57] The total is clearly incomplete, not least because there is a genuine problem in detecting tide mills: even the term itself is modern, medieval documents usually not differentiating them from other watermills, and only on occasion using the contemporary name 'sea mill'.[58] More seriously, the list shows no sign of the substantial decline

[57] W. E. Minchinton, 'Tidemills of England and Wales', *Trans. of the Fourth Symposium of the International Molinological Soc., 1977* (1982), pp. 339–53.
[58] For instance at Fareham, Hampshire: *The Pipe Roll of the Bishopric of Winchester 1210–1211*, p. 109.

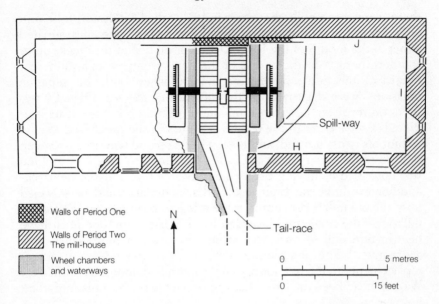

Walls of Period One

Walls of Period Two
The mill-house

Wheel chambers
and waterways

N

Spill-way

H

Tail-race

0   5 metres
0   15 feet

Figure 7 The Abbey Mill, Abbotsbury. Reproduced from the
Proceedings of the Dorset Natural History and Archaeological Society,
1986, **108**, by kind permission of the excavator Alan Graham.

in milling activity that took place after 1350, which at once raises the
suspicion that the increasing quantity of tide mills might be a false
perception, based on nothing more than the general increase in
documentary sources.[59] When, instead of simply being listed, these
mills are looked at in as much detail as the documentation allows, it
becomes obvious not only that the previously accepted chronology for
their development demands drastic revision, but also that their
usefulness was decidedly limited. If tide mills were most plausibly a
development of the Ancient World, it was also the case that there was
no steady growth in their numbers from the eleventh century onwards;
indeed it appears that by the thirteenth century their value was being
called into question.

This we can see illustrated at Walton in Suffolk, a manor which is
fortuitously well-documented for the decades before 1300. In 1269

---

[59] It is also the case that as only secondary works are cited as evidence for Minchinton's
medieval tide mills, their dating may be more uncertain than he suggests.

there were three mills there; a windmill called Godeston mill, and Gulpeler mill and Lestanston mill which were both tide mills, situated either at the mouth of the River Deben or on one of the creeks on its southern bank.[60] In the course of the next twenty years an inherent hazard of the tide mill became evident when both, on separate occasions, were destroyed by the violence of the sea. Over £4 was spent on repairing Lestanston mill in 1276, but only three years later there is a terse entry in the reeve's account of rope purchased to haul its timbers to dry ground, and meanwhile a second windmill had been built to replace it at a cost of £3. 14s 4d.[61] In 1289 Gulpeler mill too was described as having been ruined by the sea, and the next year another windmill was built, using what materials could be salvaged from the old mill.[62] For centuries the tide had been used at Walton for milling – the single mill recorded for the manor in 1086 must have been a tide mill – and now at last there was a more satisfactory alternative.[63] The abandonment by 1300 of the tide mill and its replacement in the manor by the windmill demonstrates that for Walton it had been the latter that had proved to be the more important innovation.

There was a similar series of events further down the coast, at Milton Hall in Essex, where the new windmill in 1299 also replaced a tide mill destroyed by the sea some years before.[64] In Norfolk, the tide mill at Lynn belonging to the Bishop of Norwich, recorded in 1325, had by 1369 been destroyed by the sea and had not been rebuilt.[65] Tide mills were still to be built during the thirteenth century, like the ruinously expensive Lydden mill on the Isle of Thanet in Kent that lasted for little more than twenty years before the sea forced its removal to an inland site, but this was self-evidently an example of conservatism rather than of innovation: windpower would have proved far less expensive, and no doubt more reliable.[66] Indeed, it is only too plain how inadequate tide mills could be. For an established watermill to be replaced by a less reliable windmill was, as has been

60 PRO, C 132/38/17; SC 6/1007/4, 6.

61 PRO, SC 6/1007/7, 9.

62 PRO, SC 6/1007/14, 15.

63 *Domesday Book*, ii, fol. 339b.

64 J. F. Nicholls, 'Milton Hall: the compotus of 1299', *Trans. Southend-on-Sea and District Antiquarian and Hist. Soc.*, 2 (1932), pp. 125, 137.

65 PRO, SC 6/1141/1, m. 3; 1141/2, m. 2.

66 See chapter 5.

shown, most unusual; yet here was a type of watermill to which the new windmill was often preferred. This, more than anything, confirms the antiquity of the tide mill in England, placing the period of its greatest growth within the context of the uneven distribution of milling capacity before reliable windmills became available during the thirteenth century: that is, in the era when even marginal watermills were considered to be worth building.

By any standards, and not merely by comparison with the tide mill and the multiple mill, the windmill was a genuine innovation that met a real need. The measurable extent of its success during its first century alone, as detailed in chapter 2, leaves no doubt at all of how profitable the windmills built in such great numbers by 1250 were to their owners. As it was essentially the application of an existing machine to a different source of power, little mechanical adaptation was necessary beyond an elementary rearrangement of the position of the millstones. This was in effect an inversion of the mechanism to take account of the position of the mill axle, which in the windmill had to be at the top of the building, the only position from which the long sails could turn; the watermill was driven by a wheel set at the building's base, the drive being transmitted upwards to millstones on an upper floor. Any problems that the millwrights faced in constructing windmills would therefore have arisen out of features that were new: the size and shape of the mill, its sails and, most troublesome of all, its foundations. The question of how to keep the sails facing into the wind had been solved by balancing the windmill on a single massive upright post, so that the whole structure could be turned around. The weak point in the solution was that the post had to be held rigid throughout the lifetime of the mill, for if it began to falter under the enormous strains placed on it, the mill would become unstable and only prompt action would prevent its falling over.

Medieval illustrations of windmills show a uniformity of construction that cannot be attributed entirely to artistic convention.[67] Obviously the windmills of the fourteenth and fifteenth centuries were very much as they were portrayed, being post mills with sails set symmetrically on four sailyards, a pointed roof, a fixed step-ladder leading to the doorway at the rear of the mill, and a long tail-pole with which the structure was turned into the wind. The oldest surviving

[67] J. Salmon, 'The windmill in English medieval art', *Journal of the British Archaeol. Assoc.*, 3rd ser., 6 (1941), pp. 88–102; Wailes, *The English Windmill*, pp. 188–93; L. M. C. Randall, *Images in the Margins of Gothic Manuscripts* (Berkeley, 1966), p. 226.

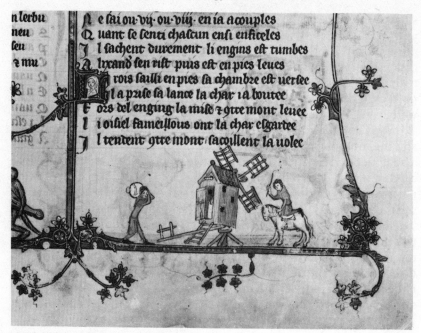

Plate 4 A fourteenth-century windmill (Ms. Bodley 264). Reproduced by courtesy of the Bodleian Library.

post mills, particularly that at Bourn in Cambridgeshire which was built by the early seventeenth century, look very similar to their medieval forebears, and the design must have been a serviceable one to merit its continued use through more than seven centuries. It would be all the more remarkable, then, if the earliest post mills had possessed quite this degree of perfection, and undoubtedly at first there was considerable trial and error in their construction as numerous deficiencies were corrected. The earliest illustration in a surviving manuscript dates only from 1270, and before then windmills may have been much less standard in design as millwrights attempted to build machines that were more powerful and more stable.[68] Only one certain example of the former has been identified, in a reference to a windmill with six sails at Framlingham, Suffolk, in 1270, and which was still in use in 1287 and 1325.[69] The identification is possible only

[68] Salmon, 'The windmill in English medieval art', p. 92.
[69] *Medieval Framlingham*, pp. 20, 22, 60.

Plate 5 England's oldest windmill, the early seventeenth-century mill at Bourn, Cambridgeshire. Reproduced by kind permission of the Cambridge Evening News.

because the manor also possessed a windmill of more orthodox design, and the clerk used the number of their sails as a way of distinguishing between them; how many more such idiosyncracies of construction are concealed in the bare details of repairs it is impossible to say.

Differences in the construction of the foundations of windmills, however, are detectable, because unlike the superstructure they survive to give substance to the documentary evidence. In comparison with the number of excavated watermills, the total of windmill sites that has been identified and examined is a large one, the result of the understandable tendency on the part of archaeologists to investigate visible remains and earthworks. Only the windmill at Mucking, Essex, was identified by aerial photographs of crop marks, all the others being found in the course of investigation of the obviously artificial mounds on which they stood.[70] As stable foundations were essential to the mill's existence, excavation usually reveals the remains of an elaborate structure consisting of a cross of massive timbers on which the post stood, and to which had been attached the sloping tie beams or quarter-bars. The effect was to provide a stout pyramid of timber to hold the post steady, an arrangement still used in modern post mills and clearly shown in manuscript illustrations.

Unlike the foundations of modern mills, the cross-trees and the base of the post were usually set firmly in the ground to give them greater stability and then a low but extensive mound was raised over . them, though the precise way in which the timbers were secured varied from mill to mill. At Bridlington, for instance, a mill dated on rather flimsy evidence to the fifteenth century proved to have had a post three feet in diameter, set into a post-hole three feet deep. The cross-trees were four separate beams of oak held firm with a packing of heavy clay and cobbles, and the mound of clay and soil heaped up over them measured at its destruction in 1970 seventy-six feet by fifty-six feet and rather more than five feet in height.[71] More often the base of the post was not itself secured in the ground but rested on two crossed timbers, one eighteen feet long and the other sixteen feet at Higham-on-the-Hill, Leicestershire, or twenty feet by twenty at

[70] W. T. Jones, 'The Mucking windmill', Journal of Thurrock Local Hist. Soc., 23 (1979), p. 42. In addition to the excavation reports cited below, see W. P. Westell, 'Sandon Mount, Hertfordshire: its site, excavations and problems', Trans. St Albans and Herts. Architectural and Archaeol. Soc., (1934), pp. 173–83; P. A. and M. H. Rahtz, 'T 40: Barrow and Windmill at Butcombe, North Somerset', Procs. of the Univ. of Bristol Spelaeological Soc., 8 (1957), pp. 89–96; S. V. Pearce, 'A medieval windmill, Honey Hill, Dogsthorpe', Procs. of the Cambridge Antiquarian Soc., 59 (1966), pp. 95–103; 'Rugby Tumulus', note in Trans. Birmingham Archaeol. Soc., 52 (1927), pp. 301–2; Bennett and Elton, History of Corn Milling, ii, p. 279.

[71] Earnshaw, 'The site of a medieval post mill at Bridlington', pp. 19, 20, 22, 24.

Bridgwater Without, Somerset, or seventeen feet by sixteen at Great Linford, Buckinghamshire, and the structure was again held in place by a mound.[72] Some mills were provided with more carefully contrived foundations, the most elaborate of which so far excavated being those discovered at Lamport in Northamptonshire. There the cross-trees of a possibly fourteenth-century mill rested on a cruciform wall of stone which when built must have stood five or six feet above the ground level. After a period long enough for the stone of the wall to weather, a mound was thrown up around it which nevertheless did not cover it, so the foundation timbers remained exposed.[73] Wall foundations of this sort have been found elsewhere, though clearly bearing buried timbers, so whilst this is the only example known of the timbers of a medieval mill resting above the ground, it was not necessarily unique.[74]

Reeves' accounts containing details of new windmills are generally reticent on the matter of foundations. Work done by the carpenter on the new mill at Newborough, Anglesey, in 1303, included the construction of the cross; in Norfolk in 1306 *crosbondes* were prepared for the lower end of the post of Halvergate mill, and a new post, complete with *crostres*, was fitted to Lopham mill.[75] At other mills the record of work performed is more cursory, as at Walton in 1291 where four trenchers were paid 3s 4d for inserting and ramming the post of the new mill, and a mound was made at a cost of 10s, or at Milton Hall where the post of the mill built in 1299 was rammed in for 2s 10d, and 7s 2d was paid for making the mound.[76] In 1326 at Wyke, Suffolk, 8d was spent on propping up the fallen mill and ramming its post with earth, a description which, like the previous two, seems to imply that the post was held steady in the ground without the aid of other timbers.[77] The arrangement was not impossible, having been found at

[72] G. C. Bellairs, 'Wooden cross found buried under a mound at Higham-on-the-Hill, Leicestershire', *Trans. Leics. Architectural and Archaeol. Soc.*, 9 (1905), pp. 18–19; 'Medieval Britain in 1971', *Medieval Archaeology*, 16 (1972), p. 211; R. J. Zeepvat, 'Post mills and archaeology', *Current Archaeology*, 71 (1980), p. 376.

[73] M. Posnasky, 'The Lamport Post Mill', *Journal of the Northants. Nat. Hist. Soc. and Field Club*, 33 (1959), pp. 66–79.

[74] C. Monkman, 'Buried cruciform platforms in Yorkshire', *Yorks. Archaeol. and Topographical Journal*, 2 (1873), pp. 69–81; see also Mortimer, *Forty Years' Researches in British and Saxon Burial Mounds*, pp. 187–8; 205–6; 338–40.

[75] Salmon, 'Erection of a Windmill at Newborough (Anglesey) in 1303', pp. 250–2; PRO, SC 6/936/17; 938/11.

[76] PRO, SC 6/1007/15; Nicholls, 'Milton Hall: the compotus of 1299', p. 136.

[77] PRO, SC 6/1141/1.

Rillington in Yorkshire, where the foundations of a mill consisted of no more than the post fixed in a stone-lined pit, surrounded by a substantial mound of clay and soil.[78]

It is tempting to conclude that there was a series of improvements in the design of post mill foundations, with the simple affixing of the post in the earth, used in the earliest windmills, giving way to the rigid timber framework buried in the ground. The Lamport mill foundations would therefore represent a transitional form, before the most stable arrangement, with the cross-trees raised above the ground on brick or stone piers, was arrived at perhaps by 1600. The difficulty with this course of development, however logical, is that the paucity of finds means that very few excavated windmills have been dated at all closely, and so no progress of evolution through time can be demonstrated; indeed, where firm dates are offered, either by documentary sources or by archaeology, they provide little support for the hypothesis. It appears on the contrary that the different ways of constructing windmill foundations might have coexisted for long periods, with each method having its adherents.

Medieval post mills, it is usually asserted, were considerably smaller than modern mills; and whilst this may not be an unreasonable assumption it is based on no other evidence than that of contemporary illustrations. Yet medieval artists made little use of scale, and the diminutive size of the windmills when compared with the human figures in the marginal embellishments of manuscripts is no guide at all to their actual size. The archaeological evidence for foundations seems also to contribute little, as the irregular dimensions and structure of the cross-trees were in all likelihood more closely related to the consistency and weight of packing over them and the caution of the millwright than to the size of the superstructure. Documentary evidence indicates the dimensions of the sails, but only very rarely indeed. Of all the many accounting entries recording purchases of new sailyards only one has been found where the length is specified — a sailyard of oak, thirty-six feet long, bought for 4s in 1269 for the mill at Halvergate in Norfolk.[79] A span of over seventy feet for the sails of a medieval mill is unlikely, as this was the largest span ever encountered in a modern post mill: the early nineteenth-century mill from Danzey

---

[78] Earnshaw, 'The site of a medieval post mill at Bridlington', p. 25, citing N. A. Huddleston, History of Rillington (1955), pp. 17 and 20–22.

[79] PRO, SC 6/936/2.

Green, Warwickshire, and now at the Avoncroft Museum of Buildings, Bromsgrove, was a very average post mill of its time and has a span of sixty feet.[80] Such massive sails can be attached to the windshaft only by means of a heavy iron casting, which was unavailable to the medieval millwright, and so it is logical to interpret the Halvergate sailyard as being intended to carry two sails: that is, it was to be jointed right through the head of the windshaft, at once the simplest construction and the strongest. Thus Halvergate mill had a span of thirty-six feet — rather less if the sailyard had been trimmed, but greater than that if extending spars had been fastened to it. The sails swept close to the ground, as common sails, made of canvas stretched over the latticework on the sailyard, must be adjusted by hand: allowing for a small clearance, therefore, the windshaft of Halvergate mill was most probably some twenty feet above the ground. To the top of the roof the mill would have stood a further five feet at least, and although this is appreciably less than the height of the Danzey Green mill, at nearly forty feet, the comparison is a misleading one. In modern post mills the foundation timbers are raised above the ground, whereas at Halvergate they were buried beneath a mound; the body or buck of the Danzey Green mill is in fact the same size as that postulated for Halvergate.

Reasonable as it may be to infer that the thirteenth-century Halvergate mill was a structure comparable in size with the post mills of later centuries, but set much closer to the ground and so with shorter sails, the evidence of one sailyard can hardly be stretched any further and corroborative evidence is negligible. Prices of new sailyards varied from 1s in 1275 at Middle Zoy, Somerset, to 5s 6d and 6s 1d at Wood Hall, Suffolk, in 1324 and 1325: probably the Halvergate sailyard was similar to those purchased for 4s 2d at Bircham, Norfolk, in 1311, and for 5s 3d at Brancaster in 1303.[81] Purchases of specified lengths of sailcloth are frequently recorded, but it seems impossible to use them to deduce the size of the sails, as the number to be made and the width of the cloth are unknown. At Walton, Somerset, thirty ells of canvas were bought for the new mill: at forty-five inches per ell, this works out at twenty-eight feet for each of four sails.[82] What is not clear is whether it was thought prudent to provide a spare sail-cloth, or

[80] R. Wailes, 'Some windmill fallacies', *Trans. Newcomen Soc.*, 32 (1959—60), p. 95.
[81] Longleat MS 11,244, m. 33; PRO, SC 6/1008/2, 3; 930/1; 931/1.
[82] Keil, 'Building a post windmill in 1342', pp. 151—4.

even a spare set. Sixty ells were supplied for the new mill at Milton Hall in 1299, and eighty yards for the new mill at Walton, Suffolk, in 1290.[83] The following year this mill needed another forty-six ells, and two years later in 1293 a further forty-eight ells.[84] These canvas sails obviously did not last long, and it must have been usual to keep some in reserve.

The windmill stands alone, as the only successful innovation in corn milling technology in the medieval period. The adaptation of existing technology to a new power source so as to bring milling to areas where waterpower had been inadequate demonstrates that medieval man lacked nothing in ingenuity, although the continued evolution of the post mill's foundations suggests that it was not until after the close of the Middle Ages that it could be accounted an entirely stable and reliable device. But there was an awareness that improvement of design was possible and, according to iconographic evidence, at the end of the fifteenth century came the development of the tower mill.[85] Both documentary and archaeological sources are entirely silent as to the event, and consequently there is nothing further to be said about it here.

[83] Nicholls, 'Milton Hall: the compotus of 1299', p. 136; PRO, SC 6/1007/15.
[84] PRO, SC 6/1007/16, 18.
[85] Salmon, 'The windmill in English Medieval Art', pp. 100–2.

9
An Industrial Revolution of the Middle Ages?

When in 1941 Eleanora Carus-Wilson published her incautiously titled article 'An Industrial Revolution of the thirteenth century', she did much to promote the view of the medieval period as an age of mechanical innovation.[1] It came at a time when several other historians were turning their attention to medieval science and technology, and her account of the introduction of the fulling mill to England before 1200 and its proliferation during the following century went to swell a growing list of publications on the subject. Starting in 1929 with Abbott Payson Usher's *History of Mechanical Inventions*, and most notably including Marc Bloch's two articles 'The advent and triumph of the watermill' and 'Mediaeval "inventions"' published in *Annales* in 1935, the literature went on to culminate, for the time being, in such massive surveys as Singer's five-volume *History of Technology* and Daumas' *A History of Technology and Inventions*.[2] But more than any other, the name that has been associated with this exploration of the many facets of medieval technological ingenuity has been that of Lynn White, Jr, the first of whose many contributions on the theme

---

[1] E. M. Carus-Wilson, 'An Industrial Revolution of the thirteenth century', *Econ. Hist. Review*, 11 (1941), repr. in E. M. Carus-Wilson, ed., *Essays in Economic History*, i (London, 1954), pp. 41−60.

[2] A. P. Usher, *History of Mechanical Inventions* (New York, 1929: revised ed., Cambridge, Mass., 1954); M. Bloch, 'Avènement et Conquêtes du Moulin à Eau', and 'Les "Inventions" Médiévales', *Annales E.S.C.*, 7 (1935), pp. 538−63, 634−43; trans. J. E. Anderson in M. Bloch, *Land and Work in Medieval Europe* (London, 1967), pp. 136−68, 169−85; C. Singer, E. J. Holmyard, A. R. Hall, T. I. Williams (eds), *A History of Technology*, 5 vols (Oxford, 1956); M. Daumas (ed.), *Histoire Générale de Techniques* (Paris, 1962), published as *A History of Technology and Invention*, 3 vols (London, 1980).

of medieval innovation, 'Technology and invention in the Middle Ages', was published in 1940.[3]

With notable exceptions, such as Bloch and Carus-Wilson, those historians who chose to write on medieval technology largely restricted their efforts to gathering together recorded instances of the use of new devices, hoping to discover when they were invented and how quickly they had spread. At a time when the very idea of medieval technical progress was inconceivable to many, this was a useful aim; unfortunately, little attempt was subsequently made to begin to assess what economic or social significance these inventions might have had. Moreover, such attempts as were made did not necessarily meet with the approval of historians whose own researches were more firmly rooted in the realities of medieval agrarian society. Severe criticism greeted Lynn White's *Medieval Technology and Social Change*, with its thesis that certain fundamental changes in feudal society were the result of technological innovations; nevertheless, the book has been a powerful influence upon most technological historians.[4]

Amongst the innovations that White described were the watermill and windmill, and he laid particular stress on the medieval application of waterpower not just to cornmilling but to industrial production as well. Medieval man increasingly saw the possibilities of the water-wheel, and by the end of the period waterpowered machines were not only fulling cloth but were being used in a wide range of manufacturing processes.[5] This role of the watermill has since been further explored and elaborated in *Stronger than a Hundred Men: A History of the Vertical Water Wheel* by Terry S. Reynolds, which as a study of the developing role of waterpower in history perhaps understandably gives rather more prominence to its application to manufacturing industry than it does to its less exciting use in grinding corn.[6]

It is a matter for regret that so many years after historians began to take medieval technology seriously it should still be possible for a study of this kind to pay so little attention to the questions of who built

---

[3] L. White, Jr, 'Technology and invention in the Middle Ages', *Speculum*, 15 (1940), repr. in L. White, *Medieval Religion and Technology* (Berkeley, 1978), pp. 1−22.

[4] L. White, Jr, *Medieval Technology and Social Change* (Oxford, 1962); R. H. Hilton and P. H. Sawyer, 'Technical determinism: the stirrup and the plough', *Past and Present*, 24 (1963), pp. 90−100.

[5] White, *Medieval Technology and Social Change*, pp. 83−4.

[6] T. S. Reynolds, *Stronger than a Hundred Men: A History of the Vertical Water Wheel* (Baltimore, 1983).

these machines, and why; how profitable they were as compared with former methods of working, and what contribution they made to overall production. These might not be easy questions to answer, but in attempting them new insights would inevitably be gained to fill out the bare details of chronology and distribution which are all we have at the moment. Furthermore, it becomes increasingly important that historians should address themselves to questions of this sort, because the absence of the results of empirical research has allowed enthusiasts for medieval technology to make increasingly extravagant claims. These have varied in detail, but in substance they may be summed up in the single statement that there was a 'medieval power revolution'.[7]

The effect of such assertions is to make it impossible to present the evidence for industrial mills in England without first establishing a more rational context for it, and to do so it is necessary to look at this 'power revolution' again. Its origins, said Reynolds, are to be sought in 'the eighth or ninth century, when European engineers began to aggressively apply water power to industrial processes', with what White called a 'mill for making mash for beer' and Reynolds called usually a 'beer mill' but at least once a 'mill for making beer'.[8] This curious device, unknown to modern brewing practice, was recorded in Picardy in 861, and White felt confident that 'a new machine was involved: a series of vertical stamps activated by cams on the axle of the water-wheel'. In fact the reference is to a grant, approved by Charles the Bald, of a combined mill and brewery — *molendinum unum cum camba*. Whilst it is logical enough to assume that the mill was primarily intended to grind malt, one is at a loss to see in this, or in the numerous examples of 'beer mills' given by A-M. Bautier, any sign of a different kind of mill, and least of all White's new machine with its

[7] An expression used by Norman Smith, for example, in an article intended for a popular readership, in which it is implied that the medieval period saw the mechanization of the greater part of European industrial production: N. A. F. Smith, 'Water power', *History Today* 30 (March 1980), pp. 38−9, and *passim*. Lynn White believed that 'the great glory of the later Middle Ages . . . was the building for the first time in history of a complex civilization which rested not on the backs of sweating slaves or coolies but primarily on non-human power': 'Technology and invention in the Middle Ages', p. 22.

[8] T. S. Reynolds, 'Medieval roots of the Industrial Revolution', *Scientific American* 251 (1984), p. 109; L. White, Jr, 'The Expansion of Technology 500−1500', in C. M. Cipolla (ed.), *The Fontana Economic History of Europe*, i (London, 1972), p. 155; Reynolds, *Stronger than a Hundred Men*, pp. 69−71.

revolutionary mechanism.[9] On the contrary, what is abundantly clear is that all these references are to the malt mill, which was like any other corn mill. Recorded receipts of multure show that English manorial mills everywhere ground both bread-grains and malted grains, an arrangement that was not entirely satisfactory, as the distinctively flavoured and sticky malt tainted subsequent grindings of meal. In communities with more than one or two mills, therefore, it was customary to separate these functions, as at Stratford-upon-Avon where two of the sets of millstones of the triple mill there were for hard grains and the third was reserved for malt.[10] Consequently, malt mills are often to be found in manorial documentation, with the 'beer mill' not an exciting invention of the ninth century but an unconscious invention of twentieth-century historians.

The tan mill — more accurately the bark mill — was another of the water-driven machines that appeared during the Middle Ages. To extract the tannin used for curing hides, the bark from which it comes must first be crushed between stones, and this must often have suggested itself as a process that could be performed using a modified version of the corn mill. Bark-crushing mills were found in the Paris region from 1138 onwards, and in the next century they existed in many parts of Europe.[11] Yet the crucial question of how commonly they were used has not been answered, as this would demand research techniques more sensitive than the simple accumulation of references. In England, as it turns out, bark mills were very rare, despite a string of references that could be quoted to suggest that they were in frequent use. The first recorded example was in Cumberland in 1165, after which they are to be found occasionally, often as ecclesiastical enterprises: for instance at Kirkstall Abbey in 1288; at Battle Abbey in the fourteenth century; at Tavistock Abbey, where two were converted to fulling mills early in the fifteenth century; at Truro where there was one mentioned in passing in 1337.[12] What is most significant is that in

[9] White, 'The Expansion of Technology 500—1500', p. 155; Actes de Charles le Chauve, ed. G. Tessier (Paris, 1952), ii, 225, p. 2; A-M. Bautier, 'Les Plus Anciennes Mentions de Moulins', pp. 601—3. The suggestion that the mill 'made beer' has confused at least one eminent historian, as G. Duby felt that its mechanism must have operated paddles: Rural Economy and Country Life in the Medieval West, p. 107.

[10] Red Book of Worcester, p. 244.

[11] Bautier, 'Les Plus Anciennes Mentions de Moulins', pp. 594—601.

[12] Pipe Roll, 11 Henry II (Pipe Roll Soc., 1887), p. 54; Carus-Wilson, 'An Industrial Revolution of the thirteenth century', p. 46; E. Searle, Lordship and Community: Battle

the large sample of manorial documentation that has been consulted in the course of this study, amongst the many hundreds of corn mills no other mention of a bark mill has been found. And that, it must be emphasized, is not because they avoided being recorded. Like other demesne assets, seigneurial bark mills would have appeared in the annual reeve's account and the manorial survey; in the event of their having been built by an entrepreneur who merely rented the water rights, the rent would be recorded in the same way. The same is true for all industrial mills of the better-documented thirteenth and fourteenth centuries.

In an article in the *Scientific American* published in 1984, Reynolds demonstrated the extensive use of waterpower in early medieval Europe by turning to the evidence of Domesday Book. Discussing the English mills of the late eleventh century, he wrote: 'Most of them probably ground grain', a form of words that implies the possibility that most did not, and the certainty that a minority were industrial mills of one kind or another.[13] His justification for making such a claim can only be that out of all Domesday Book's 6,000 mills there were four, at Lexworthy in Somerset, that paid their rent not in cash or in grain but in blooms of iron. There were quite a number of such rents for lands in Gloucestershire and Somerset, so there is no certainty at all that these were mills that were being used in the smelting of iron ore, their water-wheels powering bellows or trip-hammers.[14]

Before the invention of the blast furnace at the end of the Middle Ages, the raw iron produced by the bloomeries needed continual reheating and hammering to remove impurities. This was heavy work, and was a process to which waterpower could clearly be applied with advantage. Hammer mills were recorded at Issoudun in France in 1116, in Catalonia in 1138 and in Sweden by the early years of the

---

Abbey and its Banlieu 1066–1538, (Toronto, 1974), p. 301; Finberg, *Tavistock Abbey,* pp. 153–4; *Caption of Seisin,* p. 73.

[13] Reynolds, 'Medieval Roots of the Industrial Revolution', p. 110.

[14] *Domesday Book,* fols 91b, 94b. Rents paid in iron are listed by Darby, *Domesday England,* p. 360. The question of whether these really were industrial mills is one to which archaeology might supply an answer. Presumably they were situated on the stream passing through Lexworthy Farm, some two miles to the south-west of Bridgwater, and whilst the sites of the buildings may no longer exist, a surviving scatter of slag and other industrial debris would indicate that iron-working had been carried on in the locality. Under the circumstances, an intensive field-survey of the area would appear to be justified.

thirteenth century. By 1400 they were to be found throughout Europe, but again the question must be asked: how common was their use?[15] In England a waterpowered forge for hammering blooms, found at Chingley in Kent, has been assigned to the first half of the fourteenth century, and the earliest dated reference to a waterpowered forge is to the hammer mill or *oliver* recorded at Warley in the West Riding of Yorkshire in 1349.[16] Other early examples were also from the northern counties: at Creskeld in 1395, and at three other locations in Yorkshire in the following century, whilst at *Byrkeknott* in Weardale around 1400 there was a well-documented iron works belonging to the Bishop of Durham.[17] An account roll for this bloomery covering part of the year 1408−9 demonstrates that waterpower contributed to the operation, though whether it was used to drive hammers, bellows or both is not disclosed. In the major iron-producing district of the Sussex Weald there were waterpowered ironworks during the fifteenth century, although there is no earlier evidence for their existence. A survey of all the identified waterpowered forges and furnaces in the district lists 189 sites, of which the overwhelming majority came into use in the course of the sixteenth century. Nevertheless, there are fewer than twenty to which origins can be assigned early in the sixteenth century or before, and it is quite obvious that the widespread mechanization of smelting in the region was beginning to come about only at the very end of the medieval period.[18]

---

[15] D. W. Crossley, 'Medieval smelting', in Crossley, *Medieval Industry*, p. 40; Duby, *Rural Economy and Country Life in the Medieval West*, p. 107; Bautier, 'Les Plus Anciennes Mentions de Moulins', p. 606, n. 1; H. Cleere and D. Crossley, *The Iron Industry of the Weald*, (Leicester, 1985), p. 106.

[16] Crossley, 'Medieval Smelting', p. 36; *Court Rolls of the Manor of Wakefield 1348−50*, ed. H. M. Jewell (Yorks. Archaeol. Soc., Wakefield Court Rolls Ser., 2, 1981) pp. xxi, 260; H. Jewell, D. Michelmore, S. Moorhouse, 'An Oliver at Warley, West Yorkshire, AD 1349−50', *Historical Metallurgy*, 15 (1981), pp. 39−40.

[17] M. L. Faull and S. A. Moorhouse, *West Yorkshire: An Archaeological Survey to A.D. 1500*, iii (Wakefield, 1981), pp. 775−6; G. T. Lapsley, 'The account roll of a fifteenth-century iron master', *English Hist. Review*, 14 (1899), pp. 509−29.

[18] Cleere and Crossley, *The Iron Industry of the Weald*, pp. 106−8, 309−67. The position with regard to the application of waterpower to the smelting processes of the other metalliferous industries is not so clear. What was described as a 'tin mill' on Bodmin Moor was excavated in 1979−80, and dated probably from the fifteenth century; in the early sixteenth century tin-smelting mills, or 'blowing mills', were built. Whether, as T. A. P. Greeves believes, the blowing mill was used in earlier centuries seems still uncertain: the only evidence he could advance is a reference to a *blouynghous*

After smelting, the iron was ready to be worked by the smith. Until recently there was no indication that the primary manufacturing processes had been mechanized in England in the Middle Ages, but excavations at Bordesley Abbey in Worcestershire have revealed the remains of a series of mills used in the manufacture of metal goods, the earliest dating from perhaps before 1200. Hearths were prominent in the mill complex, and so hot metal was definitely worked by waterpower; again, though, it is not clear whether powered hammers, bellows or both were involved.[19] It would be surprising if there had not also been a powered grindstone, as the use of waterpower for sharpening knives and all manner of edged tools is known elsewhere. Of all the industrial uses of the watermill, this must have been the most obvious: the very first miller of all was surely tempted to sharpen his knife on the edge of the spinning millstone. To drive a grindstone by belting or to mount it directly onto a turning shaft would have been easily contrived, and sharpening-mills or blade mills may have existed long before they were reported in 1204 at Évreux in Normandy.[20]

Although such mills were recorded frequently thereafter, this is not to say that they were widely used; in England they remained rarities until the sixteenth century. John Langdon's search through the manorial documentation of the West Midlands counties produced only one example of a sharpening-mill, in Caen Abbey's manor of Minchinhampton around 1306; none has been found in the large amount of documentation for eastern England that has been consulted; northern records, too, have failed to produce any examples.[21] In the

---

at Lostwithiel in the fourteenth century, and an inferred shift in smelting techniques in the thirteenth. It appears that the medieval lead industry made no use of waterpower: 'Medieval Britain in 1980', *Medieval Archaeology*, 25 (1981), p. 226; J. Hatcher, *Rural Economy and Society in the Duchy of Cornwall 1300–1500* (Cambridge, 1970), p. 239; T. A. P. Greeves, 'The Archaeological Potential of the Devon Tin Industry' and I. S. W. Blanchard, 'Lead Mining and Smelting in Medieval England and Wales', in Crossley, *Medieval Industry*, pp. 85–95, and 72–84.

[19] 'Medieval Britain and Ireland in 1985', *Medieval Archaeology*, 30 (1986), p. 153. For medieval smithing in general see R. F. Tylecote, 'The Medieval Smith and His Methods', and I. H. Goodall, 'The Medieval Blacksmith and His Products', in Crossley, *Medieval Industry*, pp. 42–50, 51–62.

[20] Bautier, 'Les Plus Anciennes Mentions de Moulins', p. 604.

[21] *Charters and Custumals of the Abbey of Holy Trinity, Caen*, ed. M. Chibnall (Brit. Acad. Records of Social and Econ. Hist., new ser., 5, London, 1982), pp. 127–8; personal communication from J. L. Langdon.

south, a smith called John Corbet possessed a sharpening-mill in 1405 and 1420 at Carhampton in Somerset, for which he paid only a shilling rent to the lord: evidently he had erected the structure himself, or bought it from another, and this rent was for water-rights only.[22] At Ecchinswell in Hampshire a smith had similarly paid a rent of a penny to have a sharpening-mill, but by the mid-fifteenth century this had long disappeared.[23]

Two mills at Winchester were enterprises on a larger scale. Situated outside the east gate, one occupied eighty feet of river bank for a rent of 1s and the other, by an eighty-year lease granted in 1428, occupied a larger piece of ground two hundred feet by twenty-eight feet for a rent of 3s 4d. Both tenants were strictly forbidden to convert their mills to any other purpose.[24] As well as sharpening newly-manufactured edged tools, it has been suggested by Derek Keene that these mills were positioned to attract trade from the numerous workshops of the cloth finishers and leather workers of the city: it seems plausible that they would indeed have needed to sharpen enormous quantities of tools to justify their building costs.[25] Even so, most sharpening in Winchester was done by hand, and grindstones standing outside smiths' workshops commonly obstructed the streets.[26] Probably only where there was a concentration of custom for a sharpening-mill could it be economically viable, and it is significant that in the Midlands the growing edge-tool industry of the Birmingham region made no use of waterpower before its rapid expansion into national markets in the sixteenth century.[27]

In medieval England, if not in the rest of Europe, the vast majority of industrial mills were fulling mills. The fulling process in which new cloth was scoured, or washed with a detergent substance to remove both dirt and the natural oiliness of the wool, while being vigorously pounded or beaten to shrink the weave and felt the fibres together, had since ancient times been performed in a variety of ways using

[22] Somerset CRO, DD/L P17/4; P18/2.

[23] Hampshire CRO, Winchester Pipe Roll 1465–6, Eccl. II, 155833.

[24] Ibid.

[25] D. Keene, Survey of Medieval Winchester, i (Winchester Studies, 2, Oxford, 1985), p. 279.

[26] Ibid., p. 279.

[27] R. A. Holt, The Early History of the Town of Birmingham 1166–1600 (Dugdale Soc., Occasional Paper 30, Oxford, 1985), p. 18; Victoria County History, Warwickshire, 7 (London, 1964), pp. 253–69.

hands, clubs and feet.[28] In early medieval Europe probably most cloth was fulled by foot, 'walked' by professional fullers or walkers in great tubs or troughs.[29] To such repetitive labour waterpower could profitably be applied, with the axle of the mill raising in series a row of falling stocks or hammers to imitate the walker's feet. The earliest unambiguous reference to a fulling mill is to one in Normandy in 1087, although there is not another until 1145 after which they were frequently to be found in France, and particularly in Normandy.[30] The earliest firmly dated English fulling mills are still the pair identified by Carus-Wilson at Newsham in Yorkshire and at Barton-on-Windrush near Temple Guiting in Gloucestershire, which were already standing in 1185 as the property of the Knights Templars; between these, however, and those identified by Reginald Lennard at Kirkby-on-Bain, Lincolnshire, and Heycroft, near Malmesbury, Wiltshire, referred to perhaps as early as 1154 and 1174 respectively, it is possible that the earliest English fulling mill was built several decades before the 1180s.[31] Exceptionally, this new device was to be widely used, and Carus-Wilson was able to identify 124 fulling mills dated to before 1327 — many in the Cotswolds and the south-west, and in the north, particularly the West Riding of Yorkshire and the Lake District. The number has since been added to, and a map showing the distribution of these early references is here reproduced. (See figure 8).[32]

Carus-Wilson was not content merely to chronicle this upsurge in the application of waterpower. She associated it with the apparent rapid decline of old-established centres of cloth manufacturing in the eastern lowlands, deducing that the fulling mills located on the rivers of the western uplands had caused the decline by drawing to themselves the primary processes of manufacturing. The cloth industry

[28] R. A. Pelham, *Fulling Mills* (Soc. for the Protection of Ancient Buildings, London, 1958), pp. 1 — 2.

[29] Carus-Wilson, 'An Industrial Revolution of the Thirteenth Century', pp. 42 — 4. So universal had fulling under foot obviously become that the word 'walk', which originally meant simply to full cloth, came in Middle English to denote ambulatory activity in general.

[30] Bautier, 'Les Plus Anciennes Mentions de Moulins', p. 582.

[31] Carus-Wilson, 'An Industrial Revolution of the Thirteenth Century', pp. 45 — 6; *Records of the Templars in England*, pp. ccxiii, 50, 127, cxxv; R. V. Lennard, 'Early English fulling mills: additional examples', *Econ. Hist. Review*, 17 (1947), pp. 342 — 3.

[32] Carus-Wilson, 'An Industrial Revolution of the Thirteenth Century', pp. 49 — 51, 60.

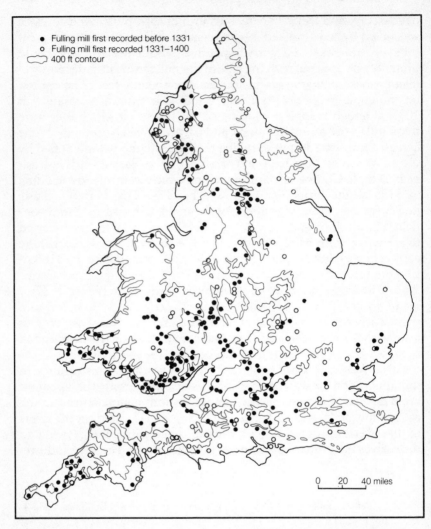

Figure 8 Early fulling mills in England and Wales. Reproduced from R. A. Pelham. *Fulling Mills* (SPAB, 1958), by kind permission of the Wind and Watermill Section of the Society for the Protection of Ancient Buildings.

was now to be a widespread rural one, no longer concentrated in the towns, for whilst at first the new mills had processed rural cloth intended for local consumption, they soon attracted the attentions of cloth merchants eager for cheaper methods of finishing town-made cloth. Inevitably, the whole industry followed, as weavers and other cloth workers came to settle near the fulling mills.[33]

Such a sequence of events has been challenged, most effectively by Edward Miller. Examining the cloth industry of the thirteenth century in rather greater depth, he has suggested that the restrictiveness of the weavers' gilds and the growth of overseas competition were powerful incentives for urban cloth merchants to direct their attentions towards both the existing low-cost rural industry and the home market for inexpensive cloths. Thus the spread of the fulling mill was not a causative factor; it reflected instead an attempt on the part of rural lords to acquire a share of the profits being made by the cloth industry which in fact was expanding in every rural district and not just in the north and west. Some of the evidence for its expansion, moreover, comes from the early years of the thirteenth century, before the effect that Carus-Wilson claimed for the fulling mill could possibly have been felt. Finally, the cost benefit to be derived from rural fulling was likely to have been minimal, as any lord who built a fulling mill did so in the expectation of receiving a good return from it.[34]

The distribution map of the fulling mill shows the greatest concentration in South Wales, which can never have been an area to receive many migrant cloth workers from the English towns. No major rural industry was to be drawn there, and the only reason why so many fulling mills were built was that, like the north, this was a region of plentiful waterpower. Carus-Wilson implied that there were so few fulling mills in the south and east because it was next to impossible to build them except on the 'swift, clear streams of the north and west'; instead, might it not be that where waterpower was limited there were other, more profitable, uses to which it could be put? Incredibly, the assertion that lords built fulling mills as 'an investment from which considerable profit could be derived' has never been tested.[35] The rents of these mills could be high, although usually they were not; most importantly they should not be considered in isolation, as the return on a fixed investment in a machine of timber and iron. There was also the price to be paid for the site of the mill, and so the profit from every new fulling mill would necessarily have been weighed

[33] Ibid., pp. 51–60.

[34] E. Miller, 'The fortunes of the English textile industry during the thirteenth century', *Econ. Hist. Review*, 2nd ser., 18 (1965), pp. 64–82.

[35] Carus-Wilson, 'An Industrial Revolution of the Thirteenth Century', p. 52.

against the potential income from a different use of the site. In practice this meant a corn mill.

The records of the great estates confirm that the fulling mill was a rarity in eastern England in the thirteenth century. In Norfolk in particular there was none belonging to the Earl, the Bishop of Norwich or the Cathedral Priory, and according to the Hundred Rolls of 1279, only two were to be found in the whole of Cambridgeshire, sharing a site with two corn mills on the river Cam in the Prior of Ely's manor of Hauxton.[36] In the same year in the Suffolk villages surveyed in the Itinerary of Solomon of Rochester there was none among the thirty-four watermills and the sixty-five windmills.[37] The Abbey of Bury St Edmunds had no fulling mill in the county, and only at the Abbey of Bec's manor of Blakenham, at Wood Hall and at the Earl of Norfolk's manor of Hollesley are single examples recorded.[38] The first was in use by 1288, and the second by 1323.

The course of events at Hollesley is instructive. The manorial corn mill in the 1290s was a windmill, and it was obviously decided to bring back into service the site of a former watermill. The millpond was accordingly patched up, and a new corn mill was built. Three years later it was leased as a fulling mill for £2 6s, which can only mean that the new mill had been a financial disaster, and in desperation it had been converted to a different use.[39] So far from this fulling mill having been built in the expectation of a considerable profit, it existed only because of its failure as a corn mill. At Wood Hall, meanwhile, it is possible to discover how profitable the fulling mill was to the demesne. In 1337 it was at farm for £3 6s 8d, whilst the two watermills and the windmill were farmed for seventy-three and a half quarters of wheat and twenty-six quarters of maslin. Wheat from the manor was sold that year mainly at 5s or 5s 8d a quarter, and maslin for 4s, so the value of the tollcorn amounted to little less than £25 — much more than the fulling mill was worth.[40]

The same marginal contribution was made by Peterborough Abbey's

[36] PRO, C 132/38/17; SC 6/1141/1; Norfolk CRO, DCN 40/13; Rotuli Hundredorum, ii, p. 550.

[37] Pinchbeck Register, pp. 30–281.

[38] Brit. Lib., Harley MS 230, fols 144–56v; Add. MS 14,849, fols 3–83; Select Documents of the English Lands of the Abbey of Bec, ed. M. Chibnall (Camden 3rd ser., 73, 1951), p. 132; PRO, SC 6/1008/2; 999/1.

[39] PRO, SC 6/998/28; 999/1.

[40] PRO, SC 6/1008/9.

fulling mill at Kettering in Northamptonshire. At farm for only £1 in 1281 when the manor's corn mills brought in £6, no mention was made of it in the estate survey made in 1321.[41] Twenty miles away, at Elton on the River Nene, Ramsey Abbey had by 1267 built the only fulling mill in Huntingdonshire, according to the Hundred Rolls; again, its profits were far less than those of the manor's corn mills.[42] All were operated by demesne servants, and in the accounting year ending in 1297 the two corn mills took in multure wheat, maslin and malt worth £6 4s, whilst the fulling mill took only £1 7s 3d, despite the abbey's enforcing suit of this mill on its tenants.[43] In 1304, when the receipts of the fulling mill were only 18s, the tollcorn was sold for over £9, and although in some later years the fulling mill did produce £2 or more, it still fell a long way behind the corn mills in profitability.[44]

The 'swift, clear streams' of the south-west did not power mills that were any more profitable. At Dunster in Somerset, a survey of the manor in 1279 recorded two watermills worth £2 13s 4d and a fulling mill worth 13s 4d; by 1331 the watermills were yielding £13 6s 8d, but the fulling mill was still at the same rent.[45] At Wrington a fulling mill annexed to an existing independent corn mill was paying a rent of just 6d in 1325; forty years later the rent was unchanged, indicating that Glastonbury Abbey had had nothing to do with the construction of the mill and claimed only a token sum for water rights.[46] There were two more fulling mills on the Abbey's lands, at Mells, which returning once more uneconomic rents of 1s and 6s 8d demonstrate that at least one great lord was unwilling to risk any capital in industrial mills, even when potential sites were available.[47] On the estates of the Bishop of Bath and Wells, at Wiveliscombe in 1309 there were three corn mills worth £10; the fulling mill returned only 16s that year, and had gone by 1329. At Wookey in the latter year one corn mill was at farm for £12, a second for £2 13s 4d and the fulling mill for £1 1s 8d; at

---

[41] Brit. Lib., Add. Charter 737; Add. MS 39,758, fol. 122.

[42] *Cartularium Monasterii de Rameseia*, i, p. 490; *Rotuli Hundredorum*, p. 656. For the dating of the Elton survey to 1267 see E. A. Kosminsky, 'The Hundred Rolls of 1279–80 as a source for English agrarian history', *Econ. Hist. Review*, 3 (1931), p. 28, n. 1.

[43] PRO, SC 6/874/2; *Select Pleas in Manorial Courts*, p. 92.

[44] PRO, SC 6/874/3, and see *Elton Manorial Records*, pp. 51, 110, 184, 230, etc.

[45] Somerset CRO, DD/L P1/1. 2.

[46] Brit. Lib., Egerton MS 3321, fols 166v; PRO, SC 11/621.

[47] Brit. Lib., Egerton MS 3321, fols 132v, 133.

Cheddar there were four fulling mills at farm for £3 12s, and one corn mill at farm for £4.[48]

The same pattern is seen in the Pennines. Among the Earl of Lincoln's mills in Lancashire in 1296 there was a fulling mill at Colne, and that year a new one was built at Burnley. But the Colne mill brought in only £1 13s 4½d, when the corn mill there was worth £12 16s; in 1305 it was worth £1 14s and the corn mill £11 2s, while the Burnley fulling mill brought in £1 4s and the corn mill £9 8s 5d.[49] Everywhere, in fact, throughout this random sample of manors, where fulling mills are to be found they returned a lower profit to their owners than corn mills did, and this was the crucial factor in their distribution pattern. In a manor with surplus water resources a lord could regard a fulling mill as a desirable investment; where resources were scarce, as in the eastern counties, to use a valuable mill site for fulling was hardly ever justifiable.

It is perfectly clear that a 'power revolution' did not occur in medieval England. It is also possible to say why it did not occur. The lords of hundreds of manors were willing, indeed eager, to invest heavily in windmills during the thirteenth century, because corn milling was profitable; they did not invest large amounts in industrial production because they did not see the same prospect of getting their money back. Few industrial commodities were made in sufficient quantities during the Middle Ages to make the mechanization of all or part of the manufacturing process feasible: leather was one, but the preparation of crushed bark was a small part of the tanning process and apparently not worth mechanizing; cloth was another, and the fulling mill could often be a realistic investment. But otherwise, industrial production was limited because this was an impoverished society in which practically all of the population directed most of their efforts towards acquiring sufficient bread: corn mills alone were generally worth building because flour was the only commodity that was always, everywhere, in demand. Of course, the ingenuity of medieval man led him to devise a range of new applications of waterpower, but the mechanization that was technically possible could not come about in practice until the growing markets and emerging capitalist enterprise of the sixteenth century ushered in an era of larger scale production.

[48] PRO, SC 6/1131/4; 1131/6.
[49] *Two Compoti of the Lancashire and Cheshire Manors of Henry de Lacy*, pp 4, 8, 15, 16, 99, 104.

10
The End of the Golden Age

Evidence from a wide range of sources shows that when the plague epidemic known as the Black Death swept through England during 1348 and 1349, it left between one-third and one-half of the population dead.[1] Moreover, it ushered in an extended period of population decline and stagnation from which the country would not emerge for at least another century. If the reasons for this are as yet imperfectly understood, its results are all too plain, as the shortage of labour, higher wages, and after the 1370s low prices of grain and other commodities, made demesne agriculture uneconomic. For much of the fifteenth century aristocratic incomes were in decline as the level of rents fell, whilst for the peasantry there was abundant land and prosperity.[2] The structure of agrarian society was beginning to change fundamentally, as customary tenure and the incidents of serfdom withered away.[3]

The manorial mill could hardly escape the effects of these long-term changes, and for most mills 1348 marked a clear divide: the point when all at once the high profits of the previous century came to an end. Thereafter milling was to be a more hazardous venture, with profits increasingly uncertain. To illustrate how this happened, it is useful in the first instance to trace the course of events on just one manor, Standon in Hertfordshire. Because of its position on the River Rib, Standon had plentiful water resources, and in 1086 there had been five mills there worth £2 5s.[4] In the 1330s there were four corn mills and a fulling mill, though the latter was of little value, producing

---

[1] P. Ziegler, The Black Death (London, 1979), pp. 224–31.

[2] J. Hatcher, Plague, Population and the English Economy 1348–1530 (London, 1977), pp. 31–54, reviews the evidence.

[3] R. H. Hilton, The Decline of Serfdom in Medieval England (London, 1969), pp 32–43, 57 and passim.

[4] Domesday Book, fol. 142d.

only £1 6s 8d rent in 1338 — its last recorded year. By 1343 there were just the four corn mills: Lottesford mill, at farm for £4 6s 8d, and the Old Mill, the New mill, and the Malt mill together at farm for ninety-two quarters of grain.[5] During the Black Death Lottesford mill stopped working for six months, and by 1355 the affect of the high death rate on the need for milling capacity was obvious. The rent of Lottesford mill had fallen to £3, one of the other three corn mills had been converted to a fulling mill rented for £2, and the farm of the remaining two mills had fallen to forty quarters of wheat.[6] After that the rents crept up again, though they went down in 1362 and 1363 because, it was said, of the second plague epidemic.[7] The underlying trend, however, was towards recovery, so that by 1375 Lottesford mill was back to a rent of £4 6s 8d, the fulling mill was farmed for £2 10s and the total of forty quarters of grain from the other two mills was all sold for £11 18s 2d. Nevertheless, at under £19 the demesne's income from its mills was still less than it must have been before 1348; ominously, repairs that year cost £10 17s 2d, and two years earlier had cost £12 13s 9d.[8] There then follows an unfortunate hiatus in the documentary record, until 1460, which obscures but cannot conceal a further deterioration in the fortunes of the Standon mills. Between those dates Lottesford mill, too, had been converted to fulling, but now stood derelict, and the remaining two corn mills and the fulling mill were together farmed for £10. Maintenance costs of £5 3s 11d brought net milling revenues down to less than £5 that year, and by 1471 the rent paid for the mills had fallen even further, to £8.[9] A decline of this order is more correctly termed a collapse, and it demonstrates how decisively the golden age of milling had come to an end.

The example of a single manor does not fully convey the scale of the immediate impact of the Black Death and succeeding epidemics. In the 1320s a vacancy account of the lands of the bishopric of Norwich listed fifteen watermills and twelve windmills; in 1369 a similar account could record only ten watermills and six windmills.[10] And in numerous individual cases it is easy to see how mills could so quickly go out of use. The windmill at Ramsay Abbey's manor of Brancaster in Norfolk

[5] PRO, SC 6/868/21, /22, 23; 869/3, /8.
[6] PRO, SC 6/869/9, /11.
[7] PRO, SC 6/869/14.
[8] PRO, SC 6/869/15, /16.
[9] PRO, SC 6/870/4, m. 1; /7, m. 1.
[10] PRO, SC 6/1141/1; 1141/2, /3.

had fallen into disrepair by 1352, and nobody would lease it. After £4 had been spent on repairs the mill worked for the remaining thirteen weeks of the financial year, but when the miller's wage of a quarter and four bushels of grain had been paid, only six bushels of tollcorn remained. The following year a total of only four quarters was received because new millstones were needed, and though subsequently the mill was at farm for twelve or thirteen quarters a year this can have been little more than half of the £4 that had to be spent on one new millstone in 1363.[11] Faced with the same need at Hilgay, the abbey was not at all certain that the expenditure was justified, and the mill there was allowed to stand idle for a whole year before a new millstone was grudgingly purchased in 1360.[12] With milling ceasing to be a profitable activity in so many places, there must have been a brisk market in the parts of dismantled mills, and in 1364 Norwich Cathedral Priory was able to purchase a second-hand millstone for its mill at Hindringham: even so, at £1 6s 10d, this was still a considerable expense.[13]

John Langdon, in his study of the West Midlands documentation, has observed a similar rapid decline in the number of mills after the middle of the fourteenth century.[14] In Cornwall the sudden depopulation seems to have had little effect on numbers, although it greatly reduced the revenues mills produced: the same state of affairs is observable in Durham and Northumberland.[15] As far as the northern mills are concerned this is not unexpected, considering how profitable they had been and thus how far their rents would have had to fall before they became no longer worth maintaining. For several of the manors of the Bishop of Durham surveyed in about 1380 a previous mill rent is given, and in each case the fall was precipitate: from £38 to £20 at Whickham, from £22 to £16 13s 4d at Gateshead, from £10 13s 4d to £6 6s 8d at West Auckland, and from £3 6s 8d to 13s 4d at Lynsak'.[16] Yet all of these mills, except the last, still produced rents that lords in the rest of England would have envied. At Hartlepool the rent of the windmill had fallen, though by how much was not stated,

[11] PRO, SC 6/931/4, /5, /6, /7, /8.
[12] PRO, SC 6/937/15.
[13] Norfolk RO, DCN 60/20/30.
[14] Personal communication from J. L. Langdon.
[15] J. Hatcher, *Rural Economy and Society in the Duchy of Cornwall 1300–1500* (Cambridge, 1970), p. 177.
[16] *Bishop Hatfield's Survey*, ed. W. Greenwell (Surtees Soc., 32, Durham, 1857), pp. 31, 53, 89, 93.

and comparison with the mutilated vacancy account of about 1300 shows further massive reductions in mill rents at Newbottle from £17 6s 8d to £8 13s 4d, at Ryton from £8 13s 4d to £4 16s 8d, and at Heighington from £26 13s 4d to £4 13s 4d. Mills recorded at the beginning of the century at Whessoe and at Bisshopley had apparently gone by 1380.[17]

The excellent series of accounts for the manor of Great Shelford (referred to in chapter 8) continues throughout this period and finishes only towards the end of the fifteenth century. It is therefore possible to trace in considerable detail the way in which changing conditions affected this one mill, although we should not assume that what happened there was entirely typical. As a powerful watermill on the even-flowing River Cam, it undoubtedly gave a more predictable return on investment than did Cambridgeshire's many windmills; although at times it was expensive to maintain, it never looked as if it would not survive. In fact it weathered the storms of the 1350s and 1360s with ease. There was a reduced but still healthy profit, and in 1371 the rent rose to £8 10s — a level not reached since the 1320s when grain prices had started to drift downwards towards a trough in the years immediately before the Black Death. A renewed uncertainty in grain prices was probably the reason why the annual rent began to fall again; in addition the mill may have been showing signs of age, as the administration of the Ely estate decided to rebuild it. By their willingness to invest they left no doubt of their belief that milling would continue to be profitable at Great Shelford, although their decision that the new mill should be a combined corn and fulling mill does show how much times had changed. Constructed at a cost of £15 12s 6d, the mill measured eighty feet by twenty feet and probably stood over the mill leat with its two water-wheels set in the centre, side by side, like the mill at Abbotsbury. Its first tenant in 1388 was one John Sturmyn, described as a carpenter: he would himself have been able to keep the machinery in repair, while the work of the combined enterprise was performed by hired hands. Despite continued falls in the price of grain into the next century, the mill provided a good return for both lord and tenant, and Sturmyn remained in charge for fifteen years paying a rent that was stable at £8 6s 8d.[18]

Conditions in the fifteenth century were to prove no more

[17] Ibid., pp. 5, 10, 18, 23, 59, 92, 160−1, 198; PRO, SC 11/1012.
[18] For details see Appendix 3; PRO, SC 6/1134/1, 2, 3. For the multiple mill at Abbotsbury, Dorset, see chapter 8.

favourable to demesne mills. The rents of many continued to fall, and even at a viable mill such as Great Shelford, where the rent remained relatively buoyant, the problem of rising costs was becoming increasingly serious. Throughout the economy labour costs were going up, and this was reflected both in the amounts now having to be paid out for maintenance and in the wages taken by mill servants. Because in the fifteenth century it was so rare for millers to be demesne employees there is very little evidence for their wages, but one known example suggests they had risen considerably. At Catesby in Northamptonshire in 1415 the miller received £1 and his assistant 2s 6d, even though the mill they served returned only £1 2s in cash and six quarters and two bushels of tollcorn. No livery of grain is mentioned in the account, which suggests that the millers' share of the tollcorn had already been deducted from the total. Catesby Priory, the owners of the mill, had to find 9s for repairs and essential running costs, including shoes for the mill horses and candles so that the mill could work in winter; accordingly the profit on this mill can have been only some three or four quarters — perhaps worth £1.[19]

The severity of the new crisis into which milling was slipping indicates that factors other than just increased labour costs were at work. The most difficult time for some mills was the 1440s, a decade of low grain prices; whereas at Shelford the only sign of this was a temporary lull in the level of rent, elsewhere the difficult time around the middle of the century was more noticeable, and contrasted sharply with the partial recovery of the previous decades.[20] Thus the mill of Farleigh Hungerford, in Somerset, had produced thirteen quarters of tollcorn just before the Black Death, although afterwards three quarters or less was usual, the mill being invariably described as broken, useless or having worthless millstones.[21] In 1414 tollcorn worth £1 18s 4d was received, even after tithes and the miller's share had been deducted, but this was evidently a false dawn as the mill was later put at farm for £1 6s 8d, and by 1466 was in the lord's hand and rented for a mere 6s 8d.[22] The mills at Elton in Huntingdonshire, at farm for £3 6s 8d in 1393, had recovered something of their former value when in 1425 Ramsey Abbey leased them as two mills in one house for a rent of £6

[19] G. Baker, The History and Antiquties of the County of Northampton, 2 vols (London, 1822—41), i, pp. 278—82.

[20] Appendix 3.

[21] PRO, SC 6/970/12—21.

[22] PRO, SC 6/971/1, 14.

13s 4d. By 1460, however, they could only be rented for £5 6s 8d, and more importantly a schedule to the account for that year reveals that the farmer, who was in the last year of his lease, still owed £11, whilst £14 was owed by previous farmers over a period of at least thirteen years.[23]

The effect of the crisis on more marginal mills was catastrophic. The once-valuable windmill at Popinho, Norfolk, that had produced twenty-five quarters of tollcorn before the Black Death, was rented for £1 13s 4d in 1418, though it had previously been worth £2. By 1441 its rent was down to £1 10s, and it had been let on the understanding that the farmer should pay for all of the maintenance. Perhaps predictably, ten years later it was derelict.[24] As far as many of these mills were concerned, there was not to be any continuation of the relative prosperity of the 1370s and 1380s into the early part of the fifteenth century, and for them the onset of the crisis came even before 1400. Ramsey Abbey's windmill at Holywell had been at farm for £1 6s 8d in 1371, and by 1392 was worth £2; already by the end of the century its value was falling again, and it was leased for seven years for a rent of only £1. In 1414 William Prykke, who was to be its last farmer, took a ten-year lease for 13s 4d, but the mill was blown down by the wind and abandoned.[25] When in 1432 Elsworth mill, less than five miles away, was granted to a new tenant he was given the millstones and cogwheel from Holywell mill; the rent that was to be paid, only 8s rather than the 16s which had been paid since 1411, was not high enough to justify Ramsey's spending anything at all on new components. Before 1453 Elsworth mill had burnt down, and had been written off.[26] Another early fourteenth-century casualty was the single survivor of the two pre-Black Death windmills at Hindolveston, Norfolk. It was thought to merit the expenditure of £3 16s 4d in 1380; by 1412, however, it had fallen down, and was not to be rebuilt. The mill at Bircham, too, last recorded in 1380, was derelict by 1404.[27]

It would be too facile to blame the fifteenth-century milling crisis on the population level, which continued to stagnate until the middle

[23] PRO, SC 6/874/17; *Liber Gersummarum*, ed. E. B. DeWindt (Toronto, 1976), p. 191; SC 6/874/27.

[24] PRO, SC 6/942/16, 20; 943/1, 2, 3.

[25] PRO, SC 6/877/21, 22, 25; 878/6; *Liber Gersummarum*, pp. 24, 118.

[26] Ibid., pp. 100, 226; PRO, SC 6/767/4.

[27] Norfolk CRO, DCN 60/18/27, 41, 43, 59; PRO, SC 6/930/34.

years of the century.[28] This second crisis, visible on some manors by
1400, on others in the 1440s, but in Cornwall, for example, only by
the 1470s, was something quite apart from the straightforward
contraction after the Black Death, to be seen on practically every
manor during the 1350s and 1360s.[29] Some other reason has to be
sought, beyond the observation that the pattern was little different
from that in other sectors of the economy. As there was a similar
decline in the exports of wool, cloth, tin and other commodities, and
in the quantities of wine that were imported, the various phenomena
were no doubt related: underlying much of this apparent economic
recession was an acute reduction in the incomes of aristocratic families
and institutions all over England.[30] With rents of demesne lands
everywhere falling or simply not being paid, it does not seem strange
that the same should have been true of mill rents. Can the
accompanying attrition of mills that we have seen be then attributable
at least in part to an inefficiency of lordship? That, by implication,
these mills were falling into ruin, not because demand for them had
fallen away to the extent that it was no longer possible for them to
operate profitably, but instead because their aristocratic owners could
no longer command the necessary level of rent to maintain them?

Some confirmation is provided by indications that the crisis was
indeed one of demesne milling. In different contexts mills could
thrive, and there was even some investment in new capacity. As we
saw in chapter 4, a high proportion of the independent mills on the
Glastonbury Abbey estates were able to weather the crises and survive
into the sixteenth century, at the same time as mills that had supposedly
been able to rely on the suit of villein tenants were going under. More
telling than this was the eagerness on the part of men who can only be
described as entrepreneurs to move into the field that lords had
vacated, and build their own mills. An early example comes from
Bibury in Gloucestershire, where the demesne mill lay in ruins soon
after the Black Death, and where during the 1370s the Bishop of
Worcester gave his permission for a tenant to rebuild the mill at his
own expense, paying only a token rent of 6d and then of 2s.[31] A

[28] Hatcher, *Population and the English Economy*, pp. 68–9.
[29] Hatcher, *The Duchy of Cornwall*, p. 177.
[30] Hatcher, *Population and the English Economy*, pp. 35–42.
[31] *Red Book of Worcester*, p. 504; PRO, E 136/13/9; Worcestershire CRO, 009:1 BA
2636/160/92052 and subsequent accounts. I am grateful to J. L. Langdon for providing
me with these references.

similar case is recorded in county Durham in the following century. The mill at *Benefeldside* was ruined by 1380, and in 1433 the Bishop of Durham allowed one John Bateson to take the site on a lifetime lease and build a new mill there, to be held for a rent of 3s 4d.[32]

Most often, it appears, the private milling activity that was permitted was the operation of a horsemill. At Alverstoke in Hampshire during the 1460s a tenant paid an annual rent of 3s 4d so that he might grind the malt of the villagers in his horsemill; in the 1450s and 1460s the villagers of Swavesey, Cambridgeshire, who had some years previously been deprived of their windmill, could legally use Richard Webbe's horsemill, licensed by the Abbot of Ramsey for 13s 4d a year.[33] In the same way the abbot did not attempt to rebuild his windmill at Chatteris, described as early as 1379 as having been dismantled, and therefore a casualty of the first, post-Black Death crisis; by 1441 there was a horsemill there, held on a life tenancy for 4s 3½d, and although seven years later it was described as ruined it was still recorded as being at work in 1461.[34] In 1466 a tenant of Nostell Priory in Yorkshire paid 3s to have a horsemill on his land at South Kirkby, and so it goes on.[35]

Inevitably, behind these few examples there must have been many more horsemills in use, unlicensed as well as licensed, so that the question arises of how far suit of mill remained a practical reality. At a time when lords found their ascendancy over their tenants under threat, it is hardly credible that it could have been enforced with its old vigour, a view which was also expressed by H. P. R. Finberg. In discussing the fulling mills built after 1400 by the abbots of Tavistock, he assumed that no attempt would have been made to force the tenants to use them, as 'the fifteenth century was no time for pressing home seigneurial rights.' John Hatcher, too, detailing the spectacular decline of the Duchy of Cornwall's mills when there were signs that independent mills were prospering, suggested that a probable relaxation of suit of mill was responsible.[36]

[32] *Bishop Hatfield's Survey*, p. 114.

[33] Hampshire CRO, Winchester Pipe Roll 1465–6, Eccl. II, 155833; PRO, SC 6/770/4, 5.

[34] PRO, SC 6/765/21; 766/7; *Liber Gersummarum*, pp. 279, 325.

[35] W. T. Lancaster, 'A fifteenth-century rental of Nostell Priory', *Yorks. Archaeol. Soc. Rec. Ser.*, 61 (1920), p. 119.

[36] H. P. R. Finberg, *Tavistock Abbey* (Cambridge, 1951), p. 154; Hatcher, *The Duchy of Cornwall*, p. 177. In the years around 1500 the court of the Bishop of Worcester's

Unable to draw adequate rents from their own mills and reluctant to invest, the lords of many manors had become resigned to taking no more than a small share of the proceeds of milling. At the same time, they concentrated the limited investment they were prepared to make into enterprises that could promise some return, such as Ramsey's mills at Elton, or Ely's at Great Shelford. Massive repair costs did undoubtedly add to their problems: £81 was spent on repairs to Barford mill, Warwickshire, between 1442 and 1444, and at Great Shelford the mill built for only £15 12s 6d in 1387 cost £29 1s 6d to renovate in 1413, and £35 13s in 1432.[37] Rather than the overall decline in milling activity, therefore, that manorial documentation seems to show, there was in reality a far more complex situation, in which perhaps the only constant factor was the general inability of lords to rely on the suit of their tenants and to charge high mill rents as they had formerly done. Incidentally, their enforced withdrawal from what were now marginal areas of milling, and a consequent substitution of small-scale milling enterprises using the horsemill, once again demonstrates how unsuited the watermill and the windmill were to ventures that were not capital-intensive. Without expensive water-control systems, or vulnerable wood and canvas sails, the horsemill could be built and repaired at low cost or by the miller himself, and could be operated in a small way yet still profitably. In a very real sense it fulfilled the same function in fifteenth-century England as the horizontal mill did at the beginning of the Middle Ages.

The concentration on larger mills that could still be made to return a profit was a successful policy, particularly as towards the end of the century there is evidence that the rents of some of them were rising. Now at last, after a century and a half of contraction, there were lords who considered the time ripe to expand the number of their mills. The rent of Great Shelford mill went up from £8 in 1450 to £10 in 1458, and to £12 in 1483, although the last increase coincided with another rebuilding of the mill costing this time £27 3s 11d. John Langdon has observed the same trend towards cautious expansion in

---

manor of Hanbury, where there was no longer a manorial mill, regularly fined the owner of a horsemill 2d for taking excessive toll. It is quite clear that by this date the Bishop was no longer attempting to reserve to himself the profits of milling, except in this marginal way: Worcester CRO, 705:7 BA 7335/64. I am grateful to C. C. Dyer for providing me with this reference.

[37] Warwickshire RO, CR 895/8/28. I am grateful to J. L. Langdon for providing me with this reference.

the West Midlands, and the examples of two estates will suffice to illustrate what was happening.[38] On the estates of the Percy family, situated not only in Northumberland but also in Cumberland, Yorkshire and Sussex, the decline in mill rents during the first half of the century was in line with the overall decline in revenues; by the last quarter of the fifteenth century, however, and certainly by 1500, some of the estate's corn mills were beginning to increase in value. Those at Petworth in Sussex, which since the 1430s had rendered less than £7, rose from £7 5s in 1475 to £8 in 1485, and to £10 in 1503. At Duncton a new mill was built to be rented for £1 6s 8d, and at Catton in Yorkshire the corn and fulling mills rented for £20 in 1492 were at £26 in 1517.[39]

A detailed terrier of Glastonbury Abbey's manors made between 1516 and 1520 for Abbot Richard Beere allows comparisons with the documentation of earlier centuries.[40] On the twenty-five manors included in the surviving sections of the terrier which had mills either in the sixteenth century or between 1300 and 1350, the number of watermills had fallen from twenty-one to eighteen, and the windmills from twelve to ten.[41] The rents that were paid confirm the extent of the recession, though most had not fallen as much as that for the windmill of Othery, down from £2 to 6s 8d, or were as low as those for the two windmills at Middle Zoy, at only 5s each. The effect of the recession can also be seen in the windmill at South Brent, rented for 6s 8d, which has every appearance of having been built either by the wealthy farmer who held it or by a previous tenant.[42] On the other hand, the signs that the recession had come to an end are equally abundant. Richard Beere, who had been abbot since 1493, had himself built four mills: a new watermill in the town of Glastonbury, rented

[38] Appendix 3; personal communication from J. L. Langdon.

[39] J. M. W. Bean, *The Estates of the Percy Family 1416–1557*, (Oxford, 1958), pp. 18–23, 25, 29, 30, 41–3, 48.

[40] Brit. Lib., Egerton MSS 3034, 3134; Harley MS 3961; Society of Antiquaries Lib., MS 653.

[41] Details of Glastonbury's mills in the early fourteenth century are to be found in Longleat MSS 10,632, 10,761, 10,801; Brit. Lib., Egerton MS 3321, fols 2, 2v, 23v, 82v, 105v, 123, 155v, 157, 166v, 183v, 190v, 206v, 226v, 227, 238v, 239, 251v; Add. MS 17,450, fols 106v, 170v, 189v; *Rentalia et Custumaria*, p. 166. Watermills and windmills are recorded in the early sixteenth century in Brit. Lib., Egerton MS 3034, fols 37v, 90, 128, 153, 188, 198, 221v–2v, 245v; Egerton MS 3134, fols 51v, 60, 149v, 166v, 196v, 226; Harley MS fols 96v, 111, 124v, 132, 146, 165v, 166v.

[42] Brit. Lib., Egerton MSS 3321, fol. 227; 3134, fols 196v, 149v, 166v; 3034, fol. 153.

for £10, and a fulling mill there rented for £1; a windmill at East Brent assigned to one of the obedientiaries; and a windmill at Winterborne Monkton rented for £1.[43] These were not the rents of two centuries before, when Abbot Beere's predecessors had built mills to such benefit to their house; nevertheless the renewal of confidence is plain to see.

Further changes are revealed in the folios of Abbot Beere's terrier. The total of all the mills taken together was in fact up, from thirty-five to thirty-nine, there having been an increase in the number of both horsemills and fulling mills, from one of each before the Black Death to five and six respectively. The single fulling mill had been at Wrington, and now there were four there, although the rents they paid — 4s 4d, 2s, 1s and 8d — tell how small a part the abbey had taken in building them. Like the new fulling mill at Glastonbury, that at *Nony* paid a realistic rent, £1 4s, and so these two had in contrast been built by the abbey.[44] The end of easy profits from corn milling made fulling mills (and no doubt other industrial mills as well) more important as revenue-earners than they had been, although details such as these confirm that lords still found their appeal limited, and that they remained worth building only where there was an already established cloth industry as well as plenty of available water.

The horsemill at Westonzoyland had been worth £1 12s in the 1330s, and the two that were there in the sixteenth century — one of them built by Beere's predecessor John Selwode (1456–92) — returned 16s and 16s 10d each. The others were at Glastonbury, Middle Zoy, and at Moorlinch, where there had previously been no mill at all.[45] Closely associated with non-seigneurial milling as the horsemill now was, it is significant that it also had its attractions for a great institution like Glastonbury Abbey. There could be no better illustration of how the course of medieval technological innovation was determined by economic and social movements, and of why there was no inexorable increase in the use of waterpower and windpower in the Middle Ages. The vertical mill and the windmill had served the purpose of English lords striving to impose a milling monopoly on

[43] Brit. Lib., Egerton MS 3034, fols 37v, 128; Harley MS 3961, fol. 96v.

[44] Brit. Lib., Egerton MSS 3321, fol. 166v; 3034, fols 207, 211v, 223, 225v, 37v; Harley MS 3961, fol. 200v.

[45] Longleat MS 10,761; Brit. Lib., Egerton MSS 3134, fols 119, 131, 109, 163; 3034, fol. 37v.

their tenants; now economic considerations dictated the use of a less powerful but cheaper machine.

On these Glastonbury Abbey manors the number of corn mills had returned almost to its earlier level: there were thirty-three where once there had been thirty-four, although as the smaller horsemill was now more in favour, overall milling capacity might have fallen rather more than the figures would suggest. The fall in their value to the abbey was greater, and was to be permanent. Alexander Savine's analysis of the income from a sample of sixty English monasteries at the eve of the Dissolution showed that the revenue from mills now amounted to 2.25 per cent of their total temporal income, or less than half the contribution that mills had made to seigneurial incomes two centuries before.[46]

But it was those earlier rents that had been the aberration, the result of a temporary combination of circumstances. The decline in the number and profitability of mills during the fifteenth century was really the mirror image of the rise in their rental value during the thirteenth century. Then, a peak of seigneurial authority coincided with increasing population pressure, and so enabled lords to exact an inflated price for grinding from the peasant customers, while paying extremely low wages to the employees who worked and maintained the mills. As a result of these circumstances, there were many mills built and made to return a profit that at any other time would not have been viable. The aftermath of the Black Death had brought about a swift adjustment of the number of mills to the level of the population; what we can observe in the fifteenth century was a longer and more painful phase of readjustment, as it became obvious how many of these marginal mills there were, and how little real need there had been for them.

[46] A. Savine, 'English Monasteries on the Eve of the Dissolution', in P. Vinogradoff (ed.), *Oxford Studies in Social and Legal History* (Oxford, 1909), pp. 126–8.

Appendix 1
Early Windmill References

Edward Kealey, after what appears to have been an exhaustive search through twelfth- and thirteenth-century charters (which are seldom dated), believes he has found evidence of fifty-six windmills that were in existence before 1200. A large number, however, can be dated only approximately to the years around 1200, some are firmly dated only after 1200, and others are dated on decidedly subjective grounds: for instance a grant of a windmill to Hickling Priory, Norfolk, was 'probably issued before 1200', because of 'its antiquated style and the generosity of its terms'.[1] Several early windmills owe their existence to Kealey's argument that since certain manors had no mill in 1086 but had a windmill in the thirteenth century, any mill recorded there between those dates must have been a windmill. So Wigston Magna in Leicestershire, where a mill was recorded in 1169, is reckoned to have had an early windmill because only a windmill existed there over a century later;[2] nearby Wigston Parva possessed a windmill perhaps by 1200, leading Kealey to conclude that the mill that had been there in 1137 must have been the earliest recorded windmill.[3] Needless to say, the evidence we have seen that there were continued attempts to develop water resources after 1086, that in eastern England in particular there were many watermills that were marginal at best, and that a small but significant proportion of watermills were replaced as soon as the windmill became a viable alternative, means that Kealey's argument is unsound.

In fact, there are twenty-three English windmills, listed below, which can be firmly dated to before 1200, nine of them newly identified by

---

[1] Kealey, *Harvesting the Air*, p. 241.
[2] Ibid., p. 227.
[3] Ibid., pp. 227–8.

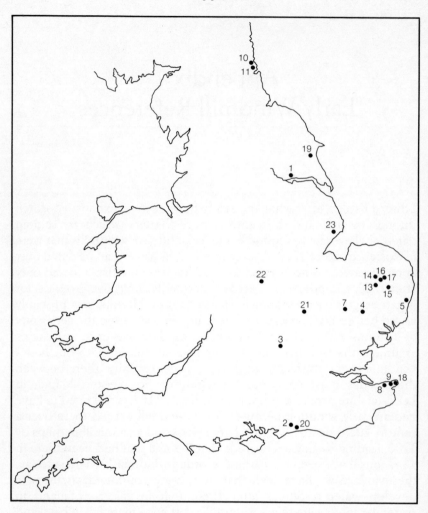

Figure 9 Early windmills (1185—1200). *note*: numbers 6 and 12 are not shown as their locations are uncertain.

Kealey. Their locations are shown in figure 9. Presumably most were older than the first references to them, and obviously the twenty-three can have been no more than a small part of the total. Nevertheless, the bunching of these early references into the last two decades of the twelfth century, and particularly into the 1190s, concurs with other evidence we have seen that the windmill was then a very recent innovation.

Of the twenty-three windmills, three are firmly dated in the 1180s:

(1)   Weedley, in the East Riding of Yorkshire, was mentioned in a survey of the lands of the Templars made in 1185.[4]

(2)   Amberley, Sussex, was granted in 1185 to the canons of Chichester Cathedral by Bishop Seffrid II who had built it since 1180.[5]

(3)   Dinton, Buckinghamshire, was granted to the nuns of Godstow by Agnes of Mountchesney who died in 1187 or shortly after.[6]

Fifteen windmills are firmly dated to the 1190s, or the undated documents that record them can be safely dated then:

(4)   *Haberdun*, Bury St Edmunds, was the site of the mill built by Herbert the Dean and which enraged Abbot Samson, who feared that the income of his own mills was threatened. The episode is conventionally dated to *c.*1190, because of the order of events in Jocelin of Brakelond's chronicle.[7]

(5)   Also in Suffolk, at Dunwich, was a windmill granted to the Templars by Richard I (1189–99).[8]

(6)   As detailed more fully in chapter 2, Pope Celestine III (1191–8) ordered the Abbot of Ramsey and the archdeacon of Ely to enforce the collection of tithes from a windmill that had been built presumably in Huntingdonshire or Cambridgeshire.[9]

(7)   A grant of the tithes of a windmill at Silverley in Cambridgeshire was made by Reginald Arsic apparently before 1194 (although there is no evidence it was made as early as Kealey supposes).[10]

(8) (9)   Between 1193 and 1195 Archbishop Hubert Walter granted

[4] *Records of the Templars in England in the Twelfth Century: The Inquest of 1185*, (Brit. Acad. Records of Social and Econ. Hist., 9, London, 1935), p. 131.

[5] *The Chartulary of the High Church of Chichester*, ed. W. D. Peckham (Sussex Rec. Soc., 46, 1946), p. 41.

[6] Kealey, *Harvesting the Air*, pp. 213–14.

[7] *The Chronicle of Jocelin of Brakelond*, ed. H. E. Butler (London, 1949), pp. 59–60.

[8] *Recs. of the Templars in England in the Twelfth Century*, pp. xxii, 135.

[9] Cheney, 'The Decretal of Pope Celestine III on Tithes of Windmills'.

[10] Kealey, *Harvesting the Air*, pp. 98–105, 216.

the tithes of two windmills in Kent, at Reculver and at *Westhallimot*, Isle of Thanet, to Eastbridge Hospital, Canterbury.[11]

(10) (11) In 1196 Thomas le Bigod and his wife Agnes sold two windmills to the east of Newcastle-upon-Tyne to Robert de Peshale.[12]

(12) In 1198 Simon de Farnham purchased half of the windmill belonging to Ralph Dun at *Hienhel*, Suffolk.[13]

(13) In 1198 the windmill of Ralph de Burg', at Attleborough in Norfolk, was mentioned in a final concord.[14]

(14) Stephen de Camais, who had died by 1198, gave a windmill at Flockthorpe, Norfolk, to Wymondham Priory.[15]

(15) Walter fitz Robert, who died in 1198, gave land at Hempnall, Norfolk, to the Abbey of Bury St Edmunds for the erection of a windmill.[16]

(16) (17) In a charter dated apparently to before 1199, William de Albini confirmed, *inter alia*, the grant of two windmills to Wymondham Priory, Norfolk.[17]

(18) Late in the 1190s William de Wode built a windmill at, Monkton, on the Isle of Thanet in Kent, which became the subject of prolonged litigation with the Prior of Holy Trinity, Canterbury.[18]

Five other windmills seem to be datable to before 1200:

(19) According to two conflicting accounts written in the late fourteenth century, a windmill at Beeford, in the East Riding of Yorkshire, was granted to the Abbey of Meaux either during the 1180s or 1190s.[19]

(20) Bishop Seffrid of Chichester (1180–1204), who built one windmill before 1185, built another at Ecclesdon.[20]

---

[11] Ibid., pp. 225, 227.

[12] *Feet of Fines, 1196–1197* (Pipe Roll Soc., 20, 1896), 1.

[13] *Feet of Fines, 1198–1199* (Pipe Roll Soc., 24, 1900), 32.

[14] *Feet of Fines for the County of Norfolk, 1198–1202*, ed. B. Dodwell (Pipe Roll Soc., new ser., 27, 1952), 203.

[15] Kealey, *Harvesting the Air*, pp. 237–8.

[16] Ibid., p. 238.

[17] Ibid., pp. 243–5.

[18] *Curia Regis Rolls*, i (HMSO), 1923), p. 16; iii (HMSO), 1927), pp. 86–7.

[19] *Chronica Monasterii de Melsa*, 3 vols, ed. E. A. Bond (Rolls Ser., 1866–8), i, pp. 164–5, 224–5)

[20] *Chichester Cartulary*, pp. 42–3.

(21)   Probably not long before 1200 the monks of Newnham Priory were granted land on which a windmill stood at Renhold, in Bedfordshire.[21]

(22)   A windmill at Wigston Parva in Leicestershire, claimed by Kealey to have existed before 1137, was first mentioned around 1200.[22]

(23)   A windmill at Friskney, Lincolnshire, was granted to the nuns of Ormsby in the years around 1200.[23]

[21] *The Cartulary of Newnham Priory*, 2 vols, ed. J. Godber (Beds. Historical Rec. Soc., 43, 1963–4), 368.

[22] Kealey, *Harvesting the Air*, pp. 75, 227–8.

[23] *Transcripts of Charters Relating to the Gilbertine Houses of Sixle, Ormesby, Catley, Bullington and Alvingham*, ed. F. M. Stenton (Lincoln Rec. Soc., 18, 1922), p. 45.

Appendix 2
The Cost of Building a Windmill

Of the manorial accounts that provide details of the building of new windmills, a useful group come from the Suffolk manors of the Earl of Norfolk, and show that in the closing years of the thirteenth century the true cost of a new windmill was around £10. Because some items were seldom accounted for in cash terms, or were missing altogether, the cost as given in the account is generally less than this. Timber was felled on the estate, for instance, and tasks that required quantities of unskilled labour were most economically performed from the labour services that were owed, as at Kelsale in 1294 when the height of the mill mound was increased.[1] Most importantly, when an existing mill was being replaced, which was often the case in a later account, there were components and materials to be reused. Thus the new windmill at Soham in 1295 in reality cost much more than the £3 8s 6d accounted for, which covered only 8s 6d for some ironwork and the fee of £3 paid to the carpenter or millwright. Leaving aside the timber, which was not valued because it had not been paid for, the most serious omission was the millstones. Obviously the pair from the previous mill were to be used, one of which was new, having been purchased only the year before for £1 10s.[2] At least a further £3, then, needs to be added to the cost of Soham mill.

Elsewhere, the sum paid to the millwright was slightly higher, and consistent, indicating not only a keen appreciation of the cost of building a windmill on the part of the Earl of Norfolk's officials but also that there was a uniform design and size of mill. At Walton in 1279 it was £3 14s 4d, and a shilling less at Framlingham in 1286 and at Kelsale in 1294; at Walton in 1291 it was £3 6s 9½d.[3] The total cost

[1] PRO, SC 6/1000/18d.
[2] PRO, SC 6/1004/10, 9.
[3] PRO, SC 6/1007/8; *Medieval Framlingham*, pp. 27–8; SC 6/1000/18; 1007/15.

of the Framlingham mill was £8 4s 5d, including one new stone at £1 13s; the cost of the second stone would have put the real total at around £10. The mill that was built at Walton in 1291 cost £6 16s 2½d, without stones, which were to come from the tide mill it replaced: if their value is estimated at £3 then again the true cost of this windmill had been £10. Three years later Kelsale mill was built for £4 16s 10¼d, and again the millstones were not included as the pair in the old mill were deemed to be serviceable. Replacement stones cost £2 each in 1301 and 1306.[4]

Two other windmills of the period cost rather more to build, a reflection perhaps of their different locations or that labour and materials were generally becoming more expensive. It is also possible that both were larger than the Suffolk mills. At Milton Hall in Essex in 1299 the millwright's fee, at £5, and the cost of the millstones which were £5 11s 4d, together contributed to the rather high total cost of £15 4s 11d; at Walton, in Somerset, the cost of the windmill built in 1342 was as low as £11 12s 11d only because a pair of inexpensive local stones costing £1 7s were used, instead of the imported stones that were usual in eastern and southern England. On this occasion the millwright's fee was £5 6s 8d.[5]

It was uncommon for a new windmill to be built after the Black Death, but in 1375 at Brandon in Suffolk a second-hand mill was purchased for £4, and fifty-two men with twenty-six carts were paid 12s 2d, almost threepence each, to bring it from Dereham.[6] It must have gone out of use when its post failed, as a new one was purchased and carried from Shipdham for 8s. Second-hand millstones and ironwork, too, were acquired for £6 13s 4d and 16s respectively. The cost of reassembling the mill, and replacing several parts including one of the sailyards, came to a further £7 18s 8d. The total cost of bringing this old mill back into service, therefore, was £20 8s 2d – or double the cost of the new windmills of a century before. At a time when the reduced population needed fewer mills, when labour costs had increased, and when mill rents had fallen, it must have been common for redundant mills to be cannibalized in this way.

[4] PRO, SC 6/1000/18, 20, 23.
[5] Nicholls, 'Milton Hall: the compotus of 1299', p. 136; Keil, 'Building a post windmill in 1342', pp. 151–4.
[6] PRO, SC 6/1304/36.

Appendix 3
The Watermill at Great Shelford, Cambridgeshire: Annual Rent and Maintenance Costs, 1319–1484

Year	PRO SC 6	Mill Farm		Expenses	
1319–1320	1132/14	9	6s 8d	13s	9½d
1322	''	10	0s 0d	1 19s	9d
1323	''	10	0s 0d	—	
1326	''	10	0s 0d	6s	11d
1327	''	8	0s 0d	4 6s	8d
1328	1132/15	6	13s 4d	4s	3d
1329	''	6	13s 4d	1s	4½d
1330	''	6	13s 4d	mutilated	
1331	''	6	13s 4d	5s	5d
1332	''	6	13s 4d	11s	5½d
1333	''	6	13s 4d	16s	7¾d
1339	1133/1	5	6s 8d	—	
1341	''	5	6s 8d		10d
1342	''	5	6s 8d	2 3s	11d
1344	''	5	6s 8d	12s	11d
1346	''	5	6s 8d	4s	5d
1347	1133/2	6	0s 0d	1 7s	9d
1348	''	6	0s 0d	19s	11d
1351	''	6	0s 0d	16s	4½d
1352	''	6	6s 8d	1 2s	6½d
1353	''	6	6s 8d	4 2s	8¼d
1354	''	7	13s 4d	6s	10d
1362	1133/3	3	6s 8d	8s	9d
1363	''	6	0s 0d	1 6s	7½d
1364	''	6	0s 0d	—	
1365	''	6	13s 4d	5s	6½d
1366	1133/3	6	13s 4d	4 2s	6d

1368	1133/4	5 10s 0d	10 16s 8d
1369	"	7 6s 8d	16s 4½d
1371	"	8 10s 0d	2 0s 0½d
1372	"	8 0s 0d	5s 3d
1375	1133/5	7 13s 4d	17s 4d
1376	"	7 13s 4d	1 17s 2d
1377	1133/5	7 13s 4d	10s 6d
1378	"	7 0s 0d	7 13s 5d
1379	"	7 13s 4d	1 6s 5½d
1380	1133/7	7 1s 6½d	3 6s 6d
1381	"	6 6s 8d	—
1382	"	6 6s 8d	4s 5d
1383	"	6 6s 8d	3 13s 6d
1385	"	6 6s 8d	3s 9d
1386	"	6 6s 8d	—
1387	1134/1	6 6s 8d	15 12s 6d
1389	"	7 13s 4d	—
1391	"	8 6s 8d	5 1s 4d
1392	"	8 6s 8d	3s 0½d
1393	"	8 6s 8d	7s 0½d
1394	"	8 6s 8d	7s 2d
1396	1134/2	8 6s 8d	5s 9d
1397	"	8 6s 8d	1 3s 10d
1398	"	8 6s 8d	4 15s 3d
1399	"	8 6s 8d	2 2s 0d
1401	1134/4	8 6s 8d	4 7s 7d
1402	"	8 6s 8d	7d
1403	"	8 6s 8d	2 2s 0d
1404	"	8 6s 8d	13s 5d
1405	"	8 13s 4d	1 8s 10d
1406	"	8 13s 4d	19s 6d
1407	"	8 13s 4d	11s 10d
1408	1134/1	8 13s 4d	5s 9d
1409	"	8 13s 4d	9 9s 5d
1410	"	8 13s 4d	19s 9d
1411	"	8 13s 4d	7s 1d
1412	"	8 13s 4d	19s 8d
1413	"	8 13s 4d	19 1s 6d
1414	1134/5	8 13s 4d	14s 7d
1415	"	8 13s 4d	17s 4d
1417	"	8 13s 4d	5 9s 1½d
1418	"	8 13s 4d	19s 6d
1419	"	8 13s 4d	2 19s 3d
1420	1134/6	8 13s 4d	6 1s 10d
1421	"	8 13s 4d	2 19s 2d

Year	PRO SC 6	Mill Farm	Expenses
1422	"	8 13s 4d	6 3s 10d
1423	1134/7	8 13s 4d	1 3s 1d
1426	"	8 13s 4d	12s 4d
1427	"	8 13s 4d	1 12s 8d
1428	"	8 13s 4d	7 19s 0d
1429	"	9 0s 0d	1 9s 8d
1430	1134/8	8 16s 0d	6 4s 3d
1431	"	9 6s 8d	6s 11d
1432	"	9 6s 8d	34 13s 0½d
1435	"	9 6s 8d	6s 11d
1440	"	10 0s 0d	14s 7d
1444	1134/9	8 0s 0d	1 13s 4d
1445	"	8 0s 0d	3 0s 6½d
1446	"	8 0s 0d	1 11s 6d
1447	"	8 0s 0d	3 7s 3d
1448	"	8 0s 0d	1 8s 0d
1450	1135/1	8 0s 0d	14s 5d
1452	"	9 0s 0d	11 17s 5½d
1455	"	9 0s 0d	1 19s 1½d
1456	"	9 0s 0d	2 8s 5d
1458	"	10 0s 0d	2 8s 1d
1467	1135/2	10 0s 0d	14 5s 11d
1468	"	10 0s 0d	7 14s 6d
1469	"	11 0s 0d	Uncertain
1470	"	11 0s 0d	5 0s 11d
1473	1135/3	11 6s 8d	1 5s 2d
1474	"	11 6s 8d	8 3s 11d
1475	"	11 6s 8d	3 11s 11½d
1476	"	11 6s 8d	1 18s 1d
1477	1135/4	11 6s 8d	5 4s 11½d
1478	"	11 6s 8d	1 15s 10d
1479	"	11 6s 8d	4 3s 2d
1481	1135/5	11 6s 8d	17s 4d
1482	"	11 6s 8d	7 12s 9d
1483	"	12 0s 0d	27 3s 11d
1484	"	12 0s 0d	19s 4½d

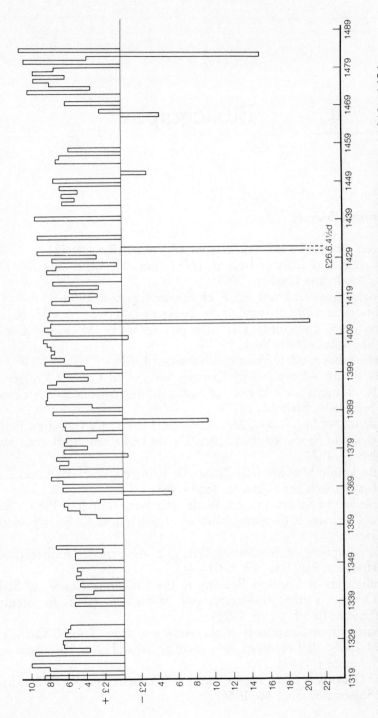

Figure 10 The watermill at Great Shelford, Cambridgeshire: annual rent and maintenance costs, 1319—1484.

Bibliography

Printed Sources

Actes de Charles le Chauve, ii, ed. G. Tessier (Paris, 1952).
The Ancient Laws of Ireland, vol. 1: *Introduction to Senchus Mor* (Dublin and London, 1865).
Anglo-Saxon Charters, ed. P. H. Sawyer (London, 1968).
Bishop Hatfield's Survey, ed. W. Greenwell (Surtees Soc., 32, 1857).
Boccaccio, Giovanni, *The Decameron*, trans. M. Musa and P. Bondanella (New York, 1977).
Boldon Book, ed. D. Austin (Chichester, 1982).
The Burton Abbey Twelfth Century Surveys, ed. C. G. O. Bridgeman (Collections for a History of Staffordshire: William Salt Archaeol. Soc., 1916, Stafford, 1918).
Calendar of Inquisitions Miscellaneous, 1219–1307 (London, 1916).
Caption of Seisin, ed. P. L. Hull (Devon and Cornwall Record Soc., NS 17, 1971).
Cartularium Monasterii de Rameseia, 3 vols, ed. W. H. Hart and P. A. Lyons (Rolls Ser., London, 1884–94).
Cartularium Saxonicum, ed. W. de Gray Birch (London, 1885–99).
The Cartulary of Cirencester Abbey, 2 vols, ed. C. D. Ross (London, 1964).
The Cartulary of Newnham Priory, 2 vols, ed. J. Godber (Beds. Historical Rec. Soc., 43, 1963–4).
Transcripts of Charters Relating to the Gilbertine Houses of Sixle, Ormsby, Catley, Bullington and Alvingham, ed. F. M. Stenton (Lincoln Rec. Soc., 18, 1922).
Charters and Custumals of the Abbey of Holy Trinity, Caen, ed. M. Chibnall (Brit. Acad. Records of Social and Econ. Hist., new ser., 5, London, 1982).
The Chartulary of the High Church of Chichester, ed. W. D. Peckham (Sussex Rec. Soc., 46, 1946).

The Great Chartulary of Glastonbury, 3 vols, ed. A. Watkin (Somerset Record Soc., 59, 1947; 63, 1952; 64, 1956).

Chaucer, Geoffrey, *The Canterbury Tales*, ed. W. W. Skeat (Oxford, 1912).

Chronica Monasterii de Melsa, 3 vols, ed. E. A. Bond (Rolls Series, London, 1866–8).

The Chronicle of Jocelin of Brakelond, ed. H. E. Butler (London, 1949).

Chronicon Petroburgense, ed. T. Stapleton (Camden Soc., old ser., 47, London, 1849).

Court Rolls of the Abbey of Ramsey and of the Honour of Clare, ed. W. O. Ault (New Haven/London, 1928).

Extracts from the Court Rolls of the Manor of Aldborough 1338–9, ed. T. Lawson-Tancred and J. W. Walker (Yorks. Archaeol. Soc. Rec. Ser., 74, 1929).

Court Rolls of Chalgrave Manor, 1278–1313, ed. M. K. Dale (Bedfords. Hist. Rec. Soc., 28, 1950).

Court Rolls of the Manor of Hales, i, ed. J. Amphlett (Worcs. Hist. Soc., 1912).

Court Rolls of the Manor of Hales, iii, ed. R. A. Wilson (Worcs. Hist. Soc., 1933).

Court Rolls of the Manor of Wakefield, vol. i: 1274–1297, ed. W. P. Baildon (Yorks. Archaeol. Soc., 29, 1901).

Court Rolls of the Manor of Wakefield, ii, 1297–1309, ed. W. P. Baildon (Yorks. Archaeol. Soc. Record Ser., 36, 1906).

Court Rolls of the Manor of Wakefield, iii, 1313–16, 1286, ed. J. Lister (Yorks. Archaeol. Soc. Record Ser., 57, 1917).

Court Rolls of the Manor of Wakefield, iv, 1315–17, ed. J. Lister (Yorks. Archaeol. Soc. Record Ser., 78, 1930).

Court Rolls of the Manor of Wakefield, v, 1322–31, ed. J. W. Walker (Yorks. Archaeol. Soc. Record Ser., 109, 1944).

Court Rolls of the Manor of Wakefield 1348–50, ed. H. M. Jewell (Yorks. Archaeol. Soc., Wakefield Court Rolls Ser., 2, 1981).

Curia Regis Rolls, i (HMSO, 1923); iii (HMSO, 1927).

Domesday Book (London, 1783).

The Domesday of St Paul's of the Year 1222, ed. W. H. Hale (Camden Soc., old ser., 69, London, 1858).

Early Yorkshire Charters, vol. vii: The Honour of Skipton, ed. C. T. Clay (Yorks. Archaeol. Soc. Rec. Ser., Extra Ser. 5, 1947).

Elton Manorial Records 1279–1351, ed. S. C. Ratcliff (Roxburghe Club, Cambridge, 1946).

Feet of Fines, 1196–1197 (Pipe Roll Soc., 20, 1896).

Feet of Fines, 1198–1199 (Pipe Roll Soc., 24, 1900).

Feet of Fines for the County of Norfolk, 1198–1202, ed. B. Dodwell (Pipe Roll Soc., new ser., 27, 1952).

Feet of Fines, Northumberland and Durham, ed. A. M. Oliver and C. Johnson (Newcastle upon Tyne Recs. Committee, 10, 1931).

Final Concords of the County of Lincoln 1244–1272, ed. C. W. Foster (Lincoln Rec. Soc., 17, 1920).

Halmota Prioratus Dunelmensis: Extracts from the Halmote Court or Manor Rolls of the Prior and Convent of Durham 1296–1384, ed. W. H. Longstaffe and J. Booth (Surtees Soc., 82, 1889).

Historia de Rebus Gestis Glastoniensibus Adami de Domerham, ed. T. Hearne, 2 vols (Oxford, 1727).

Historia et Cartularium Monasterii Sancti Petri Gloucestriae, ed. W. H. Hart (Rolls Ser., 3 vols, 1863–7).

Abstracts of Inquisitions Post Mortem for Gloucestershire, iv, ed. S. J. Madge and E. A. Fry (British Rec. Soc., 30, London, 1903).

Inquisitiones Post Mortem for the County of Worcester, i, ed. J. W. W. Bund (Worcs. Hist. Soc., 1894).

The Kalendar of Abbot Samson of Bury St Edmunds, ed. R. H. C. Davis (Camden 3rd ser., 84, London, 1954).

The Langley Cartulary, ed. P. R. Coss (Dugdale Soc. Pubs., 32, Stratford-upon-Avon, 1980).

The Ledger Book of Vale Royal Abbey, ed. J. Brownbill (Lancs. and Cheshire Rec. Soc., 68, 1914).

Liber Gersummarum, ed. E. B. DeWindt (Toronto, 1976).

Liber Henrici de Soliaco: An Inquisition of the Manors of Glastonbury Abbey of the Year 1189, ed. J. E. Jackson (Roxburghe Club, London, 1882).

Manorial Records of Cuxham, Oxfordshire, c.1200–1359, ed. P. D. A. Harvey (Historical Manuscripts Commission, JP23/Oxfordshire Rec. Soc., 50, London, 1976).

Medieval Framlingham: Select Documents 1270–1524, ed. J. Ridgard (Suffolk Records Soc., 27, 1985).

Ministers' Accounts of the Earldon of Cornwall, 1296–1297, ii, ed. L. M. Midgley (Camden 3rd ser., 68, 1945).

The Minor Poems of John Lydgate, ed. H. N. MacCracken (Early English Text Soc., London, 1934).

Pedes Finium, Commonly Called Feet of Fines, for the County of Somerset, 1196 to 1307, ed. E. Green (Somerset Rec. Soc., 6, Taunton, 1892).

The Pinchbeck Register, 2 vols, ed. F. Hervey (Brighton, 1925).

Pipe Roll, 11 Henry II (Pipe Roll Soc., 1887).

The Pipe Roll of the Bishopric of Winchester 1210–1211, ed. N. R. Holt (Manchester, 1964).

The Political Songs of England, from the Reign of John to that of Edward II, ed. T. Wright (Camden Soc., old ser., 6, London, 1839).

Records of the Templars in England in the Twelfth Century: The Inquest of 1185, ed. B. A. Lees (Brit. Acad. Records of Social and Econ. Hist., 9, London, 1935).

Register of Edward the Black Prince, 4 vols (HMSO, 1930–3).

Register of the Priory of St Mary, Worcester, ed. W. H. Hale (Camden Soc., old ser., 91, London, 1865).

Rentalia et Custumaria Michaelis de Ambresbury, 1235–1252, et Rogeri de Ford, 1252–1261, ed. C. J. Elton (Somerset Rec. Soc., 5, 1892).

Rotuli Hundredorum, ii, ed. W. Illingworth and J. Caley (Record Commission, London, 1818).

Select Documents of the English Lands of the Abbey of Bec, ed. M. Chibnall (Camden 3rd ser., 73, London, 1951).

Select Pleas in Manorial and Other Seignorial Courts, ed. F. W. Maitland (Selden Soc. Pubs, 2, 1889).

Statutes of the Realm, vol. 1 (Record Commissioners, London, 1810).

Two Compoti of the Lancashire and Cheshire Manors of Henry de Lacy, Earl of Lincoln, 24 and 33 Edward I, ed. P. A. Lyons (Chetham Soc., old ser., 112, 1884).

Vitruvius, *On Architecture*, 2 vols, ed. F. Granger (London, 1931–4).

Walsingham, Thomas, *Gesta Abbatum Monasterii Sancti Albani*, 3 vols, ed. H. T. Riley (Rolls Ser., London, 1867–9).

Secondary Works

N. W. Alcock, 'An East Devon manor in the later Middle Ages', *Trans. of the Devonshire Assoc.*, 102 (1970), pp. 141–87.

H. Amouric, 'De la roue horizontale à la roue verticale dans les moulins à eau' *Provence Historique*, 33 (1983), pp. 157–69.

F. Atkinson, 'The horse as a source of rotary power', *Trans. Newcomen Soc.*, 33 (1960–1), pp. 31–55.

M. Baillie, 'Dendrochronology — the Irish view', *Current Archaeology* 73 (August 1980), pp. 61–3.

G. Baker, *The History and Antiquties of the County of Northampton*, 2 vols (London, 1822–41).

A. Ballard, *British Borough Charters 1042–1216* (Cambridge, 1913).

P. Bauters, 'The oldest references to windmills in Europe', *Trans. of the Fifth Symposium of the International Molinological Soc.*, 1982 (Saint-Maurice, 1984), pp. 111–19.

A-M. Bautier, 'Les Plus Anciennes Mentions de Moulins Hydrauliques Industriels et de Moulins à Vent', *Bulletin Philologique et Historique*, 2 (1960), pp. 567–626.

J. M. W. Bean, *The Estates of the Percy Family 1416–1557*, (Oxford, 1958).

J. and R. Bedington, 'The "Norse" watermills of Shetland', *Wind and Water Mills*, 5 (1984), pp. 33–8.

O. Bedwin, 'The excavation of Batsford Mill, Warbleton, East Sussex, 1978', *Medieval Archaeology*, 24 (1980), pp. 187–201.

G. C. Bellairs, 'Wooden cross found buried under a mound at Higham-on-the-Hill, Leicestershire', *Trans. Leics. Architectural and Archaeol. Soc.*, 9 (1905), pp. 18–19.

H. S. Bennett, *Life on the English Manor* (Cambridge, 1937).

J. A. W Bennett, *Chaucer at Oxford and Cambridge* (Oxford, 1974).

R. Bennett and J. Elton, *History of Corn Milling*, 4 vols (London and Liverpool, 1898–1904).

I. S. W. Blanchard, 'Lead mining and smelting in medieval England and Wales', in Crossley, *Medieval Industry*, pp. 72–84.

M. Bloch, 'Avènement et Conquêtes du Moulin à Eau', and 'Les "Inventions" Médiévales', *Annales ESC*, 7 (1935), pp. 538–63, 634–43; trans. J. E. Anderson in M. Bloch, *Land and Work in Medieval Europe* (London, 1967), pp. 136–68, 169–85.

J. K. G. Boucher, 'Watermill research and development in Nepal', *Wind and Water Mills*, 5 (1984), pp. 43–8.

K. M. Briggs, *A Dictionary of British Folk-Tales*, Parts A and B, 4 vols (London, 1970–1).

A. A. M. Bryer, *The Empire of Trebizond and the Pontos* (London, 1980), pp. 405–11 of Section VII, 'The Estates of the Empire of Trebizond'.

E. M. Carus-Wilson, 'An Industrial Revolution of the thirteenth century', *Econ. Hist. Review*, 11 (1941), repr. in E. M. Carus-Wilson (ed.), *Essays in Economic History*, i (London, 1954), pp. 41–60.

M. G. Cheney, 'The decretal of Pope Celestine III on tithes of windmills, JL 17620', *Bulletin of Medieval Canon Law*, New ser., 1 (1971), pp. 63–6.

P. Clay, 'Castle Donington', *Current Archaeology*, 102 (1986), pp. 208–11.

H. Cleere and D. Crossley, *The Iron Industry of the Weald*, (Leicester, 1985).

G. G. Coulton, *The Medieval Village* (Cambridge, 1925).

D. W. Crossley (ed.), *Medieval Industry* (Council for British Archaeology, Research Report 40, London, 1981).

W. Cunningham, *The Growth of English Industry and Commerce during the Early and Middle Ages* (Cambridge, 1905).

E. C. Curwen, 'The problem of early water-mills', *Antiquity*, 18 (1944), pp. 130–46.

H. C. Darby, *The Domesday Geography of Eastern England* (Cambridge, 1952).

H. C. Darby, *Domesday England* (Cambridge, 1977).

H. C. Darby and E. M. J. Campbell, *The Domesday Geography of South-East England* (Cambridge, 1962).

H. C. Darby and R. W. Finn, *The Domesday Geography of South-West England* (Cambridge, 1967).

H. C. Darby and I. S. Maxwell, *The Domesday Geography of Northern England* (Cambridge, 1962).

H. C. Darby and I. B. Terrett, *The Domesday Geography of Midland England* (Cambridge, 1954).

M. Daumas (ed.), *Histoire Générale de Techniques* (Paris, 1962), published as *A History of Technology and Invention*, 3 vols (London, 1980).

L. Delisle, *Études sur la Condition de la Classe Agricole et l'État de l'Agriculture en Normandie au Moyen Age* (Évreux, 1851/Paris, 1903).

P. Dockès, *Medieval Slavery and Liberation* (Chicago, 1982).

G. Duby, *Rural Economy and Country Life in the Medieval West* (London, 1968).

C. C. Dyer, *Lords and Peasants in a Changing Society: The Estates of the Bishopric of Worcester, 680–1540* (Cambridge, 1980).

J. R. Earnshaw, 'The Site of a Medieval Post Mill and Prehistoric Site at Bridlington', *Yorks. Archaeol. Journal*, 45 (1973), pp. 19–33.

D. L. Farmer, 'Some grain price movements in thirteenth-century England', *Econ. Hist. Review*, 2nd ser., 10 (1957), pp. 207–20.

M. L. Faull and S. A. Moorhouse, *West Yorkshire: An Archaeological Survey to A.D. 1500* (Wakefield, 1981).

H. P. R. Finberg, *Tavistock Abbey* (Cambridge, 1951).

E. A. Fuller, 'Cirencester — Its Manor and Town', *Trans. Bristol and*

Gloucestershire Archaeol. Soc., 9 (1885), pp. 298–344.

D. W. Gade, 'Grist Milling with the Horizontal Waterwheel in the Central Andes', Technology and Culture, 12 (1971), pp. 43–51.

E. Gauldie, The Scottish Country Miller 1700–1900 (Edinburgh, 1981).

J. Gimpel, The Medieval Machine: The Industrial Revolution of the Middle Ages (London, 1977).

T. Glick, Islamic and Christian Spain in the Early Middle Ages (Princeton, 1979).

I. H. Goodall, 'The medieval blacksmith and his products', in Crossley, Medieval Industry, pp. 51–62.

G. Goudie, 'On the horizontal water mills of Shetland', Procs. of the Soc. of Antiquaries of Scotland, new ser., 8 (1885–6), pp. 257–97.

A. H. Graham, 'The old malthouse, Abbotsbury, Dorset: The medieval watermill of the Benedictine Abbey', Procs. of the Dorset Nat. Hist. and Archaeol. Soc., 108 (1986), pp. 103–25.

T. A. P. Greeves, 'The archaeological potential of the Devon tin industry', in Crossley, Medieval Industry, pp. 85–95.

J. Hatcher, Rural Economy and Society in the Duchy of Cornwall 1300–1500 (Cambridge, 1970).

J. Hatcher, Plague, Population and the English Economy 1348–1530 (London, 1977).

C. Henderson, Essays in Cornish History (Oxford, 1935).

H. J. Hewitt, Medieval Cheshire (Chetham Soc., new ser., 88, 1929).

R. H. Hilton, A Medieval Society (London, 1966).

R. H. Hilton, The Decline of Serfdom in Medieval England (London, 1969).

R. H. Hilton, Bond Men Made Free (London, 1973).

R. H. Hilton and P. A. Rahtz, 'Upton, Gloucestershire, 1959–1964', Trans. Bristol and Glos. Archaeol. Soc., 85 (1966), pp. 70–146.

R. H. Hilton and P. H. Sawyer, 'Technical determinism: the stirrup and the plough', Past and Present, 24 (1963), pp. 90–100.

M. Hodgen, 'Domesday Water Mills', Antiquity, 13 (1939), pp. 261–79.

R. A. Holt, The Early History of the Town of Birmingham 1166–1600 (Dugdale Soc., Occasional Paper 30, Oxford, 1985).

R. A. Holt, 'Whose were the profits of corn milling? An aspect of the changing relationship between the Abbots of Glastonbury and their tenants 1086–1350', Past and Present, 116 (1987), pp. 3–23.

N. A. Huddleston, History of Rillington (1955).

J. G. Hurst, 'The Wharram research project: results to 1983', Medieval

Archaeology, 28 (1984), pp. 77–111.

P. Hyde, 'The borough of Witney', *Oxfordshire Rec. Soc.*, 46 (1968), pp. 89–107.

H. Jewell, D. Michelmore, S. Moorhouse, 'An Oliver at Warley, West Yorkshire, A.D. 1349–50', *Historical Metallurgy*, 15 (1981), pp. 39–40.

G. F. Jones, 'Chaucer and the medieval miller', *Modern Languages Quarterly*, 16 (1955), pp. 3–15.

W. T. Jones, 'The Mucking windmill', *Journal of Thurrock Local Hist. Soc.*, 23 (1979), pp. 42–6.

S. L. Kaplan, *Provisioning Paris: Merchants and Millers in the Grain and Flour Trade during the Eighteenth Century* (Ithaca and London, 1984).

E. J. Kealey, *Harvesting the Air: Windmill Pioneers in Twelfth-Century England* (Woodbridge, 1987).

I. Keil, 'Building a Post Windmill in 1342', *Trans. Newcomen Soc.*, 34 (1962), pp. 151–4.

D. Keene, *Survey of Medieval Winchester*, i (Winchester Studies, 2, Oxford, 1985).

I. Kershaw, 'The great famine and agrarian crisis in England 1315–1322' in R. H. Hilton (ed.), *Peasants, Knights, and Heretics* (Cambridge, 1976), pp. 57–132, repr. from *Past and Present*, 59 (1973).

E. A. Kosminsky, 'The Hundred Rolls of 1279–80 as a source for English agrarin history', *Econ. Hist. Review*, 3 (1931), pp. 16–44.

E. A. Kosminsky, *Studies in the Agrarian History of England in the Thirteenth Century* (Oxford, 1956).

W. T. Lancaster, 'A fifteenth-century rental of Nostell Priory', *Yorks. Archaeol. Soc. Rec. Ser.*, 61 (1920), pp. 108–35.

J. Langdon, *Horses, Oxen and Technological Innovation* (Cambridge, 1986).

G. T. Lapsley, 'The account roll of a fifteenth-century iron master', *English Hist. Review*, 14 (1899), pp. 509–29.

R. V. Lennard, 'Early English fulling mills: additional examples', *Econ. Hist. Review*, 17 (1947), pp. 342–3.

R. V. Lennard, *Rural England 1086–1135* (Oxford, 1959).

A. T. Lucas, 'The horizontal mill in Ireland', *Journal of the Royal Soc. of Antiquaries of Ireland*, 83 (1953), pp. 1–36.

H. S. Lucas, 'The Great European Famine of 1315, 1316, and 1317' in E. M. Carus-Wilson (ed.), *Essays in Economic History*, ii, (London, 1962), pp. 49–72, repr. from *Speculum*, 5 (1930).

W. A. McCutcheon, 'Water Power in the North of Ireland', *Trans.*

Newcomen Soc., 39 (1966 – 7), pp. 67 – 94.

J. McDonald and G. D. Snooks, *Domesday Economy: A New Approach to Anglo-Norman History* (Oxford, 1986).

J. Mann, *Chaucer and Medieval Estates Satire* (Cambridge, 1973).

M. Mate, 'Property investment by Canterbury Cathedral Priory 1250 – 1400', *Journal of British Studies*, 33 (1984), pp. 1 – 21.

S. Maxwell, 'A horizontal water mill paddle from Dalswinton, and some notes on the occurrence of this type of mill in Scotland', *Trans. Dumfriesshire and Galloway Nat. Hist. and Antiquarian Soc.*, 3rd ser., 33 (1954 – 5), pp. 185 – 96.

'Medieval Britain in 1957', *Medieval Archaeology*, 2 (1958).

'Medieval Britain in 1971', *Medieval Archaeology*, 16 (1972).

'Medieval Britain in 1980', *Medieval Archaeology*, 25 (1981).

'Medieval Britain and Ireland in 1984', *Medieval Archaeology*, 29 (1985).

'Medieval Britain and Ireland in 1985', *Medieval Archaeology*, 30 (1986).

E. Miller, *The Abbey and Bishopric of Ely* (Cambridge, 1951).

E. Miller, 'The fortunes of the English textile industry during the thirteenth century', *Econ. Hist. Review*, 2nd ser., 18 (1965), pp. 64 – 82.

E. Miller, 'England in the twelfth and thirteenth centuries: an economic contrast?', *Econ. Hist. Review*, 2nd ser., 24 (1971), pp. 1 – 14.

W. E. Minchinton, 'Early tide mills: some problems', *Technology and Culture*, 20 (1979), pp. 777 – 86.

W. E. Minchinton, 'Tidemills of England and Wales', *Trans. of the Fourth Symposium of the International Molinological Soc., 1977* (1982), pp. 339 – 53.

C. Monkman, 'Buried cruciform platforms in Yorkshire', *Yorks. Archaeol. and Topographical Journal*, 2 (1873), pp. 69 – 81.

L. A. Moritz, *Grain-Mills and Flour in Classical Antiquity* (Oxford, 1958).

J. R. Mortimer, *Forty Years' Researches in British and Saxon Burial Mounds of East Yorkshire* (London, 1905).

J. Muendel, 'The horizontal mills of Pistoia', *Technology and Culture*, 15 (1974), pp. 194 – 225.

J. Muendel, 'The distribution of mills in the Florentine Countryside during the Late Middle Ages', in J. A. Raftis (ed.), *Pathways to Medieval Peasants* (Toronto, 1981), pp. 83 – 115.

J. F. Nicholls, 'Milton Hall: the compotus of 1299', *Trans. Southend-on-Sea and District Antiquarian and Hist. Soc.*, 2 (1932), pp. 113 – 67.

S. V. Pearce, 'A medieval windmill, Honey Hill, Dogsthorpe', *Procs. of the Cambridge Antiquarian Soc.*, 59 (1966), pp. 95–103.

R. A. Pelham, *Fulling Mills* (Soc. for the Protection of Ancient Buildings, London, 1958).

M. Posnasky, 'The Lamport post mill', *Journal of the Northants. Nat. Hist. Soc. and Field Club*, 33 (1959), pp. 66–79.

P. A. Rahtz, 'The Saxon and medieval palaces at Cheddar', *Medieval Archaeology*, 6–7 (1962–3), pp. 53–66.

P. A. Rahtz, *The Saxon and Medieval Palaces at Cheddar: Excavations 1960–62* (BAR, British ser., 65, London, 1979).

P. A. Rahtz, 'Medieval Milling', in Crossley, *Medieval Industry*, pp. 1–15.

P. A. and M. H. Rahtz, 'T 40: Barrow and Windmill at Butcombe, North Somerset', *Procs. of the Univ. of Bristol Spelaeological Soc.*, 8 (1957), pp. 89–96.

P. Rahtz and D. Bullough, 'The Parts of an Anglo-Saxon Mill', in P. Clemoes (ed.), *Anglo-Saxon England*, 6 (Cambridge, 1977), pp.

L. M. C. Randall, *Images in the Margins of Gothic Manuscripts* (Berkeley, 1966).

Z. Razi, 'The Struggles between the Abbots of Halesowen and their Tenants in the Thirteenth and Fourteenth Centuries', in T. H. Aston, P. R. Coss, C. C. Dyer and J. Thirsk (eds), *Social Relations and Ideas: Essays in Honour of R. H. Hilton* (Cambridge, 1983), pp. 151–67.

T. S. Reynolds, *Stronger than a Hundred Men: A History of the Vertical Water Wheel* (Baltimore, 1983).

T. S. Reynolds, 'Medieval Roots of the Industrial Revolution', *Scientific American* 251 (1984), pp. 108–16.

J. E. Thorold Rogers, *Six Centuries of Work and Wages* (London, 1884).

'Rugby tumulus', note in *Trans. Birmingham Archaeol. Soc.*, 52 (1927), pp. 301–2.

J. Russell, 'Millstones in wind and water mills', *Trans. Newcomen Soc.*, 24 (1943–5), pp. 55–64.

J. Salmon, 'Erection of a windmill at Newborough (Anglesey) in 1303', *Archaeologia Cambrensis*, 95 (1940), pp. 250–2.

J. Salmon, 'The windmill in English medieval art', *Journal of the British Archaeol. Assoc.*, 3rd ser., 6 (1941), pp. 88–102.

P. Salway, *Roman Britain* (Oxford, 1981).

A. Savine, 'English Monasteries on the Eve of the Dissolution', in P. Vinogradoff (ed.), *Oxford Studies in Social and Legal History*

(Oxford, 1909).

P. H. Sawyer, *Medieval Settlement* (London, 1976).

E. Searle, *Lordship and Community: Battle Abbey and its Banlieu 1066–1538* (Toronto, 1974).

G. Sicard, *Les Moulins de Toulouse au Moyen Age* (Paris, 1953).

C. Singer, E. J. Holmyard, A. R. Hall, T. I. Williams (eds), *A History of Technology*, 5 vols (Oxford, 1956).

N. A. F. Smith, 'Water power', *History Today* 30 (March 1980), pp. 37–41.

E. Stone, 'Profit-and-loss accountancy at Norwich Cathedral Priory', *Trans. Royal Hist. Soc.*, 4th ser., 12 (1962), pp. 25–48.

F. F. Strauss, '"Mills without wheels" in the sixteenth-century Alps', *Technology and Culture*, 12 (1971), pp. 23–42.

L. Syson, *British Water Mills* (London, 1965).

J. Tann, 'Multiple mills', *Medieval Archaeology*, 11 (1967), pp. 233–5.

J. Z. Titow, *English Rural Society 1200–1350* (London, 1969).

R. F. Tylecote, 'The Medieval Smith and His Methods', in Crossley, *Medieval Industry*, pp. 42–50.

K. Ugawa, 'The economic development of some Devon manors in the thirteenth century', *Trans. of the Devonshire Assoc.*, 94 (1962), pp. 630–83.

A. P. Usher, *History of Mechanical Inventions* (New York, 1929: revised edn, Cambridge, Mass, 1954).

Victoria County History, Warwickshire, vol. 7 (London, 1964).

R. Wailes, *The English Windmill* (London, 1954).

R. Wailes, 'Some windmill fallacies', *Trans. Newcomen Soc.*, 32 (1959–60), pp. 93–109.

R. Wailes, 'The "Greek" and "Norse" waterwheels', *Trans. Fourth Symposium International Molinological Soc. 1977* (1982), pp. 163–4.

W. P. Westell, 'Sandon Mount, Hertfordshire: its site, excavations and problems', *Trans. St Albans and Herts. Architectural and Archaeol. Soc.*, (1934), pp. 173–83.

L. White, Jr, 'Technology and Invention in the Middle Ages', *Speculum*, 15 (1940), repr. in L. White, *Medieval Religion and Technology* (Berkeley, 1978), pp. 1–22.

L. White, Jr, *Medieval Technology and Social Change* (Oxford, 1962).

L. White, Jr, 'The Expansion of Technology 500–1500', in C. M. Cipolla (ed.), *The Fontana Economic History of Europe*, i (London, 1972).

Ö. Wikander, *Exploitation of Water-Power or Technological Stagnation? A Reappraisal of the Productive Forces in the Roman*

Empire (Scripta Minora Regiae Societatis Humaniorum Litterarum Lundensis, Lund, 1984).

Ö. Wikander, 'Archaeological evidence for early water-mills — an interim report', *History of Technology*, 10 (London, 1985), pp. 151—79.

R. J. Zeepvat, 'Post mills and archaeology', *Current Archaeology*, 71 (1980), pp. 375—7.

P. Ziegler, *The Black Death* (London, 1979).

Index

The numerous passing references to *mill*, *watermill*, and *windmill* have not been indexed. Place names are listed county by county.